Mat McLachlan is one of Australia's leading battlefield historians and media presenters in the history space. He is the author of *Walking with the Anzacs* and *Gallipoli: The Battlefield Guide*, and the founder of Mat McLachlan Battlefield Tours, which sends thousands of Australians to visit battlefields around the world each year, including Cowra.

As a media presenter, Mat is a regular on TV and radio and in print. His *Living History* podcast reaches more than 30,000 Australian history enthusiasts each week, and he produces the *BattleWalks* and *Pete & Gary's Military History* podcasts. Mat also produces and presents history documentaries for various networks. He appears regularly as a history expert on all major Australian television and radio networks, and reaches over five million people on YouTube each year. He lives in Sydney with his wife and children.

Also by Mat McLachlan

Walking with the Anzacs
Gallipoli: The Battlefield Guide

The
COWRA
BREAKOUT

The
COWRA
BREAKOUT

MAT McLACHLAN

hachette
AUSTRALIA

Published in Australia and New Zealand in 2022
by Hachette Australia
(an imprint of Hachette Australia Pty Limited)
Gadigal Country, Level 17, 207 Kent Street, Sydney, NSW 2000
www.hachette.com.au

Hachette Australia acknowledges and pays our respects to the past, present and future Traditional Owners and Custodians of Country throughout Australia and recognises the continuation of cultural, spiritual and educational practices of Aboriginal and Torres Strait Islander peoples. Our head office is located on the lands of the Gadigal people of the Eora Nation.

A catalogue record for this
work is available from the
National Library of Australia

ISBN: 978 0 7336 4762 8 (paperback)

Cover design by Luke Causby / Blue Cork
Cover and internal photographs courtesy of the Australian War Memorial unless otherwise specified
Map by Laurie Whiddon, Map Illustrations
Typeset in Simoncini Garamond by Kirby Jones
Printed and bound in Australia by McPherson's Printing Group

MIX
Paper from
responsible sources
FSC® C001695

The paper this book is printed on is certified against the Forest Stewardship Council® Standards. McPherson's Printing Group holds FSC® chain of custody certification SA-COC-005379. FSC® promotes environmentally responsible, socially beneficial and economically viable management of the world's forests.

CONTENTS

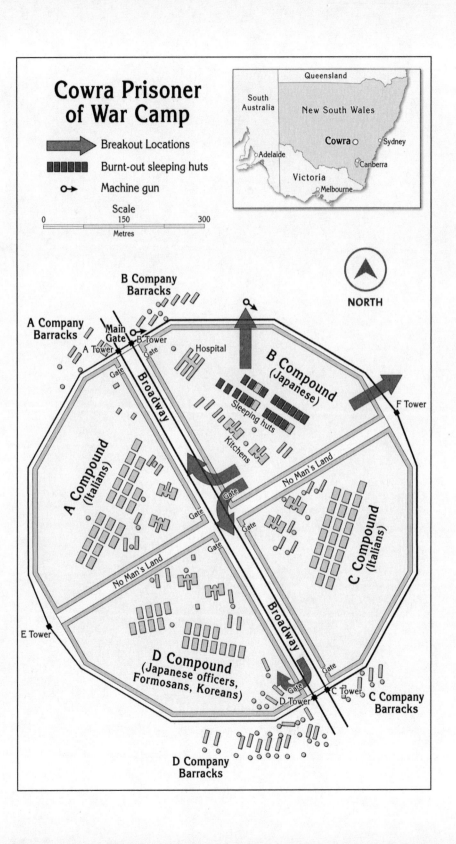

Cowra Prisoner of War Camp

Breakout Locations

Burnt-out sleeping huts

Machine gun

Scale
0   150   300
Metres

Queensland

South Australia

New South Wales

Cowra ○   ○ Sydney

○ Adelaide

○ Canberra

Victoria

○ Melbourne

NORTH

B Company Barracks

A Company Barracks

Main Gate

A Tower   B Tower

Gate

Hospital

B Compound (Japanese)

F Tower

Broadway

Sleeping huts

A Compound (Italians)

Kitchens

Gate

No Man's Land

C Compound (Italians)

Gate

Gate

No Man's Land

E Tower

Broadway

D Compound (Japanese officers, Formosans, Koreans)

Gate

Gate

D Tower   C Tower

C Company Barracks

D Company Barracks

INTRODUCTION

It's tough country out Cowra way. Even the first people to live here, the Wiradjuri, didn't seem particularly enamoured with the place. They called it *Ngoura*, which loosely and unaffectionately translates to 'place'. The first European to encounter it was George Evans, an explorer who has been largely forgotten but in his day was something of a trailblazer, both figuratively and literally, when he became the first European to cross the Great Dividing Range and explore the fertile grazing land along the Lachlan River (the more famous party led by Blaxland, Lawson and Wentworth had not actually crossed the main range). He christened the river after the governor of the colony, Lachlan Macquarie, and named the area Oxley Plains after his boss, surveyor-general John Oxley. Oxley was a man who knew good farming country when he saw it, but this area didn't impress him; during an expedition along the Lachlan in 1817 he was so disheartened by the 'swamps', 'quicksands' and 'bogs' he encountered that he swiftly returned to Sydney convinced that the entire interior of the country was submerged under a giant inland sea.[1] Settlers didn't arrive in any great numbers for another 20 years, and corrupted the Aboriginal name when they called the first township 'Caura Rocks'. The name was well chosen – rocks are a key and unrelenting feature of the landscape in this rural corner of New South Wales. Vast sheets of granite outcrops form small escarpments, boulders huddle in conspiratorial groups across the landscape, and loose scree carpets the slopes and chokes the gullies.

The soil is actually pretty good, but to get a decent crop from it takes skill and sweat. None of the paddocks are flat – they all roll like a bay under a decent swell, and the ground is dry and scoured with washaways. Scorching in summer, freezing in winter, it's the sort of country where a farmer never finishes a day's work without taking off a dusty hat and running a forearm across a sweaty brow, and staring out across the land he's just worked as if staring down a vanquished foe.

Yet in spite of all that, in spring the wheat and canola grow lushly, the gold-brown and daisy-yellow patchwork stretching to the distant horizon. Plump sheep munch on new grass between the rock piles, wandering aimlessly, content in the chilly morning air.

In one of these paddocks the sheep graze not around rocks but stark slabs of concrete and brick, rough foundations of buildings long since vanished. Rough dirt tracks cross the site, and slender trees in the distance mark an indistinct perimeter. There are signs, too, directing the visitor to various corners of the paddock, while others warn the unwary not to venture off the paths, lest they encounter a snake in the ankle-high grass. The signs don't lie – there are snakes here, lots of them. You see them basking in the warm embrace of the long grass, slithering across the paths and, mostly, coiled in the cracks and crevices of the old foundations. And these aren't small and harmless – no tree snakes or carpet pythons here. These are eastern browns, two metres long and thick as a grazier's wrist, and packing a deadly punch.

It's fitting to find them here. The serpent, that harbinger of death, the betrayer of Eve and catalyst for the downfall of man, belongs in this paddock, among all others. Perhaps they detect the faintest scent of blood in the parched soil, perhaps the air tastes heavy with grief; perhaps they just sense that ghosts walk here and they feel content among them. For this is the site of Number 12 Prisoner of War Group, a place that should be forgotten to history. Other former POW camps across the country have vanished without trace, from both the landscape and memory, and Cowra should have joined them. But of course, because of what went on here, it never will.

What went on here on a frosty winter's night in August 1944 was brought about by a clash of cultures, a tempest of misunderstanding, animosity and shame that eventually couldn't be contained, and erupted into violence. At the time it was covered up, dismissed as an aberration, a senseless waste of life in a war that was defined by senseless wastes of life.

But over time the Cowra Breakout has come to mean something more – it's come to represent the heavy burden borne by all who participated in the Second World War, the importance of crossing cultural bridges and the beauty of reconciliation. Even after 80 years, the ghosts of Cowra have an important story to tell.

1

'TENNOHEIKA BANZAI!': THE GREAT ATTACK

Seaman First Class Tatsumi Hanada was awakened by a trumpet call at 4 a.m. and rolled out of his bunk. He had slept fitfully, just as he had so many times as a youth the night before an important baseball match. Through half-sleep his mind had raced with thoughts about the upcoming day, and his role in it; he had rehearsed every step of his duties and was determined to perform honourably for his navy, his country and his Emperor. He dressed quickly – on any other day he would have donned the same filthy uniform he had been wearing for the past week, the khaki fabric crusted with oil, salt and sweat. But today, the day of the Great Attack, he dressed in fresh clothes – khaki shorts and a button-down short-sleeve shirt, over a white undershirt and underwear. He completed the ensemble with his well-worn woollen summer cap. It was a cool morning, but it would be hot before long, and there would not be time to change. In the crew mess he ate a quick breakfast, then joined his crewmates in the cavernous midships hangar and set to work.

Hanada had been in the navy for more than four years, and most of that time had been spent working as an aircraft mechanic and learning the intricacies of attack aircraft, particularly their powerful but temperamental radial engines. Since joining the crew of the aircraft carrier *Hiryu* two years earlier, he had worked almost exclusively on the Zero, and knew every panel and rivet of the formidable fighter. He and a dozen crewmates had worked for months on the same *Zero-sen* under the watchful gaze of their *seibicho*, the maintenance petty officer.

Hanada and his crewmates set to work fuelling and arming their plane. They unfurled metal hoses and began brimming the aircraft with high-octane aviation fuel. A 275-litre external drop tank (designed to be dropped from the plane when empty) was unfastened from clips on the bulkheads, attached to the aircraft and fuelled. As the Zero's tanks filled, Hanada detected the familiar, yet slightly unsettling, aroma of fuel vapours. Unlike the open-sided hangars on their American equivalents, hangars on Japanese carriers were completely enclosed, providing protection from the elements but creating a noxious environment for fumes. No amount of fastidious cleaning could remove the odour of fuel, grease, paint and motor oil that were trademarks of the operation of military aircraft. Huge ventilation units, built into the deck to better clear the heavier-than-air vapours, laboured noisily to suck the noxious fumes away.

While the fuel tanks were filling, armourers were busy feeding belts of 7.7 mm machine-gun ammunition into the twin turrets on the nose of the Zero and cramming 60-round cannisters into the wing spaces for the two 20 mm cannons. Around them, the hangar teemed with crews working to fuel and arm their own Zeros, as well as the Type 99 dive bomber, which would play a crucial role in the upcoming attack. Several decks above them, other crews completed the same tasks on fighters, dive bombers and torpedo bombers that had been stowed on the flight deck and would launch in the first wave – the air fleet had been substantially increased for this attack, and there simply wasn't space to store all the aircraft below decks.

As he worked, Hanada glanced admiringly at his plane. The Zero had looked sleek and shiny when it first rolled off the assembly line; but now, after nearly two years of seaborne operations, it was bearing a few scars, the chipped paint and oil streaks giving it a sinister demeanour in the crowded hangar. But even in this weather-beaten state, it was a formidable offensive weapon. The Zero was innovative in design, and brutally effective in operation. In order to preserve structural strength, a necessity to deal with the gut-wrenching manoeuvres that were a trademark of expert pilots, its designers had eschewed the fully folding wings typical of other carrier aircraft, deeming the mechanism to operate them too heavy, and representing an unacceptable sacrifice in performance. Only the wingtips of a Zero folded up, a meagre concession to space-saving, and one begrudgingly made to ensure that the planes fitted on the narrow carrier elevators.

The result was that the Zero was magnificent in the air, but frustratingly difficult to store and manoeuvre in the cramped confines of a carrier hangar. Each plane took up a disproportionate amount of valuable hangar real estate, and it took a highly trained crew to service and move the planes. Even getting a Zero onto the flight deck was a chore – a dozen crewmen were needed to manhandle a single plane onto one of the carrier's aircraft elevators and to roll it several dozen metres into position on the flight deck, an arduous physical challenge even for an experienced crew.

Their carrier, the *Hiryu*, was a somewhat peculiar vessel. Launched in 1937, she was a victim of a confusing period in the 1930s when post–First World War treaties limited the size and armament of naval vessels.[2] In an effort to conform to the treaties while still experimenting with new technologies, the Japanese had essentially built a carrier fleet by trial and error. Even as their first carriers rolled down the slipways, these vessels were already struggling to perform the job they had been built to do – aircraft technology was advancing so rapidly that planes became faster and heavier (and therefore required longer flight decks) more quickly than carriers could be built to accommodate them. This meant that the early Japanese carriers had to be constantly modified during their construction and in their early days at sea, resulting in a fleet that was certainly capable, but also possessing a range of compromises that made each of its ships unique, and slightly inadequate.

In the case of *Hiryu*, an experimental exhaust system could only be installed on the starboard side of the ship, in the place where a carrier's 'island' (the tower containing the bridge) would normally be located. Consequently, the island had to be shifted to the port side, a modification that only a handful of carriers would employ during the entire war. The port-side island didn't just look odd – pilots complained that it resulted in dangerous air turbulence on the flight deck, but investigations by Japanese naval authorities failed to confirm this. *Hiryu* carried a complement of 73 aircraft and was home to more than 1100 sailors. She was a small city at sea.

Before long Hanada and his crewmates heard the constant low rumble from the flight deck as the first attack wave departed. They untethered their Zero from its assigned place in the hangar and removed the wheel chocks. They waited as the crews in front of them began the tedious process of manually pushing each aircraft into the elevator and lifting it to the flight deck. The whole process was excruciatingly slow – by the time each aircraft was manhandled to the elevator, precisely loaded, elevated to the flight deck, unloaded and the elevator returned to the hangar, as much as a minute had passed per plane. It could take 20 minutes to move a hangar full of aircraft to the flight deck – not such an issue now in the calm of a surprise attack, but a nerve-shredding experience in the heat of battle, when every lost minute meant another chance for a torpedo to slam into the carrier.

Finally it was Hanada and his crewmates' turn. Grunting and sweating, they rolled their Zero to the elevator and positioned it under the barked orders of the crew chief. They then rode with the aircraft to the flight deck, unfolding the wingtips during the trip. Once topside, they repeated the process of rolling the aircraft off the elevator and hauling it to its assigned position on the flight deck, with fighters forward and bombers aft. The plane was retethered and the wheels chocked.

As Hanada climbed into the cockpit of the Zero, he noted armourers scurrying around the dive bombers on the rear of the flight deck, wheeling carts containing 250-kilogram armour-piercing bombs to their aircraft and attaching them to the plane's belly. Hanada settled into the cramped cockpit of the Zero and began the process of warming up the engine. This was a vital step and could not be cut short – radial engines were powerful and temperamental, and if not properly warmed up they could fail spectacularly (and for the pilot, fatally) under the stresses of a full-power take-off. In this process Hanada was at a distinct disadvantage to his opposite numbers on US carriers – their open hangars meant that aircraft engines could be warmed up below decks. It was not uncommon for American planes to taxi from the elevator to the flight deck under their own power, saving both precious time and the backs of the pusher crew. The poor ventilation in the enclosed hangars of Japanese carriers meant that its crews had no choice but to warm up engines on deck.

As Hanada prepared to fire up the engine, damage control teams surrounded the plane armed with fire extinguishers – a fire on a crowded deck among heavily fuelled and armed planes could spell disaster for the entire carrier. Hanada flicked the ignition switches, and a crewmember hand-cranked the engine from the right-hand side. As the engine began to turn over, the crank man urgently retreated and, with a shout of '*Kontaaku!* (Contact!)', Hanada engaged the engine. With a cough and burst of white smoke, the 14-cylinder, thousand-horsepower powerhouse roared to life.

Hanada kept the engine idling in low revs as he allowed time for oil to fully circulate, and checked the gauges to make sure all was as it should be. He then cautiously opened up the engine to full power. As the engine bellowed, the plane strained furiously against its chocked wheels – Hanada was thankful he wasn't performing this procedure on land, where he would have had to use all his leg strength to hold the plane's brakes against the powerful forward thrust. He let the engine roar at full power for over a minute while he checked the radios and surface controls. All across the flight deck dozens of other engines were roaring into life, and the din became ferocious, all-consuming. By the time Hanada eased the power back to idle, confident that the plane was ready for take-off, he had been in the cockpit for more than 15 minutes, and was soaked with sweat. The pilot appeared as Hanada was climbing down from the aircraft, and brushed past him with barely a nod. The airman had other things on his mind.*

— —

Petty Officer Hajime Toyoshima ate breakfast in the crew briefing room with his fellow pilots at 3 a.m. The room was cramped and hot; there were no windows, and the thick air carried a peculiar aroma of fresh paint, gasoline fumes and sweat. The squadron leader briefed them on their role in the upcoming attack – to his immense disappointment, Toyoshima would not be flying in the attack waves. His Zero had been assigned to Combat Air Patrol – he would spend the morning in the skies above the carrier fleet, protecting it from enemy attack. It was vital work – no carrier could operate without a protective screen of fighters – but Toyoshima felt a pang of disappointment flare in his chest when he heard the news. Regardless, he was a loyal airman, and he would do his duty as he had been called to. There was no bigger day for the Japanese Navy, and he knew the eyes of the entire Empire were upon them.

The command of 'Airmen, line up!' blared through the loudspeakers and Toyoshima sprang to his feet. He joined his squadron as they climbed the companionway up to the flight deck, their faces set in a mix of concentration and tension. This was the first combat mission for most of them, and their nerves showed.

As they stepped into the glare of the flight deck, they were already sweating in their heavy cotton flight suits and helmets. Aircraft engines roared all around them, and flight crews

---

* Hanada's war would be a short one. He was lost along with more than 350 crewmates when *Hiryu* was sunk during the Battle of Midway in June 1942.

scurried between chocked planes. The pilots crowded around blackboards on the edge of the flight deck as their officer issued final details and instructions – he had to yell to be heard above the din of the flight deck.

Then, with a cry of *'Tennoheika Banzai!* (Long live the Emperor!)' and a collective cheer, the pilots turned and ran to their steel steeds. From now on, they would be on their own. Toyoshima did not notice the crewman who brushed past him as he headed for his plane. He climbed the ladder and settled in to the cramped grey-green cockpit, running a hand over the familiar surfaces and lightly gripping the control stick. The engine growled – the crew had done a good job preparing the plane – and Toyoshima could feel the ferocious power of the machine surging through his seat, straining to be unleashed. His time had come.

2

'I JAMMED THE THROTTLE WIDE OPEN': THE FLYGIRL

Cornelia Fort met her student on the runway beside the Interstate Cadet aircraft that she used for most of her flying lessons. The small, fabric-covered plane looked fragile compared to the muscled military aircraft that often surrounded it, but it was a solid flying platform and the perfect craft for teaching nervy students the mechanics of flight. Since arriving in Honolulu, on the island of Oahu, three months before, Fort had logged more than 300 hours of flying time, nearly all of them in this Cadet, and most of them as an instructor.

Fort was tall and athletic, and had grown up as the only daughter of a wealthy family in Nashville. But she had never been much of a debutante, and from an early age had dreamt of adventure far beyond the claustrophobic social circles of her hometown. By the time she was 15 she wanted to fly, and by 19 she had qualified as a pilot. Now, at 22, she was one of a handful of female flight instructors in the USA.

Her student was a defence worker named Ernest Suomala, who had completed several lessons and was soon due for a solo flight. Today they would be practising touch-and-go landings, and Fort had set an early take-off time – 6.30 a.m. – to take advantage of the still morning air and to avoid the 'crowds of Sunday afternooners who wanted to go flight-seeing around the island'.[3]

Soon after take-off, Suomala was at the controls and was lining up his approach when Fort saw an aircraft, fast-moving and obviously military, coming at them from the sea. As her aircraft was clearly civilian and had right of way, she instructed Suomala to stay his course. The military plane closed the gap until it was close – too close.

Fort had seen this sort of thing before. Oahu was home to five military air bases, and most of them were made up of young, new pilots. A combination of overconfidence, inexperience and an immortality complex was a dangerous cocktail in the young fliers, and close encounters were not uncommon. But even by those standards, this guy was being cocky. He was coming straight at them, and fast.

'I jerked the controls away from my student and jammed the throttle wide open to pull above the oncoming plane,' Fort later recalled. 'He passed so close under us that our celluloid windows rattled violently, and I looked down to see what kind of plane it was.'[4]

She was startled to see not the familiar stars and bars of the US Army Air Corps on its wings but the red disc of the Empire of Japan. An instant later she saw dark tendrils of smoke curling above the naval base at Pearl Harbor, less than half a kilometre away, blotting out the morning sun and painting the sky in an eerie fog of grey and red. A formation of silver bombers was coming in high overhead, unleashing its deadly payload on the ships below. Fort recognised what was happening, and the danger she and her student were in. She banked hard for the airstrip and descended quickly. Suomala, unaware of the situation unfolding around them, asked when he would be able to fly solo. 'Not today, brother!' came the terse reply, and Fort dived for the runway. They landed hard, skidding to a halt beside the hangars, and as she and Suomala ran from the plane a Japanese Zero strafed the runway, the cannon fire sending up splintered chunks of asphalt. By the time they reached the safety of the hangar, wide-eyed and gasping, Pearl Harbor was already in flames.*

— —

In the blindingly blue skies above *Hiryu*, Hajime Toyoshima banked his Zero and began another circuit over the fleet. He scanned the water and sky for ships or planes. Being alone in an aircraft over a huge expanse of ocean, nerves taut with the anticipation of encountering the enemy, was an exceedingly lonely job, and Toyoshima was tempted to put a call out over the radio, just to hear the comforting sound of another voice. He resisted, but some of his fellow fliers were not as disciplined and his radio buzzed with nervous and unnecessary chatter.

---

*   Cornelia Fort left Hawaii in early 1942. In September 1943 she became one of the first recruits in the newly formed Women's Auxiliary Ferrying Squadron. Her new role gave her the opportunity to fly a range of military aircraft from factories to airbases across the US, and she was ecstatic to be contributing to the war effort. 'The heavens have opened up and rained blessings on me,' she wrote in a cable to her mother. 'The army has decided to let women ferry ships and I'm going to be one of them.' She only flew with the squadron for five months – she was killed in an air crash in March 1943, aged 24, and is buried in the family plot in Nashville. Her headstone bears the inscription 'Killed in the service of her country'.

'Takahashi, how does it look out your way?'
'Looks like some clouds rolling in from the east.'
'Radio check. Can you read me?'
'I'll bet the Americans don't feel so cocky now ...'

Eventually the flight officer stepped in and ordered radio silence. With so much mindless chatter clogging the airwaves, there was a genuine risk that an all-important sighting report of enemy ships or planes would be missed, a potentially fatal scenario for the fleet. The silence was unnerving. Toyoshima continued scouting, and continued scanning.

Four hours later, he was back on the deck of *Hiryu*. The ship buzzed with pilots recounting stories of screaming bombing dives and wavetop torpedo runs. Nearly all the pilots had returned – the attack had been a complete surprise and had obviously been devastating for the enemy. Toyoshima had not seen an enemy plane – the attack had been carried out so successfully that the Americans never worked out where the Japanese fleet even was – but no matter. He knew he was part of something big, and that he would get more opportunities in this war. He ate a quick meal, and then retired to his bunk where he fell into a deep and contented sleep.

3

'THE HARBOUR AN INFERNO': THE BOMBING OF DARWIN

Jack Mulholland was a 19-year-old bank teller from Sydney when he enlisted in the Australian Imperial Force (AIF) in 1940. Now, two years later, he was a gunner on an ancient 3-inch anti-aircraft gun, tasked with protecting the most inhospitable outpost in Australia – the port town of Darwin. Darwin was as far from civilisation as a town could be – closer to Singapore than it was to Sydney, in the 1940s it existed only as a waypoint for ships plying the Arafura and Timor seas. Merchantmen, heavy with spices, rubber, teak and oil from the Dutch East Indies, found refuge from savage tropical tempests in its welcoming harbour, and a telegraph line snaked into the sea on the foreshore, connecting Singapore to the far-flung outposts of the former British Empire in Adelaide and Melbourne.

In 1942 Darwin was the only place in Australia that could be considered truly multicultural, and was 'peopled by Aborigines, Chinese, Japanese, Greeks, Afghans, Eurasians, Europeans and so on',[5] Mulholland recounted in his memoir.

17

'They appeared to be living in harmony, most likely bonded together by their isolation and the adverse conditions under which they worked and lived. It was as if they were a separate race of people with their own administration, interpretations of the law and general lifestyle.'

The town had been established in the mid-nineteenth century, basically because a town had to go *somewhere* to administer the vast territory that ran from South Australia to the northern coast of the continent. Named by the commander of HMS *Beagle* in 1839 after the famous naturalist who had sailed with the ship on its previous voyage, Darwin offered a good anchorage, a supply of fresh water and pretty much nothing else. The telegraph line brought workers from the south, and the discovery of gold (when postholes for the telegraph line sheared into the rich reefs) brought prospectors from everywhere else. By the middle of the twentieth century, Darwin was a melting pot of fishermen, mine workers, pearl divers, timber-getters and businessmen.

It's an understatement that Jack Mulholland didn't like the place. In fairness, you can't blame him – when he arrived in December 1940 Darwin was hot, rough, remote and dull. It was also a very long way from the war – this was the time when German and British bombers were exchanging blows on nightly raids over the cities of Europe, and Allied and Axis forces were massing in North Africa. War with Japan was a year away, and Darwin couldn't have been further from the action. 'To me, Darwin appeared to be one of our last colonial frontier towns or settlements,' Mulholland wrote decades later, with just a forgivable dash of hyperbole.

According to the Oxford dictionary, 'Colonial' seems to be the correct description. Frontier is defined as that part of a country that borders on another. That definition did not apply to Darwin but to me it did border on the unknown in all directions and was unlike anything else I knew in Australia ... Darwin is still a long way from anywhere but in 1940 it was a great deal further.[6]

It wasn't just the town's remoteness that left its mark on Mulholland. The environment was harsh and unpredictable, and the vagaries of a tropical wet season were completely alien to a boy from Sydney.

The town was scruffy, dirty and hot. Air conditioning and swimming pools were things of the future and the town baths were a fenced-in area of the harbour at the foot of the cliff close to the Oval. At high tide there was plenty of water for swimming, but at low tide the water's edge was hundreds of yards beyond the mud flats as high and low tides varied by up to about 30 feet. The troops often swam in the open sea especially when on the beaches filling sand bags. No-one was aware of the dangers of Box Jellyfish or Stone Fish.[7]

Fat tropical mosquitoes were a constant irritant, and the weather at the height of the wet season stretched men to their limits. 'The humidity was already a cloying blanket of invisible moisture,' Mulholland wrote. 'It seemed to have so much substance that I felt that I could almost bite off a chunk of the atmosphere. It was an all-enveloping and unrelenting addition to the perpetual heat.'[8]

By the end of 1941 Mulholland and his gunner mates had been in Darwin for a year, and the diversions of the town had well and truly worn thin. Mulholland's days were made up of drilling and digging, and the nights of mind-numbing guard duty. Days off were devoted to laundry, letter-writing and the odd game of cricket, hockey or football. It was a tedious war. About the only entertainment worthy of the name came from watching drunks get tossed out of the Darwin Hotel across the road from the gun site at the town oval. At least the old First World War–era guns had been removed, and new and efficient 3.7-inch anti-aircraft guns were installed in their place. If the war ever reached them, at least now they would have something to shoot back with.

And then, suddenly, shockingly, in December 1941 everything changed. Looking back, Mulholland couldn't recall exactly when the news of the attack on Pearl Harbor reached them, but when it did it prompted a flurry of activity. As news of the Japanese advance through the Pacific filtered in, Darwin was thrust from isolated outpost to front-line bastion. Its sleepy harbour and airfield were suddenly recast as vital assets in the new Pacific War, and their defence became a priority. Mulholland and his mates were ordered to carry sidearms with them wherever they went in the town, and were set to work beefing up the defences of the gun pits. The population of Darwin began to swell as army, navy and air force personnel were shipped in to form the front line of defence in Australia's new war. Civilians were evacuated and, for the first time, Mulholland heard American accents among the throng of voices in the mess halls. US ships soon crowded the harbour, and the stars-and-bars insignia of their warplanes became a common sight on the airfield. The meagre infrastructure of the town couldn't cope with the influx of personnel, and soon food began to run short. Worse still, cold beer became impossible to find, and a black market for both food and alcohol was soon doing a brisk trade, but then even that source ran dry. 'The prospect of life without a cold ale or two in the evenings', wrote Mulholland, 'did nothing to enhance life in the Top End. We had previously thought life was lacking in many things but now we realised it was going to be much worse.' In 1941 Christmas and New Year's Eve celebrations were dull affairs in Darwin.

The morning of 19 February 1942 dawned hot and bright. It would almost certainly rain that afternoon, but as he manned his post in the gun pit, Mulholland was happy to feel the sun on his face. Life in the Top End wasn't exactly enjoyable, but it was bearable.

Mulholland and his gun team had eaten an unpalatable but filling breakfast of powdered eggs, and had begun the seemingly never-ending job of strengthening the gun pit. As Mulholland and his mates stacked sandbags, another crew nearby was practising sighting on distant targets. One man peered down the telescope, scanned the skies for something to aim at, and was happy to spot a group of aircraft closing in from the south-east. Assuming them to be a flight of Kittyhawks or Wirraways from the airfield, he adjusted the focus knob to bring them sharply into view. 'Hell!' he called out. 'They've got bloody red spots on their wings!' At about the same time a radioman heard urgent shouts over the airwaves from a US pilot who was being attacked by enemy planes over the ocean. The line went dead. The radioman wasted no time and sounded the alarm. It was 10 a.m.

Mulholland and his crew took their positions on the gun with haste but not alarm – they had been through dozens of false alarms since the Pearl Harbor attack, and Mulholland was relieved he'd grabbed a pack of smokes and a paperback western as he'd rushed to the gun. At least he'd have something to do while waiting for the all-clear. Both the book and the smokes would remain untouched that morning.

As the alarm continued to wail, the air suddenly filled with the roar of aircraft engines. There were hundreds of them – far more than Mulholland had heard before, and far more than he knew the Allies had stationed in Darwin. 'The sky seemed to be full of white crosses as the heavy bombers streamed across in their formations,' he said. 'The clear skies over Darwin are always so blue and the enemy planes looked like a neat cemetery advancing across a blue field.'[9]

His crew didn't need to be given orders – they swung into action, training and instinct instantly kicking in. They had never fired their gun before, but they knew what to do. The first shots from the gun battery arced skywards and passed the first wave of falling bombs in mid-air. The guns began to fire fast and independently as they homed in on a seemingly limitless number of targets above them. At the same time, bombs began crashing into the town and harbour. The noise became ferocious, drowning out the sirens that were now blaring across Darwin. It was impossible to distinguish the blast of falling bombs from the roar of the firing guns. Mulholland's crew worked furiously to load and fire the gun:

> The gun pit was a frenzy of half naked sweaty bodies doing what they had been trained to do.
>
> 'Fire!', was called by the Number One, and Number Five forced the firing lever to the rear. The whole gun seemed to jump with the long barrel recoiling and the spent case being extracted to the rear. Those who were at the rear of the gun did a 'soft shoe shuffle' as they dodged the hot, empty cases, then picked them up and hurled them over the top of the revetment. The pit was hotter than usual, the air foul with the fumes of burnt explosives, dust and smoke – the whole dominated by the thunderous roar of gunfire and exploding bombs.[10]

The buildings in Darwin were designed to provide comfort in the tropical heat, and were only lightly constructed – they could stand up to a tropical storm, but nothing like this. Masonry and fibro were flung into the air as the bombs smashed into the heart of the town. Government House took a couple of heavy hits, then the post office disintegrated. Mulholland watched a dozen bombs fall in a perfectly straight line, the trail of destruction heading straight towards him and his gun site. 'A pattern of bombs stopped just short of our guns,' he said, 'the last being close enough to shower us with rocks and debris. One rock smashed the top of our wall and bounced through the gun pit without hitting anyone.'[11]

It wasn't just the town that was copping a pounding. The warships in the harbour were the key prize for Japanese bombs, and dive bombers, crewed by the same pilots who had set Pearl Harbor ablaze only ten weeks before, began screaming out of the sky. Zero fighters swooped in low and fast, strafing the burning ships and wharf with cannon fire. From his clifftop position at the oval, Mulholland had a grandstand view of the destruction.

The harbour was a storm of water rising like geysers and a good area of it was covered with burning oil. Ships were at anchor and could not, or did not have time, to take evasive action. Many ships were being hit by the dive bombers causing columns of smoke to rise in the air.[12]

Mulholland's crew lowered their gun to aim at the dive bombers streaking towards the ships. They had no hope of hitting such small targets – all they could do was fire a protective curtain of shells above the ships. The muzzle of the gun was eventually so low that dirt flew up from the revetment each time they fired.

'As a bomber pulled out of its dive,' Mulholland later wrote, 'one of our shells burst near its nose, sending the crippled aircraft side slipping into the harbour.'

Mulholland's whole world was consumed in a cacophony of noise – roaring aircraft engines, planes screaming into dives, exploding bombs and gunfire from the shore as every anti-aircraft gun, artillery piece and rifle in Darwin unloaded at the mass of Japanese aircraft.

Then suddenly, all was quiet. Mulholland couldn't pinpoint the moment the Japanese called off the attack, but within minutes the bombing stopped, and the enemy formations were disappearing over the horizon. One minute the aircraft were spewing death and destruction, and the next minute they were gone. 'All that remained of their visit were the fires, smoke, dust, the harbour an inferno and an uncanny dazed feeling that it was all unreal.'

Mulholland and his crew emerged zombie-like from their gun pit, their eyes stinging from fumes and dust, their ears ringing from the roar of the guns, their throats hoarse from shouting. They surveyed the scene – the smoke, the dust, the burning ships, the shattered buildings. After the savage ferocity of the attack the whole chaotic scene was eerily quiet. Mulholland lowered his face into his filthy hands.

4

'I WAS THE FIRST ONE TO SEE THE JAPANEE MAN': THE ZERO PILOT

In the skies above Darwin, Petty Officer Hajime Toyoshima banked his Zero fighter north and began the long flight back to his carrier. Smoke curled skyward in lazy columns all around him, and the sea below wore a thick coat of oil. The attack had obviously gone very well. Toyoshima was slightly disappointed that he had not had the opportunity to play a greater role – he and the 35 other Japanese fighters had been primarily tasked with engaging enemy fighters to protect the bomber force. Problem was, there hadn't been any enemy fighters to engage with. At one point Toyoshima had glimpsed an enemy plane lifting off from an airfield in the distance, but his fighter comrades had swarmed on it like angry bees, and it hadn't even completed its climb before crashing to earth in flames. Toyoshima had gained a measure of satisfaction from strafing the wharf and a couple of enemy ships with his 20 mm cannons, but at the end of the raid he had only exhausted half his ammunition – with luck he would come across an enemy plane on the return journey and give the cannons an opportunity to do the job they were designed for.

His Zero had performed well – like all navy planes that had seen a lot of service, it had a few peculiar peccadilloes, but Toyoshima knew the plane and its quirks well. At one point during the raid he had swooped low over the enemy airfield and had been caught off guard when a burst of anti-aircraft fire had sliced close to his starboard wing – a little too close, if he was honest with himself – and he suspected that a few rounds may have kissed the Zero's underside. Just another minor repair to be made by the flight mechanics once back on deck.

He adjusted his heading towards the carrier group, and confirmed his bearings on his map as he approached a large, scrub-covered island, the same one he had flown over on the approach run. He adjusted the throttle and eased back in his seat. A quick scan of the dials revealed all was as it should be; his oil pressure was a little low, but that was pretty standard for this Zero. It drank like a thirsty carp.

Suddenly the Zero began to shudder violently. Tendrils of ugly brown-black smoke began to curl from under the nose cowling, and the engine began to whine shrilly. Within seconds the noise was deafening, drowning out the low roar of the radial engine. The control stick jerked in Toyoshima's hand, and the whine from the engine seemed to grow even louder. Toyoshima knew something was seriously – perhaps fatally – wrong with his aircraft, and he instinctively began a slow descent. Thank God he was over the island now – if the worst happened, at least he wouldn't have to ditch in the ocean. The whining grew in pitch and volume, and then the engine of the Zero disintegrated. Toyoshima didn't know it, but one lucky .303 round fired from the anti-aircraft machine-gun had struck the nose of the plane, passing completely through the fuselage and blowing out the opposite panel. It had also sliced clean through the line that fed oil to the engine – for the past ten minutes the Zero had been leaking lifeblood.

As the last of the oil seeped from the engine, the 14 cylinders seized, and the engine tore itself apart. Jagged chunks of severed metal ripped through the aircraft's nose. With a tortured howl the propeller jerked to a stop, vibrated violently and groaned for half a second, and then sheared off completely. Toyoshima briefly considered bailing out but realised that the plane was still marginally in his control, although gliding towards the island at a disconcerting speed. Deciding that a belly landing was the best of his limited options, Toyoshima fought to keep the nose up as he scanned the scrub beneath him for a safe landing spot. He kept the undercarriage raised, knowing that the aircraft's wheels were useless in this situation, and fearful they would dig in on impact and flip the plane. He tightened his harness straps, held the nose as high as he dared, and braced for impact.

The Zero came in hard, bouncing off a patch of mangrove scrub and pitching nose-first into the dirt. The starboard wing connected with a thin stringybark, and the entire plane spun to the right. Toyoshima was thrown against the canopy, then back in his seat, and then violently forward, his face colliding heavily with the gunsight. The plane lurched to a stop. After the fury of the crash, Toyoshima was engulfed in sudden silence, the only noise the low chirping of insects and a soft *tick-tick* from the shattered engine.

Toyoshima lay dazed for several minutes, passing in and out of consciousness. Eventually he came to and surveyed his situation. The plane was obviously wrecked, but he was still in one piece. His head throbbed, and when he ran a hand across his face it came back soaked with blood from a deep gash above his right eye. But apart from that, miraculously, he was uninjured. He grabbed his map and his .32-calibre pistol, and stuffed them into pockets in his flying suit, then slid the canopy open. He knew that his plane and its pilot would be highly prized possessions for the enemy so early in the war, and he was eager to put as much distance between himself and the wreck as possible. He also knew that his fellow Zero pilots would have seen his stricken aircraft plunging to earth, and that a search party would be dispatched to look for him. He needed to get to the coast.

Unfortunately for Toyoshima, the coast was a long way away. Melville Island isn't just big – it's enormous. It's the second-largest island in Australia (after Tasmania) and comprises 6000 square kilometres of unrelenting tropical torment. Thick eucalypt forests blanket much of the island, and dense scrub covers the rest. Rivers and creeks crisscross the island like scars, and sodden mudflats and mangroves ring the coast. Saltwater crocodiles grow big and angry in the estuaries, gorging themselves on a bountiful diet of barramundi and water buffalo. The island's insects are fat and aggressive, and delight in sinking a barbed stinger or razor-sharp mandible into human flesh. Bats swoop overhead, and snakes slither underfoot. The island's native people, the Tiwi, have lived there for thousands of years, their genetics and culture moulded by their isolation into a society unique in the world. Even they struggle to tame this rugged outpost in the Arafura Sea. In short, Melville Island is a bad place to be stranded.

Toyoshima briefly considered trying to torch the wreck of his plane, but quickly abandoned the idea. Although the fuel tanks were still half full, he had nothing to light a fire with, and would waste valuable time on what was probably a futile endeavour. For all he knew the enemy had seen the crash, and search parties would be closing in on him with every minute that passed. He struck out from the wreck site, heading roughly northwards, towards where he thought the coast would be. He was bruised and sore but, apart from the cut above his eye, he appeared to have survived the crash landing with barely a scratch.

The going was tough in the thick bush – Toyoshima had to constantly change direction to move around fallen trees and thick patches of acacia scrub. The sun was merciless, even under the thick canopy of the paperbarks, and he was overjoyed when a sudden wet season downpour allowed him a much-needed drink. On the first day he strode with purpose, confident he would soon reach the coast and make contact with a rescue party. By the second day he walked more slowly, losing both motivation and direction. His flight suit was ripped by thorns, his body ached, and he was getting hungry. He sustained himself on a meagre diet of mud snails and bush plums, but by the third day he was growing delirious and desperate.

That afternoon he lurched into a clearing by a small creek; in front of him stood a small child, about nine or ten years old, cradling a baby in his arms. A group of women and more children stepped into the clearing from the far side – Toyoshima had stumbled on a group of local Tiwi women who were collecting honey from wild bees' nests. It's difficult to say who was more startled – the Japanese pilot half mad from thirst and exposure or the local women, confronted by a filthy stranger in a bulky flight suit. The encounter was so exciting for the Tiwi women that one of them, 'Missus Aloysius', did something she had never done before – she wrote a letter to friends who had missed the action.

I was the first one to see the Japanee man. My friends were out looking for honey nest. I was minding all the babies. The babies were all playing and when one boy see the Japanee he yelled. Then that Japanee came to me and he salute me. I got properly big fright, all right. I ran away from the Japanee man. He picked up a baby and went into the bush with him. I found my friends and went looking for that Japanee man and we found him with that baby in his arms. One of my friends went to him and took her baby away from him. He asked if the baby belongest to her, and he put his hand in his pocket and took out a watch and gave it to the boy. We asked him where are all his friends, but he didn't answer.[13]

The women and children retreated into the bush, apparently with some haste – 'we never give our legs a chance to stop running,' said Beatrice Piampireiu.[14] The exhausted Toyoshima collapsed against a tree. He slept fitfully throughout the night. In the morning, just as the sun was rising, he saw a group of local people approaching him through the clearing. The women had reported their strange encounter and sought help; now a group led by 21-year-old Matthias Ngapiatulwai returned to search for the stranger. They didn't have to look far – Toyoshima was right where the women had left him the previous day. The Tiwi people had met Japanese before – pearl divers were common in Darwin and the islands in the days before the war – and through sign language they indicated to Toyoshima that he was now a prisoner; Ngapiatulwai prodded Toyoshima in the back with the handle of a tomahawk until he put his hands up. The exhausted airman gave up without a fight, and Ngapiatulwai relieved him of his pistol and map. Somewhat comically, he also forced Toyoshima to remove his flight suit – Toyoshima's humiliation was now complete as he was marched through the bush by the Tiwi men clad only in his cotton undershirt, underwear and flying boots. Toyoshima begged for the map to be returned to him so he could destroy it, but his captors refused to acquiesce. He was escorted back to the Tiwi camp near the coast, and then bundled into a small canoe. He was rowed across Apsley Strait to neighbouring Bathurst Island, where there was a small Australian airfield. 'We came to RAAF [Royal Australian Air Force] place,' Ngapiatulwai later said.

> Might be five or six Australians there. Wireless him there. Jap put inside on chair, he get tucker ... I put camera, map cloth on table then go and sit outside. I could not understand. I thought they would shoot him for Jap humbugging Darwin and mission [i.e. bombing Darwin and the Catholic mission on Melville Island]. Father McGrath rides up on horse; he said in my language 'Yirringkirityiri'. That is, 'he got properly ugly face'. I have a good laugh.

Toyoshima was handed over to Australian Army Sergeant Les Powell, who had been sent to Bathurst Island to plant mines in the airstrip, with orders to blow the place sky-high in the event of a Japanese landing. A photo taken that day shows a triumphant Powell, shirtless with Toyoshima's pistol in hand, standing alongside the dejected pilot, still clad in his undergarments, his face bandaged and bloodied. Over the next couple of days Toyoshima lived with the Australians at the airstrip under loose guard. They communicated via hand signals and 'pidgin Japanese', and Toyoshima wrote basic English phrases and their Japanese equivalents on a scrap of paper – his first English lessons. After two days he was transferred under guard to Darwin, where he was held for a week or so and interrogated on at least three occasions.

Toyoshima was a shrewd operator – he knew that a Zero pilot would be an intelligence coup for his enemy, and that he would be interrogated relentlessly about his aircraft and its capabilities, so he had spent his days roaming Melville Island concocting a story to disguise his true identity. He was also beginning to feel the first pangs of shame at having been taken prisoner, and was determined that his family in Kanagawa did not learn of his fate. He presented himself as Sergeant Major Tadao Minami – it's unclear how he came up with the surname, but one of his brothers at home was called Tadao.

The story he fed his interrogators was improbable, to say the least. He told them he was an army air gunner on a land-based bomber that had flown out of Ambon and caught fire on the approach run to Darwin, forcing its crew to bail out. The new Minami claimed he did not recall using a parachute and had swum to Bathurst Island, where he was picked up by the Tiwi group. He assumed the rest of the crew had been killed.

Ostensibly this was a clever cover story: he had given a close approximation of his naval rank and hadn't tried to cover up the fact that he was an airman. And a large force of army bombers *had* taken part in the Darwin raid – it was plausible that one or more may have crashed en route to the target. Where the story started to unravel was in the detail – understandably Toyoshima had extremely limited knowledge of an aircraft he had never flown in, and the information he revealed was rudimentary, and often plain wrong. It seems that he couldn't even decide exactly what type of aircraft he had flown in, and settled on a strange hybrid. He variously referred to it as a 'Type 96' or 'Type 97' bomber (no doubt inspired by the Type 97 navy bombers he was familiar with that flew off the carriers). He described it as having twin rudders and engines, seemingly basing his recollections on the Type 96 land-based bomber (which coincidentally had participated in the Darwin raid), but there was no Japanese aircraft in operation that accurately matched his description. His detailing of the operation of his machine-gun, including its field of fire and an inclination to frequently misfire, as well as the bomb loadout of the plane, appears to have been completely made up. When pressed about distinguishing features of different aircraft types, his story unravelled. His interrogators reported that the prisoner

'did not know any way of distinguishing between the various models of the same type of aircraft. He had never heard of a "Type 97 Mark I", "Type 97 Mark II", and so on. If any improvements were made, he did not know how this fact would be indicated.'[15]

That's a fair statement for someone who has no working knowledge of an aircraft he professes to operate; for a genuine crewman whose life depended on knowing the capabilities of his plane, that suggestion is ludicrous.

When asked if he had experience with any new models of aircraft, he responded that he had seen a new bomber in action that was called the 'Shinjubaku'. The literal translation of that word, the report noted without apparent suspicion, was simply 'New Heavy Bomber'. His description of Japanese squadron structure and aircraft call signs was fairly accurate – probably because it was simply too complex to invent on the fly. Strangely, he was questioned about whether there were any German pilots in the Japanese forces, or German instructors training Japanese airmen. Toyoshima's surprise at being asked about this unlikely scenario was no doubt completely unfeigned. Finally, he was asked what he knew about New Guinea – his response, that he 'had never heard of it', should have raised more than a few red flags. The suggestion that an airman who had flown out of an Indonesian island had never even heard of the largest landmass in the area, located only 500 kilometres from his base, stretches incredulity levels to breaking point. The game should have been completely given away when interrogators found among Toyoshima's small quantity of possessions a good-luck token with the word 'Hiryu', the name of Toyoshima's aircraft carrier, written on it. Toyoshima explained it away by saying it had been a gift from a crewmember of that ship, a clearly bogus story that the Australian interviewers swallowed with gusto.

Fortunately for Toyoshima, Australian intelligence about Japanese aircraft characteristics and air operations was extremely limited this early in the war (which was precisely why Toyoshima was so determined to hide his true role from his captors), and so his story was accepted without too much scrutiny. His interrogators also appear to be suffering from a preconceived bias based on the propaganda of the 'primitive Jap', which made them gullible to Toyoshima's fabrications. 'He talked easily, was unselfconscious, and gave the impression of speaking the truth so far as he knew it,' his interrogator reported. 'His knowledge of his own job was adequate; his knowledge of and, apparently, interest in extraneous matters practically nil. This is considered to be consistent with his type – a peasant farmer.'[16]

When asked about his life before the war, Toyoshima claimed that he hated being in the army and longed to return to civilian life – which explains why he had paid so little attention to the technicalities of his training.

When asked about how he felt about becoming a prisoner, Toyoshima dropped the charade. 'The P.O.W. did not wish to be sent back to Japan,' the report stated. 'He thought that his friends would not want to have anything to do with him because he had been taken prisoner, and that he would not be regarded as a good character … He asked if [we] intended to kill him.'

What Toyoshima didn't know is that his efforts to throw the Australians off the trail of his Zero were in vain – about the same time that he was offering vivid accounts of a life he had never lived, his wrecked aircraft was discovered by local people near a place called Kaprimili Creek, and within days they had escorted a team from the RAAF to the site. This was the first largely intact Japanese Zero to fall into Allied hands, and it is impossible to overstate the interest it generated among Allied nations. The manufacturer's plate revealed that it had rolled off the assembly line of the Mitsubishi Heavy Industry Company in Nagoya on 4 October 1941, with serial number 5349. Its tail markings ('BII-124') revealed that it was a navy aircraft, so must have flown off a carrier, but the code did not reveal precisely which carrier the plane belonged to.

The plane was broken down and lugged out of the bush, eventually arriving back on the mainland where it was thoroughly examined, and extensive intelligence was gained about the capabilities of the Japanese fighter. Curiously, a drop tank was also examined along with the Zero's wreckage – it's unclear whether this came from Toyoshima's plane or was recovered separately. It's conceivable it may have come from Toyoshima's Zero – contrary to popular belief, Japanese drop tanks were not routinely jettisoned when a plane went into action. They were very highly engineered (probably over-engineered) and therefore expensive and difficult to replace, particularly at remote Pacific bases on the outer limits of the Japanese Empire. Pilots were ordered to jettison drop tanks only in emergencies, and even the nimble Zeros (whose manoeuvrability would be compromised by the drop tank and whose pilots, therefore, were the most likely to jettison them) routinely returned from missions still carrying their expended tanks. Toyoshima's crash landing would certainly constitute an emergency, but in the panic of a forced landing, jettisoning a fuel tank would have been the last thing on his mind.

Unbelievably, Australian authorities never linked Toyoshima with the recovered Zero, and never woke up to the glittering intelligence prize that, thanks to a small group of Tiwi people, they now held in their hands. It seems inconceivable: within the space of a few days, a lone Japanese airman had been captured wandering around in the bush, and a pilot-less Zero fighter had been recovered from almost the same spot. And yet no Australian appears to have joined the dots. No one even seems to have pondered what happened to the pilot who crash-landed the Zero. It wasn't until the 1960s that Japanese researchers even discovered that Toyoshima and Minami were the same person. (This was confirmed when Japanese survivors of the Breakout were shown photographs of Toyoshima taken before his capture and confirmed this was the man they had known as Minami at Cowra.)

Now that Australian authorities had a Japanese prisoner, they appeared to be somewhat at a loss for what to do with him. Toyoshima was taken into custody with prisoner number PWJ 110001, signifying that he was the first Japanese to be taken prisoner by Australians in the Second World War. After being interrogated in Darwin, he was sent to Melbourne, where he was confined in the cells at Army Headquarters at Victoria Barracks. There he formed an unexpected, and somewhat touching, friendship with an Australian guard.

Leading Aircraftman Sam Shallard had been a teacher and real estate agent before the war, and had enlisted in the RAAF in 1941. At 32 he was older than most of the men he signed up with, and during his training it was noted that he was a 'particularly good type of N.C.O. Has quiet, efficient manner, good appearance, very sincere type.'[17] He had joined the RAAF's Service Police and in 1942 was posted to Melbourne, where he was put in charge of guarding the new Japanese prisoner who had just been brought in. His quiet manner and sincerity apparently shone through because he quickly endeared himself to Toyoshima, and over the course of four weeks the two men formed an unlikely bond. Shallard taught Toyoshima basic English phrases, which Toyoshima scribbled in Shallard's diary, expanding the basics of English he had picked up on Bathurst Island. The men played badminton together, and shared stories about their families and lives before the war. In a relaxed moment, Shallard snapped a picture of Toyoshima standing outside his cell, his head shaved but the airman looking fit and healthy.

When students of the Cowra Breakout study Hajime Toyoshima, he is often depicted as a menacing and brooding character, a dangerous fanatic who lived by a strict code of military discipline. He glares defiantly at the camera in the few photos that exist of him after his capture. But Sam Shallard encountered a very different man. To Shallard, Toyoshima was fit and athletic; he was intelligent and personable, with a knack for languages that enabled him to learn rudimentary English in the short time he spent in Melbourne.

In quiet moments Toyoshima spoke to Shallard about his life before the war. He 'always spoke of the impossibility of returning to Japan, whatever the outcome of the war', Shallard recalled decades later, 'as he had disgraced his country, Emperor and family by being captured and there would be no place for him in the future of his country or family'.[18]

At the end of his brief stay in Melbourne, Toyoshima took the diary he had been using to practise his English and wrote a touching note to Shallard, which hints at the fate that awaited him in Cowra. The note was written informally, so several interpretations have been made of its English translation, but it most likely says:

Dear Sam Shallard,
Thank you very much for your help in recent times. I really appreciate your kindness and hospitality. I have enjoyed my time with you, especially our Japanese lessons. Well, good health and please work for your country. I would like to thank you for all the help you have given me during my stay. I have lived a very healthy life, but I am ready to die soon. I think of my mother back home and I hear her wish that I die with grace. So farewell. If you pity a death at 25, you will pity dying at 50, and even if you live to be 100, you will think you have had a short life. If you do not die in a worthwhile way, you can never die a good death. I shot down two twin-engine aircraft, so I have no regrets.[19]

He signed the note in Japanese, and then added in neat lower-case script the English version of his false name: *minami tadao*. Next to this he added in Japanese the words of possibly the most famous Japanese haiku, composed by the poet Matsuo Basho in 1686: 'The old pond, a frog leaps in, sound of the water.' Why did Toyoshima choose these words? The haiku is often interpreted as a metaphor for deep inward reflection; this would certainly be appropriate in Toyoshima's case – after more than a month in captivity, he had had plenty of time to reflect on his new life and future. There is no doubt the entire letter reveals that Toyoshima was in a deeply philosophical frame of mind by the time he left Melbourne.

There has been much speculation over the decades as to the meaning of the letter. The gratitude for the kind treatment he received from Shallard is clear, but parts of the letter are less easy to decipher. Toyoshima's reference to 'Japanese lessons' could possibly be an inside joke with Shallard, who of course taught Toyoshima English, not the other way around. Another explanation, given by Harry Gordon is his book *Voyage from Shame*, is that Toyoshima actually said 'the story of Japan', which Gordon took to mean that Shallard had been giving Toyoshima updates from the newspaper about Japan's progress in the war. Given that Japan's progress in early 1942 comprised inflicting a succession of crushing defeats on the Allies, it seems unlikely that an Australian soldier would be keen to share this devastating news with a Japanese prisoner, no matter how friendly they were.

The reference to Shallard working for his country appears to be a nod to duty from one warrior to another – they may be friends, but Toyoshima recognises that Shallard has an obligation to his country, and Toyoshima wishes him well in this endeavour.

The most intriguing part of the letter is the final sentence, where Toyoshima boasts that he shot down two planes. There's little reason for him to be making this up – the letter was private correspondence with a trusted confidant – and this revelation doesn't necessarily blow Toyoshima's cover. An air gunner on a bomber would have had nearly as many opportunities to shoot at enemy planes as a fighter pilot. The question is, when did this occur? Toyoshima hadn't fired a shot during the Pearl Harbor attack, and it's unlikely he had any airborne targets to shoot at over Darwin. His carrier had taken part in a number of smaller operations between the two, so perhaps Toyoshima's kills came at the expense of a couple of lonely Catalina crews over Wake or Palau. It's a question that can never be answered.

Regardless of these small mysteries, the letter is a fascinating insight into Toyoshima's state of mind after his capture. His philosophical mindset and resignation to his fate reveal a deep emotional trauma, but one he appears to have confronted and come to terms with. The reference to his mother and his conclusion that she would wish to see him die honourably are telling, and touching.

Toyoshima handed the diary back to Shallard, the two men shook hands, and parted ways. They never saw each other again. Shallard carried the diary and snapshot, along with his fond memories of his unlikely friend, with him for many years. It was only in the 1970s that he had the letter translated.

There is another fascinating chapter to Toyoshima's Melbourne stay that reinforces a thoughtful and sensitive side to his nature. By March 1942 word of his capture and arrival in the Victorian capital had spread quickly among the local population, and caused a buzz of excitement. Lionel Bell, a 12-year-old boy from Melbourne's eastern suburbs, was captivated by all the wartime aircraft activity in the skies over Melbourne. When he heard that a genuine Japanese airman was in his hometown, Lionel did what young boys have always done when a celebrity comes to town – he wrote Toyoshima a letter. Astonishingly, a week later the postman knocked on the front door of the Bell residence and handed young Lionel a reply, written in neat, classical Japanese characters. The translated letter reads like a reply to fan mail. 'I would like to thank everyone in Melbourne,' Toyoshima wrote, 'for all your help and support over these weeks. Thank you very much for your kindness. Please be well and take care until the coming of peace in the Pacific. Goodbye.'[20] It is astonishing that in early 1942 a Japanese prisoner, in the midst of his despair at his captivity, would take the time to pen a respectful missive to a child of his enemy, delivering well wishes and hopes for a happy future. It appears Hajime Toyoshima was not quite the brute that history has often painted him.

After leaving Melbourne, Toyoshima was sent to a prison camp at Hay in regional New South Wales. The camp had been hurriedly constructed in 1940 on the site of the town's racecourse and showground, and had been built to house civilian internees – German refugees who had fled the Nazis, Italian undesirables who had been in Australia when war was declared, and Japanese businessmen, fishermen, farmers, gardeners, laundry workers and pearl divers, mostly shipped in from northern and western Australia. Australia's internment program is a fascinating and overlooked chapter of the Second World War. Internees from Australia's European enemies were detained based on their perceived likelihood to cause trouble – members of the Nazi or Fascist parties were particularly targeted. When it came to the Japanese, however, Australia wasn't taking any chances – in May 1941 the War Cabinet had declared that, in the event of war, *all* male Japanese nationals in Australia aged 16 and over would be taken into custody.[21] Women were considered less of a threat, but it was decided to throw them into the mix as well to avoid them suffering unnecessary 'hardships' in the absence of their men (although policies were put in place to repatriate Japanese women as soon as practicable). Children were not specifically mentioned in the legislation, but it was obvious that they would have to remain with their interned parents.

These harsh decisions were made partly due to a general xenophobia towards all Asian people, but specifically because it was felt that the Japanese, viewed as a militaristic and fanatical people, would represent a security risk regardless of age or occupation. Japanese nationals in Australia were also considered not to have assimilated into society to the extent that Europeans had, and their 'outsider' status increased the likelihood of them engaging in subversion against Australia. At the outbreak of war, in scenes that would have been distressingly familiar to refugees from Europe, platoons of heavily armed soldiers could be seen sweeping through Japanese communities across Australia, rounding up Japanese nationals and transporting them to temporary enclosures where they could be 'concentrated'. After being identified and sorted, they were shipped to camps in New South Wales, Victoria, Queensland, South Australia and Western Australia.

Entire families were interned, and the age range of internees was correspondingly wide, from babies to the elderly. Rules for internment were strict and applied without leniency – many internees had been born in Australia to Japanese parents, had never been to Japan and didn't even speak Japanese. Longevity in Australia was no protection – an elderly laundry worker from Rockhampton was sent to a camp despite having lived in Australia for decades and having a son fighting with the Australian 8th Division in Malaya. Sho Takasuka had arrived in Australia as a five-year-old and had been a resident for 37 years when he was interned. He was eventually released (one of only four men who gained their freedom in 1942), but this was most likely due to the fact that he owned a large tomato farm that employed 20 workers and supplies of food were running short. As a condition of his release Takasuka was not allowed to venture more than ten miles from his farm, a restriction that was still in place in 1946.

Even being a natural-born Australian was not enough to save you from the wrath of the authorities. Rose Allkins was born in Melbourne in 1881. In 1907 she had married a Japanese man, Moshi Inagaki, and thereby forfeited her British citizenship and was forced to register as an alien in her own country. At the outbreak of the Second World War she narrowly avoided being interned, but her husband, a lecturer at the University of Melbourne, was not so fortunate. In 1942 he was sent to the internment camp at Tatura, in Victoria, where he was held for the rest of the war. Rose was still lobbying for his release when she died in 1943. On his release in 1946, Inagaki was swiftly deported. Their only daughter, Mura, was allowed to remain in Australia, where she lived until her death in 1989. The internment process remained in place for the entire war – at its peak in 1943, more than 12 000 civilians were being held in the camps.

As a prisoner of war, Toyoshima was a novelty when he first arrived in the camp, to internee and guard alike, and the other Japanese treated him as something of a celebrity. They gave him gifts of clothes and books, and urged him to recount his tales of derring-do.

Life was pretty good for the young flier in Hay. The camp had only been intended to hold civilian internees, so was more like a relocation centre than a prison – security was fairly relaxed, the food was good, and internees were able to leave the camp on work parties in the district. (It should be noted that adjusting to life in the camps was significantly easier for POWs than it was for civilian internees. Military prisoners were used to the aspects of camp life: living with large groups of strangers in cramped spaces, strict rules and regulations, keeping the mind occupied during long periods of tedium and the general privations that come with life on the battlefield. Most civilian internees had no experience with imprisonment, and found the ordeal extremely distressing – high rates of depression and even the occasional suicide were not uncommon.) Toyoshima's English continued to improve as he practised with the civilian internees, and his military status made him a natural leader. Before long he was acting as a de facto representative for the Japanese internees and helping Australian authorities with small translating jobs. Toyoshima's new life had begun.

5

'OUR AIRCRAFT TURNED TO FACE THE ENEMY': THE NAVY FLIERS

Lieutenant Bob 'Blackie' Buel pulled back on the stick in his P-40 Kittyhawk to gain altitude. He had to use considerable strength to get the plane's nose up – the Kittyhawk was notoriously heavy in a climb, but once he had gained height and begun a slow bank the plane responded nimbly. The Kittyhawk was a good kite – not as manoeuvrable as the Japanese Zeros he was likely to come up against, and not as hardy as the Wildcat fighters that flew off the American aircraft carriers, but still a solid performer. The cockpit was spacious compared to other fighters, and the plane was rugged and solidly built. It was also armed with six .50-calibre machine-guns, so it brought a lot of teeth to any fight it entered.

Buel, 24 years old and hailing from California, was an inexperienced pilot. He had flown to Darwin from Brisbane with the US Army Air Force 3rd Pursuit Squadron in early February 1942, but engine trouble had forced him and another pilot, Lieutenant Bob Oestreicher, to remain behind in Darwin while the remainder of the squadron flew on to Timor, where Japanese forces were squeezing the life out of the outnumbered Australian and Dutch defenders. Now, a week later, he and Oestreicher's Kittyhawks were the only planes defending all of Darwin, and when an emergency call came in and Oestreicher's plane could not be contacted, Buel was on his own. The call had come from a seven-ship convoy led by the USS *Houston*, which had left Darwin shortly after midnight to ferry supplies and reinforcements to the beleaguered garrison at Timor. It was now 220 kilometres west of Darwin and under attack by an enemy plane. The convoy needed fighter assistance, and fast.

The Japanese plane was a four-engined Kawanishi flying boat, known to the Allies as a 'Mavis'. It was a large and lumbering beast, but boasted exceptional range – 24-hour missions were not unheard of – and was the eyes and ears of Japanese forces in their advance through the Pacific. The eight-man crew had taken off from Ambon in the early hours, spotted the Allied convoy mid-morning and shadowed it for three hours, dodging in and out of cloudbanks to minimise detection. Now, with fuel running low, the crew launched a half-hearted attack with tiny 60-kilogram bombs, failed to damage the convoy and turned for home.

Shortly after, Buel radioed to Darwin that he had spotted the convoy. Turning north, he sighted the enemy plane as it began its homeward track.

The Mavis's navigator was Sergeant Marekuni Takahara, a 21-year-old from Kobe. The crew was relaxing and preparing lunch after their tussle with the convoy when 'a single-engined fighter, which looked like a Spitfire, approached us from the front on the right. All the crew rushed to their posts ... Our aircraft turned to face the enemy.'[22]

Buel raked the flying boat with fire from his .50-calibre machine-guns, wounding the radio operator and setting the plane on fire. Overshooting his target, he turned tightly and charged at the Mavis from the rear. But this was a fatal mistake. The Mavis had a sting in its tail – at the first sign of the enemy fighter, Takahara had rushed to his post in the tail of the flying boat and was now lining up the Kittyhawk with his 20 mm cannon, a ferocious weapon that fired a stream of explosive shells. He couldn't miss.

As [the Kittyhawk] came at us I blazed away with my cannon. At the same time shots from the fighter tore through the fuselage of our flying boat. When the attacker was right on us we saw white smoke issuing from its tail. As it fell towards the sea I fired a complete magazine of some 50 rounds into it.[23]

Buel's burning Kittyhawk speared into the sea. His plane and his body have never been found.

Takahara's excitement at scoring his first kill was short-lived. As he clipped a fresh magazine into the gun he felt the aircraft plunge into a steep dive, and heard the pilot frantically shouting to brace for impact. The stricken Mavis hit the water, hard, and Takahara was briefly knocked out. When he came to he was in the water, and two of his crewmates were dead. 'Six of us managed to clamber aboard a rubber dinghy,' he later recalled, 'just as our plane slipped below the surface.'[24]

The pitiful band of fliers was now stranded in the vast expanse of the Timor Sea. They had no radio, no food, no water, no hope. The wounded radio operator soon died. Takahara was still emotional about the ordeal when he recounted it more than five decades later: 'For days we drifted, without oars, towards the east, at the mercy of the wind and the tide. We saw many sharks circling about. Looking back, nothing was frightening, because everything was frightening.'[25]

Their excruciating journey continued for four days. In daylight the sun was scorching, at night the seas rose and threatened to swamp their tiny craft. Ferocious wet-season storms lashed them every afternoon. They were famished, and survived only on the small amount of rainwater that pooled in the boat. Takahara was becoming delirious, and on the fourth day he thought he was hallucinating when he saw the skies darken as a large formation of Japanese aircraft passed high overhead. This was no hallucination – Takahara had just witnessed a wave of Japanese bombers on their approach run to Darwin, as part of the devastating attack on the harbour town.

On the afternoon of the fifth day, unexpectedly, miraculously, they spotted land. The craft washed ashore on a large island. Whether it was held by friend or foe, they could not say. (They were in fact on Melville Island where, coincidently, Hajime Toyoshima had crash-landed the previous day. Two parties of downed Japanese airmen were now stranded on the island.)

For the next few days Takahara and his bedraggled comrades trudged listlessly through mangrove swamps and thick scrub. They sustained themselves on a pitiful ration of raw crabs and muddy rainwater, and squabbled about their next move. Takahara was weak from the ordeal at sea and at one point collapsed beside a creek and refused to move, insisting that his crewmates abandon him. They refused, and eventually dragged him to his feet and cajoled him into carrying on.

For more than ten days their aimless procession continued, until one morning they saw shadowy figures moving towards them through the scrub. They had encountered a group of Indigenous people from the adjacent Bathurst Island, who, after a frustrating exchange of sign language and gesticulating, convinced the Japanese to come with them to the mission at Bathurst Island. After crossing Apsley, as above.ley Strait in small canoes, the Japanese were startled to discover that the mission and its adjoining airstrip were occupied in strength by the RAAF.

'We stepped out and surprised five very sorry-looking Japanese,' said Sergeant Les Powell, the same airman who had taken custody of Toyoshima only a few days before. 'They started to talk among themselves, and to get them to put their hands on their heads I fired a shot at their feet.'

The exhausted Japanese were flown by military transport to Darwin. During their meander around Melville Island they had concocted a story to disguise their roles as naval aviators. Under interrogation, they claimed they were lowly fishermen whose vessel had been sunk by an American submarine. The only problem was, none of the Japanese had the first clue about seamanship or fishing, and their story was laughably implausible. Questioned separately, none of them could agree on the size of the ship, with estimates ranging from 300 tons to 3000. At one point one of the 'fishermen' forgot the name of his own ship, and spent 'some time tracing characters on the table before recollecting it'.[26]

Luckily for the Japanese, the Australian interrogation was as inept as their play-acting. The interrogators, although swiftly concluding that the story was a fabrication, dismissed the prisoners as an 'unintelligent type … who, moreover, were not employed in jobs from which they could ascertain any real information as to the purpose of their cruise'.[27] It seems the hogwash about a life at sea had been lapped up by the gullible Australians, and the prized trophy of a Japanese naval aircrew, a potential source of a wealth of valuable intelligence, went unrecognised.

It was bad enough that the Australian intelligence officers didn't figure out who they had actually captured, but the situation then became farcical as they got completely carried away with themselves. Trying to deduce a plausible explanation for a Japanese 'fishing boat' roaming around the waters north of Darwin, they wandered off into a fantasy that was not only completely wrong, but could have caused panic had it been taken more seriously. 'Having regard to … the presence on board the ship of 60 labourers equipped for building, and for clearing land,' they surmised in their report, 'it is possible that a landing was intended in Darwin's near North for the purpose of clearing roads or aerodromes or both, probably as the preliminary to a sudden incursion of troops or aircraft.' You can almost feel the intelligence officer's excitement bouncing off the page as he revels in the details of the dastardly Japanese plan he has just uncovered. Unfortunately for him, it was all rubbish (and a significantly more embellished story than the humble Japanese prisoners had ever hoped for). As an example of a comprehensive failure of intelligence, this document stands unrivalled.

As their final act in this whole sorry saga, the Australians accepted the false names given to them by the Japanese without question. With the stroke of a pen, Marekuni Takahara became Ichiro Takata. He gave honest answers about his date and place of birth because, he said later, 'it is so difficult to remember unnecessary lies'.[28]

The airmen were briefly detained at a military POW camp in Adelaide River, before travelling south by rail and road to the internment camp in Hay. Here they met Toyoshima and, as the only military occupants of the camp, the six struck up an instant friendship. In hushed tones they shared their true identities and the circumstances of their capture, and then vowed to never speak of it again. From now on, to the world and each other, they would be an 'air gunner' and five 'sailors'.

In December, authorities decided to separate military prisoners from civilian internees, and made plans to transfer the six Japanese military men to Number 12 Prisoner of War Group. The first Japanese prisoners were on their way to Cowra.

6

'A TORMENT WORSE THAN DEATH': THE INFANTRYMAN

Lance Corporal Masaru Moriki was lost in a vivid dream. In it he imagined he could hear a bell chiming, and realised he was late for sword dance practice at his local youth centre in Kawauchi. He tried to spring to his feet, but couldn't move. Was he asleep? He didn't think so. He tried to stand and a searing pain in his right leg thrust him out of his imagined world of peaceful gardens and ringing bells. When he opened his eyes he saw not the blue skies of a spring day in Tosa province, but an ugly green-grey canopy of tropical foliage; he realised with despair that he was far from his hometown in Japan. He was in the jungles of New Guinea.

Fragments of memories returned to him, as hard to grasp as the wisps of the dream that still clouded his weary mind. He remembered his platoon charging, the ferocious roar of the enemy machine-guns, the heroic cries of *'Banzai!'* as his comrades surged forward, and the screams of the dying as they were cut down by bullets. Moriki had been on the left flank, had seen the Australians sheltering in their shallow foxholes, had gotten close enough to see their faces, wide-eyed and sweaty, and set with grim determination as they poured fire into the mass of charging men. Then a sledgehammer smashed into his right thigh, and he went down hard. Other men trampled him as they rushed towards the Australian line, and then fell on him as the bullets found their mark, their limbs collapsing as if made of string. How was he alive? No man could have survived that torrent of fire. And yet here he was – he could feel the damp mud beneath him, could smell the thick pungent aroma of the fecund forest. His leg seared with pain, and he could feel blood – so much blood – soaking his pants and pooling beneath him. He closed his eyes and waited peacefully for the death that was surely close. He passed out.

Moriki awoke to the sound of low voices. When he opened his eyes he saw ghostly figures all around him, and realised a patrol must have returned to tend to the wounded. Perhaps the attack had been a success after all? He brought his attention to the nearest figure. This man was not clad in the drab khaki of the Japanese Army; he was wearing green. And he was tall. This man was not Japanese – he was Australian. 'I was about to receive treatment from enemy soldiers,' he wrote in his memoirs. 'Cold shivers went through my spine and I felt my blood curdle. I yelled as hard as I could but I made no sound. "Kill me! Kill me!" I kept yelling.'[29]

But the Australians didn't kill him. In fact, they did something worse; much, much worse. They began to treat him. 'I've become a POW.' The thought was almost too much for Moriki to bear. 'I can't begin to describe the pain of this realisation. It was like being pulled into a torment worse than death and all my family were trying to follow me, crying.'[30]

The Australians put Moriki on a stretcher and carried him off the battlefield. He realised he was being taken towards Kokoda village, away from the Japanese forces. Hope leached from him with each step away from his countrymen. He wanted to die, was desperate to die; but how could he accomplish it in his weakened state? He noted that the Australians were all carrying guns, and were watching him closely. All he had to do was get off the stretcher, and they would surely kill him. When the stretcher bearers lowered him, Moriki's moment had come. He grasped the sides of the stretcher, preparing to leap to his feet. But his arms would not respond. Not only could he not jump off the stretcher, he couldn't even sit up. He collapsed in despair, and passed out again.

For hours the Australians carried him through the jungle. When they grew tired, New Guinean porters took over. And throughout the journey Moriki was distraught. He begged for water. An Australian medic gave him an injection. And all the while they carried him further from his comrades, and closer to the shame of captivity.

At the next rest stop he saw more native porters, clad only in loincloths, gathering around the stretcher and watching him with interest. Moriki knew a small amount of English, so understood when one of the Australians said, 'They are cannibals waiting for you to die ... So you must not die. If you do you will be eaten.' Moriki couldn't tell if the Australian was joking or not; he didn't care – he longed for death and wasn't concerned if he was buried, burnt or eaten afterwards. He pointed to the Australian's gun, then put a finger to his own chest and mimed pulling the trigger. The Australian was aghast at the thought, and ordered the New Guineans to pick up the stretcher and resume the journey.

As they departed, Moriki noted the graves of both Australians and Japanese in the clearing. Both friend and foe had been buried with care. He wondered if his Japanese comrades would have treated their enemies with such respect.

At a river crossing, the going was too tough for a stretcher. A burly Australian shouldered his rifle and, with a grunt and a curse, hoisted Moriki onto his back. Moriki screamed in pain, but was thankful that the Australians were finally going to finish him off. Instead, the Australian waded into the swollen river and carried the wounded Japanese across. Moriki's feelings of hatred and humiliation began to soften.

In Kokoda village he received first-aid treatment in a field hospital alongside Australian and Japanese wounded. During his first night he heard a plane flying overhead, and prayed that it was a Japanese bomber that would blow the hospital to oblivion and release him from his torment. But death didn't come that night, or the next one.

Then he was loaded onto a plane and flown out of the mountains to Port Moresby, the objective that Japanese forces had been coveting for months. Moriki had often dreamed of his arrival in the town, but it was not supposed to be like this, wounded and carried in by his enemies on a stretcher.

At a large hospital he was tended to by pretty and considerate nurses, the first women Moriki had seen in as long as he could remember. They removed his filthy clothes and bathed him, 'as if they were handling babies'. Being clean and clad in comfortable cotton pyjamas did not make Moriki feel better – it only added to his shame, and he fell into a deeper pit of despair. The Australians operated on him, and an orderly handed him the bullet they had removed from his leg. Moriki gripped it and cursed his fate: 'Why didn't the bullet hit a place that could kill me, instead of my leg?' After a few days he was flown to Townsville, to another military hospital, where his wasted body began to recover until he could taste the milk that the nurses tenderly invited him to sip.

From there he went to Brisbane, on a hospital train with other Japanese wounded. As they were transported through the city in the back of hospital trucks, he expected the local people to jostle and jeer, but instead they looked at the Japanese prisoners with quiet fascination, with no malice in their eyes.

At the Brisbane military hospital, his attitude towards his former enemies softened further, when he received kind and considerate treatment from the Australian guards. One he called 'Tailor', as this had been the man's occupation before the war. The other was a former jockey, who amused the prisoners by pretending to ride his rifle around the ward like a hobby horse. In a quiet moment, he told Moriki that if he did not wish to return to Japan after the war, he would be welcome to come and stay on the family farm in Australia. Moriki choked back tears, overwhelmed at this unexpected kindness. It was a memory that would stay with him for the rest of his life.

It was about this time that Moriki befriended another Japanese lance corporal, who came from Hiroshima and had been wounded and captured in New Guinea a month before Moriki. His name was Juichi Kinoshita and the two men bonded quickly as they lay in adjacent beds in the hospital ward. Kinoshita had worked as a haberdasher before the war, and had delighted in sewing intricate and beautiful kimonos for the ladies of his district. In 1942 he was 30 years old, about six years older than Moriki, and had left a wife and young children in Hiroshima. He was, according to Moriki, 'a man of well-rounded character with elegant manners', who spoke frequently and emotionally about his life in Japan, and expressed his profound sadness at never being able to return to it after having been captured. 'All of us were tormented by being POWs,' Moriki recalled decades later. 'However Mr Kinoshita was more so because of his nature. I was a regular soldier but he became a soldier as a result of conscription. His torment should have been much lighter than us. But that was not the case with him.'

After a month in the Brisbane hospital, Moriki was transferred to Goulburn in New South Wales, where a former psychiatric ward had been repurposed as a hospital for Japanese POWs. He was delighted when Kinoshita joined him two weeks later. The two men were slowly recovering from their wounds and, if not quite accepting of their life as prisoners of war, certainly adapting to it. They still wanted to die, but the desire was something they pushed to the back of their minds – it could wait until later. For now there was a strange, almost ethereal, detachment from their former lives as Japanese soldiers.

For two months they enjoyed Goulburn's hot summer weather. Moriki's leg had healed enough that he could walk with the aid of a crutch around the grounds, and the trees and hills around the hospital reminded him of similar scenes in Japan. In March 1943 the two men were told they would be moved again, this time to a more permanent home. After a six-hour drive they

> stopped in front of a big gate with barbed wire around the area. Looking down from the window, I could see the huts lined up on the slope of the hill below; we didn't need to be reminded that these were the POW camp buildings. Inside the gate, three or four Japanese POWs wearing red uniforms were waiting for us. The impression of the red uniform was strong.

Moriki and Kinoshita knew they too would soon be wearing that red uniform. They had arrived in Cowra.

7

'GOOD ORDER AND MILITARY DISCIPLINE': THE POW CAMP

The site of the former POW camp at Cowra feels a long way from anywhere, and that's exactly the point. When Australian military authorities discussed establishing a POW camp in New South Wales in May 1941, as a direct result of the vast number of Italian prisoners taken during the fighting in North Africa, Cowra was the ideal spot. Close enough to Sydney to be well serviced by rail and road, it was also far enough away that any foreign inmate housed there would feel he was in the middle of nowhere – and a hell of a long way from home. His sense of utter isolation, it was hoped, would sap whatever fighting spirit he still possessed. Cowra was already home to an infantry training base, and this ready resource of armed soldiers made the choice even easier.

The site was the second cheapest of four proposed options,[31] probably because the land was rocky, sloping and sited next to a former night soil depot, where the pungent contents of Cowra's toilets had been dumped for decades. It was also smack-bang in the middle of the firing lanes for Cowra's new rifle range, and some frenzied and officious telegrams were exchanged between the army and Cowra council before the town reluctantly agreed to hand over the site. It was estimated the land acquisition and set-up costs would amount to about £3400, a relative bargain for a site that could eventually hold more than 4000 subdued Italian warriors. Construction on the site would be swift – on the same day the site was selected, a call was put out for local labour to begin construction work and for timber-getters to supply thousands of cypress poles to build the perimeter fencing. The first prisoners were due to arrive in June. In mid-1941 the camp was for Italians and non-combatant enemies of the state – war with Japan had not even been contemplated.

The design of the camp was brutally efficient – no luxuries were expected or needed for vanquished foes taken on the field of battle. An early suggestion for the camp to be constructed of tents was quicky abandoned, but the final design was still simple and utilitarian. The camp covered about 100 acres in total, and comprised four compounds, each forming a quarter slice of a roughly shaped pie. The camp appeared to form a large circle, but in fact the perimeter fence had no curves – 12 long, straight sections of perimeter ringed the camp, ranging in length from 150 to 280 metres. Each compound, designated A, B, C and D, featured accommodation for up to 1000 men in wooden buildings, with separate ablution blocks, latrines, hospitals, kitchens and workshops. Each sleeping building was a 'double', comprising two identical 20-metre × 6-metre rooms separated by a central wall, with entry doors at both ends of each room. Each of these separate rooms was designated a 'hut' and was numbered from one to forty. Each hut accommodated about 25 to 30 men who slept in individual cots. The huts were cooled by louvre windows during Cowra's scorching summers, and heated by wood-burning braziers during its icy winters.

The camp was bifurcated by a wide thoroughfare, 700 metres long and 40 metres wide, which ran north–south through the heart of the camp. This thoroughfare was brightly and perpetually lit, and was irresistibly christened 'Broadway' by the garrison. A second thoroughfare, running east–west and forming a bare strip of land that separated A and B Compounds to the north from C and D Compounds to the south, was known as 'No Man's Land'.

Each compound had a set of gates at each end, opening directly into Broadway. At the northern and southern ends of Broadway were two sets of solid gates set into the perimeter fencing – this was the only way into or out of the perimeter. To exit the camp, prisoners were funnelled into Broadway and then through the access gates at either end. Barracks and support buildings for the garrison troops were located outside the perimeter to the north, south and west of the camp.

From the outset, arrangements for securing prisoners in the camp seemed relaxed, to say the least. Perhaps the authorities were influenced by reports that the Italian prisoners being taken in North Africa were exceedingly docile and unlikely to attempt escape. Original plans called for the perimeter fences at the Cowra camp to be low and strung with single-strand barbed wire, little more than the fences farmers in the district used to contain their flocks of sheep. This plan was soon discarded, but the final fences that were built lent more to quantity than quality. Just under two metres high, three lines of fences ten metres apart were tightly strung with barbed wire. Three coils of concertina wire (known as 'Dannert wire' in the parlance of the time) snaked around the middle fence, and the space between the middle and outer fences was choked with densely tangled coils of wire to a height of about 1.5 metres. It was a decent deterrent to any prisoner casually tempted to scarper, but it was never going to create much of an obstacle to a determined escape attempt.

Once constructed, the camp seemed to offer a cursory nod, rather than a dedicated commitment, to security. Six towers guarded the perimeter (in itself a surprisingly small number) and four of these overlooked Broadway. A solitary tower guarded each of the east and west perimeters, meaning the guards within had to oversee more than 650 metres of perimeter fence from their lonely perch. F Tower, guarding the entire eastern perimeter, was especially isolated, located on the far side of the camp from the garrison barracks, and facing open fields that stretched away from the direction of town. It also overlooked B Compound, which housed the Japanese enlisted men and non-commissioned officers (NCOs). This was always going to be the weakest point in the camp's flimsy defences, and the obvious spot for an escape attempt, yet it was typically manned by a single guard, armed with a hodgepodge of whatever spare weapons were available. A scattering of sentry boxes and searchlights completed the security arrangements, but given that the garrison had to keep an eye on an area of around 100 acres, these were never going to be enough.

The occupants of the camp were an eclectic bunch. Compounds A and C, the north-west and south-east segments, contained Italians, the once-proud warriors of Mussolini who had surrendered by their thousands in North Africa and who seemed content to see out the war in the relative comfort of captivity. They were resigned to their fate, and went about life in a pacified, almost carefree state – the majority had always been poor soldiers, reluctant to fight and even more reluctant to die, and now there was something slightly comical about their demeanour and outlook. In these compounds, baking, gardening and singing were the order of the day, and the Italians demonstrated a zest for life that bemused their Australian overseers. The food was good, and they supplemented their rations with Australian claret traded with the townsfolk, or grappa made in crude stills within the camp. Prison authorities turned a blind eye to this breach of protocol – the Italians were docile, and the alcohol actually made them more agreeable. They were passionate and dramatic, and the guards occasionally had to break up a wine-fuelled fracas, but for the most part the Italians were model prisoners. On balmy summer evenings they played mandolins and sang, heartily and well – so well, in fact, that the townspeople often gathered around the camp to listen in on impromptu performances.

Such cultural diversions were rare, and welcome, in rural Australia in the 1940s. A Japanese prisoner described the Italians in words that could have been written by an Australian:

> Although we were both soldiers of the Axis Powers wearing the same burgundy PW clothing, we could not even in our most generous moments regard them as a strong military force. They were cheerful, amiable, easy-going fellows. From morning till night the strains of the mandolin, the guitar and the violin emanated from their Compound. I suppose you could say that they maintained some semblance of a military organisation; but one and all they wanted nothing more to do with the War. They were much better off than at the front. They didn't care who won or lost. They spent their time wishing for a speedy end to the war and to be reunited with their fiancées back home.[32]

Australian authorities recognised that many of the Italians were from rural backgrounds and in 1943 introduced a system of work programs for Italian prisoners in farming communities across Australia. At first many of the Italians were reluctant to participate, concerned that the program would directly support their enemy's war effort, but after the fall of Mussolini and the Italian capitulation, those concerns melted away and the ranks of Italians willing to exchange the tedium of camp life for a hard day's work swelled.[33] This unexpected free labour force was a boon to Australia's food production industry, which was struggling to meet wartime demands, and authorities did all they could to foster it, even going so far as to offer the Italians English lessons and distribute newsletters with updates from home to the prisoners. Within the camp at Cowra, the Italians tended vegetable gardens and chopped wood, repaired drains, even mended the perimeter fences that contained them.

Before long, Italian POWs were working unsupervised on local farms, and the Italians showed a willingness to conform to their orders and an aversion to freedom that bordered on the absurd. On one occasion a group of Italians was returning to camp after a long day in the fields when their truck threw a tyre. It was well after dark by the time the repair was made and the camp was locked down for the night. The Italians were forced to bang on the main gates to rouse the Australian guards, who dutifully let them into the camp and back into captivity.

Although more than 2000 Italians remained imprisoned in the camp, many hundreds more were billeted on local farms, living and working with the family, sleeping in spare rooms, even regularly joining the locals for a night on the town.

Although the Italians ingratiated themselves fairly easily with Australian civilians, relations weren't always cordial. Private Mario Soliani, a 24-year-old cobbler from a small town north of Bologna, had been captured in April 1941 during the East African campaign and had spent three years in a POW camp in India. In early 1944 he was shipped to Melbourne, and then sent with a large contingent of Italians by train to Cowra. Soliani recalled that during the journey the train stopped at a small station and, as the Italians sought relief from the heat by hanging out of the windows, a belligerent young Australian strode along the platform demanding to know if any of the Italians had fought at Tobruk. When one prisoner unwisely admitted that he had, he received a punch squarely in the face. 'That's for my brother,' the Australian said. 'He was killed at Tobruk.'[34]*

Although the Italians were relatively compliant prisoners, they did seem to have a knack for getting up to mischief and causing headaches for their Australian overseers. Their motivations don't seem to have been particularly malicious, or even to have been doing much to further their war effort. The Italians were simply trying to get the most out of life. On one occasion an Italian prisoner was discovered enjoying a film at the Cowra theatre, accompanied by the son of a local farmer and dressed in civilian clothes he had borrowed from the family. On another occasion a sergeant from the camp was dispatched to round up Private Antici Marcello, a 23-year-old clerk from Rome, who was late returning from work duty. On arriving at a local house, the sergeant found the Italian sitting in the lounge room in darkness, with the 19-year-old daughter of the house curled up in his lap. Apparently the dalliance had been going on for some time; when questioned the girl revealed that Marcello, 'who speaks good English, had asked her to marry

---

* Soliani returned to Italy after the war, but then emigrated to Australia in the 1950s. He set up a shoe repair business in Griffith, New South Wales, where he raised a family and was a prominent member of the Italian community until his death in 1997.

him and that she consented'. Marcello was swiftly marched back to camp, spent 28 days in detention and was then transferred to a camp in Victoria and later Western Australia. He returned to Italy in 1946 – the young lovebirds were never reunited.[35]

The sudden influx of charming European young men had an obvious effect on the wives and daughters of the local farmers, many of whom had never seen the lights of Sydney let alone met a charmer from Florence or Catania. The Italians were naturally charismatic, and had been deprived of female company throughout several years of military service and imprisonment. Romantic dalliances were common, and usually problematic, for farming family and POW alike.

In May 1944 an Italian prisoner named Eustacchio Vivilecchia, known as Vito to his friends, made a statement to camp authorities that would have provided ample source material for the most melodramatic of soap operas. The report is a bizarre combination of scandalous revelation and prudish censorship; the interviewer evidently had delicate sensibilities – you can feel him blushing on every typed page. The report describes in embarrassing detail an affair between Vivilecchia and the wife of the farmer with whom he was billeted. The report was made not because the affair had occurred, but simply because Vivilecchia was so traumatised by the whole thing that he could no longer wrestle with his conscience, and it ends with him begging to be transferred to another farm. The interviewer has changed the names to protect the not-so-innocent, replacing the family name with 'Smith', and it's hard not to squirm as the interviewer does his best to reconcile an account of Mrs Smith's unsubtle advances with his own sensibilities. At one stage, according to the report, Mrs Smith showed Vivilecchia a calendar and indicated the more than five weeks since her husband had 'loved' her (Vivilecchia had actually said 'had intercourse with', but this was apparently more than the prudish interviewer could handle, and the typed phrase was crossed out and amended in pen). Over several more pages of excruciating detail that no one asked for, Vivilecchia described how he was pursued relentlessly by Mrs Smith, only succumbing to her advances when she pretended to faint and Vivilecchia noted an 'absence of nether garments' as she fell to the floor. The most curious aspect of the whole sordid affair was how compliant the farmer was with it – he eventually resorted to sleeping in the car while Vivilecchia shared the marital bed with his wife. Eventually it all became too much for poor Vivilecchia who pleaded to return to the camp. The final chapter of the sorry saga saw Mrs Smith running alongside the truck and shouting tearful farewells as Vivilecchia was whisked away.[36]

Although most of their infringements were minor, one serious and persistent problem among the Italian prisoners was Fascism. The Fascists only made up a small part of the Italian population, but they were disproportionately outspoken, militant and rebellious. They wanted to make trouble, and took every opportunity to do so, even after the Fascist government had been overthrown in Italy. An Australian intelligence report in June 1944 noted:

> Evidence that some PW still vaunt their fascist views comes to hand from time to time. It is of course understandable that men who have had a creed instilled into them from early youth should find it difficult to change their opinions, but it is also difficult to imagine that a PW, who knows that his transfer to a farm depends upon his good behaviour, cannot suppress his feelings in order to bring about such transfer. Therefore it can only be assumed, and it is in fact true, that

those who persist in expressing fascist views either do not wish to go to farms or are useless for farm work.[37]

Fascist prisoners mostly contented themselves with a small and ineffective revolution that chiefly involved distributing homemade propaganda and writing letters hoping for a glorious Fascist victory in their home country. But over time they began intimidating other prisoners, particularly those they viewed as traitors for not upholding the Fascist cause, or for working for the enemy. The victims of this intimidation became so concerned for their safety that in May 1944 a group of Italian leaders wrote to the camp intelligence officer pleading that Fascist miscreants not be returned to the general population after being punished for subversion. 'We hold,' they wrote,

that [camp authorities] should continue to exercise firmness towards all [prisoners] who continue to disseminate Fascist propaganda amongst their companions. Hence we desire that all those who have been punished for any military insubordination, disobedience of orders and/or acts of Fascist subversiveness not be readmitted into the compound at the conclusion of their detention. We express the opinion that the above is the only manner whereby it can be assured that good order and military discipline will be maintained.[38]

The problem became so bad that by 1944 camp authorities had built a prison within the prison and began isolating Italian troublemakers in a special compound known as 'Middle D'. This seemed to quell the problem, and life in the Italian compounds returned to its former happy state.

While Australian authorities were distracted by quashing rebellion among Fascists in the Italian compounds, a far deadlier, and far more underestimated, threat was brewing under their noses. The number of Japanese prisoners in B Compound was reaching a critical mass, and with each new arrival the level of collective tension was rising. Could the Australians contain the problem before it boiled over?

8
'FIRM AND CAREFUL HANDLING': THE JAPANESE AT COWRA

Hajime Toyoshima, Marekuni Takahara and the other flying boat crewmembers arrived in Cowra on 8 January 1943, and the experience was surreal. The camp was bursting at the seams with Italian prisoners in two of the four compounds, but the Japanese compound was eerily quiet. Although only containing a handful of prisoners, who had been brought together from internment camps across the country, the compound consisted of more than 25 buildings, including 40 sleeping huts with space for 1000 men. It was a mini-city, currently without inhabitants, but the empty huts just waiting to be filled with new prisoners was an eerie omen for the newly arrived inmates.

At first the Japanese compound was made up of a ragtag assortment of downed airmen, shipwrecked sailors and army stragglers. But as the weeks turned into months, the quality and quantity of Japanese prisoners began to change. On 11 March 1943, there were 119 Japanese prisoners in the camp. By August 1944, that number had ballooned to an unsustainable 1104.

In early 1943 the population of the camp could be used as a barometer of Japan's fortunes in the war, and with every truckload of new arrivals it became harder for the prisoners to persuade themselves that the war was going well for the Empire. First came army troops wounded in the advance on Port Moresby. Others racked with dysentery from the brutal campaign at Kokoda arrived next. And then the floodgates really began to open – malnourished infantrymen taken by the Australians and Americans at Buna and Gona, and other army troops overwhelmed as the Allies pushed along the north coast of New Guinea. The stories these men brought with them to Cowra shocked the prisoners, many of whom had naively convinced themselves (contrary to all evidence) that Japan would somehow turn its fortunes around. Reports from New Guinea revealed an army in danger of falling apart. Masaru Moriki recalled hearing horrific details about the desperate evacuation of the Japanese base at Giruwa, where he had fought earlier in the war:

The jungle became a burnt field in no time, the dead bodies piled up, the white bones scattered and the smell of dead bodies covered the whole area. On the final day, numbered boarding passes were issued to the wounded depending on the seriousness of their injuries and the patients crawled to the beach hidden by the darkness of the night, expecting to be picked up by barge … Naturally, on the way, there were some unconscious, some groaning and some already dead, etc. It was a ghastly scene. However, the seriously wounded who had made it to the beach gathered in one group and awaited the arrival of the barge, every minute heaving heavily. Finally the last barge they were waiting for came to the shore. As soon as it touched the shore, the still strong soldiers rushed to the barge disregarding the boarding numbers. Soon the barge was taken over by them. While angry roars and shrieks swirled, cruelly, the barge began to leave shore at the order of the stronger ones. At the same time, suddenly the sound of gunfire pierced the dark night. The wounded soldiers fell one after another piling up on the beach. Even then, some hung on to the edge of the barge with all their might. At that moment, military swords fiercely shined in the dark of night. Arms and bodies which were hanging on to the barge were separated at once. The bodies sank into the sea, but a few arms still clung to the barge. However, as the barge increased speed those arms also came undone and disappeared beneath the waves.[39]

While the army prisoners brought shocking tales about defeats on land, through it all came a constant flow of airmen, both navy and army, whose aircraft had been shot out of the skies over New Guinea and the Solomons, and sailors whose ships had been sunk beneath them in the Coral, Arafura and Timor seas. Then in March, a new kind of prisoner began to arrive – soldiers from the Japanese 2nd Division, the powerful force that had been doing battle with the Americans on Guadalcanal; and they brought with them even worse stories of privation, desperation and defeat. The net result was that even the lowliest infantryman in Cowra, who lacked the most basic understanding of grand strategy, now realised that defeats on so many fronts, against so many enemies, spelled disaster for the Japanese cause. It was a mortal blow to the prisoners' already fragile state of mind. Each man now had to deal with a dual trauma, one intensely personal and one existential – his shame at having been captured, and the knowledge that Japan was in real danger of losing this war. To men already tormented by their individual circumstances, the thought that it could all be for nothing – that the grand vision they had signed up for and pledged their lives to defend – could all come crashing down, was overwhelming. This realisation bred a moodiness and discontent that went far beyond shame.

Australian authorities struggled to understand the depth of despair and self-loathing felt by the Japanese prisoners in their custody. They certainly understood that the Japanese military code forbade capture and that military men had been indoctrinated to follow that code to the death, but they simply couldn't get their heads around the fundamental concept that Japanese prisoners would prefer, indeed expected, to die rather than be taken prisoner. Why would they? They had endured the most torturous ordeals in the jungles of New Guinea and Guadalcanal, under constant threat of death, and now they were safe and warm behind the lines, enjoying good food and spending their time playing baseball and gardening. An Australian soldier in those conditions, while recognising the vague military obligation to attempt escape if feasible (and in almost all cases it wasn't), would be resigned to his fate and would recognise that his contribution to the war was over. Why would a Japanese prisoner be any different? And this was the fundamental issue with the gulf of misunderstanding that existed between Japanese captive and Australian guard. The Australians could only view the Japanese through their own lens, and that distorted perspective bred a dangerous complacency.

Private Matsuoka Ryoju had been captured by US forces near Buna in February 1943, and revealed an attitude under interrogation that was typical of Japanese prisoners:

The PW expected to be killed on capture and would have preferred that to the disgrace of being a PW. Although, as a human being, he would naturally like to see his people again, he felt at present that, like all Japanese soldiers under similar circumstances, he would not return. In any case, it had always been the case to execute men on their return and he doubted whether any allowance would be made for the fact that he was young. Although parents would be glad to see their sons again they would, nevertheless, not expect them to remain alive after disgrace or capture.[40]

But why was this the case? No matter how often the military doctrine was drilled into them, how could men possibly convince themselves that death was preferable to captivity, especially at the moment when capture was imminent and this tenet of the military code became substantially more than just a theory?

Steven Bullard offers an explanation in his excellent account of the Breakout, *Blankets on the Wire*. The Japanese attitude of servitude to the state and Emperor was encapsulated in the Field Service Code (*Senjinkun*), which was first distributed on 8 January 1941.

The Field Service Code contained a set of moral prescripts by which a Japanese soldier was to live, fight and die. These emphasised his duty as a soldier to uphold the 'Imperial way' and to act as one in body and spirit in loyalty to the emperor. The Field Service Code provides examples of how a Japanese soldier should act on the battlefield, and expanded on the lofty idealism of the Imperial Rescript to Soldiers and Sailors which was promulgated by Emperor Meiji in 1882.[41]

The section of the Field Service Code that deals with captivity falls under the heading 'Value honour' and states: 'Strong is he who comprehends shame. Be always mindful of the reputation of your community and family, while making every effort to fulfil their expectations. Do not in death leave to posterity a stain on your honour by having suffered in life the disgrace of being a prisoner.'[42]

As Bullard points out, this passage doesn't expressly command a soldier to kill himself when faced with captivity, but for most Japanese in uniform it was a moot point. They recalled stirring examples of captured samurai lieutenants committing ritual suicide rather than suffering the ignominy of serving under a new master, and also more recent accounts from the war in China of the same fanatical ideal. (It is also important to distinguish this concept of ritual suicide from the view of suicide we generally hold today. Today the concept of suicide carries a stigma, an undertone of personal failure, of inability to cope. To the Japanese of the Second World War, ritual suicide in the face of imminent capture was seen as highly courageous and noble. Decades after the war, some Cowra survivors – even those who had not been in favour of the Breakout in the first place – still looked back with pride on their comrades who had chosen to commit suicide.)

The mention in the Field Service Code of community and family is vital, and probably helps to explain the Japanese attitude of 'death before dishonour' better than anything else. When a Japanese man volunteered or was conscripted to fight in the Second World War, the elaborate farewell celebrations from family and friends when he left his home were as much a tribute to his imminent death as they were to his service. When a Japanese man left for the front, no one expected him to return. The commitment to upholding family honour was so ingrained in the Japanese military psyche that cries of 'okasan' (mother) were as commonly heard in the last moments of charging soldiers as the famous 'Banzai!'[43]

The Field Service Code spelled out how a Japanese soldier was expected to behave, and violent indoctrination during training ensured that he complied. By the time a Japanese soldier reached the battlefield (particularly an enlisted man), any notion of individuality or independent thought had long been extinguished, and the military code was the only moral rule book that shaped his behaviour. This goes a long way towards explaining not just the attitude to capture, but also the Japanese soldier's apparent predilection for committing atrocities against both civilians and soldiers. (This philosophy also explains why Japan refused to ratify the Geneva Convention – Japanese authorities felt that since no Japanese soldier would allow himself to be taken prisoner, it was unfair to expect them to wear the cost of caring for enemy prisoners in their hands. They were also none-too-keen to agree to regulations that would require them to feed and clothe prisoners to a higher standard than their own troops enjoyed.)

It is clear that the strict Japanese attitudes to surrender were not simply a philosophy – they were embraced almost universally by the men serving in the Japanese military. A document found in New Guinea in 1944 summarised the official Japanese tally of soldiers who had been taken prisoner during fighting in China: none in 1940, two in 1941, two in 1942 and 18 in 1943. 'By any but Japanese standards,' an Australian intelligence officer commented, 'this would seem a very low figure for nearly four years of war, but the document states that "It is a really serious situation".'[44] The unwavering belief that Japanese combatants would refuse to be captured was so unshakable that a Japanese soldier taken at Hollandia in April 1944 claimed to be a pilot in the mistaken belief that this would result in his immediate execution. 'His reason for this', a report into the incident claimed, 'was that he thought he was the only Japanese POW. He did not want to die when he discovered there were many others.'[45]

The result of all this was that the Japanese soldiers imprisoned in Cowra saw themselves as ghosts, trapped between the world of their comrades who had died on the battlefield and their former lives with friends and family to which they could never return. They well knew that Japanese authorities had informed their families that they had died in battle, and that their names had been etched on headstones in family shrines. Although Japanese prisoners were allowed to contact their families back in Japan, no records exist of a Japanese prisoner ever doing so – to shatter the illusion that they had met a glorious death on the battlefield with the truth that they were instead languishing in an enemy prison camp was unthinkable.

This tumult of emotions led to another mindset that the Australian authorities in the camp completely misread. Intelligence officers believed that knowledge of Japanese defeats would sap the energy and fighting spirit of the prisoners – it had certainly worked that way with the Italians – and so they readily shared information about Japanese reversals with the prisoners. In fact, it had the opposite effect. For men already riven with resentment and personal doubt, news that the Empire was in danger of falling didn't sap their strength – it crystallised their anger. They now had a common cause to rally behind – the question of what they could do to contribute to the war effort. Takahara recalled prisoners declaring 'we cannot sit idly by and watch Japan go down. Now is the time for us to take resolute action.'[46]

Life for the Japanese prisoners in the camp was a surreal half-dream. Most had never contemplated the thought of capture, so didn't know how to behave or feel when they found themselves behind the wire. This made them compliant interrogation subjects. As Japanese soldiers were expected to die rather than be captured, they had never received training in counter-interrogation techniques, and therefore spoke loquaciously about their military units, training and former operations. For many the decision to be captured had been made for them – many were army men who had been too wounded or sick to resist, or airmen and sailors marooned far behind enemy lines.

The realisation that they had become prisoners crept up on many of them slowly. On his arrival at the camp, Moriki was suddenly confronted with the grim reality of his situation, even though he had been in Australian hands for months:

> Until now, we were POWs but at the same time we were wounded soldiers and we were treated with such kindness that we felt almost strange. We never spoke together (about the torment we felt) and kept the pain in our hearts to ourselves, but the people around us tried not to remind us that we were POWs. However, this time that wouldn't be the case. By wearing that red uniform, we were branded as POWs.[47]

Newly arrived prisoners were surprised at how well they were treated by their Australian captors, as they were handed ample blankets, clothing and personal-care items. More than one prisoner pondered if their comrades back in Japan would treat Australian prisoners this well if the situation were reversed. Moriki was so impressed with the kit he received on arrival that he listed it in his memoirs (uniform, overcoat, hat, socks, singlets, underpants, blanket, razor, shaving brush, soap and a pair of shoes). 'The red colour was not only for our uniforms but blankets too,' he added. 'It seemed this colour was dyed with our bloody tears.'[48]

Probably the greatest shock for men who had grown accustomed to the privations of life in the jungles of New Guinea and the Solomons was the quantity and quality of food they received at the camp. Japanese prisoners at Cowra received the same rations as the guards (a belly-bursting 3753 calories per day), which included rice, meat, fish, bread and vegetables. The meat often came from plump Cowra lambs (still to this day considered some of the best in the country), and the fish was so fresh that the prisoners used it to make sashimi and consumed it raw. In an effort to find work for idle hands, camp authorities encouraged the Japanese to cultivate their own vegetables, a task they embraced with relish. The fertile soils of the compound were soon bursting with Chinese cabbages, radishes, watermelons, lettuce, spinach, turnips, cauliflower and onions. This meant that, in practice, the prisoners were now enjoying a greater range of food, in more quantity, than their Australian overseers.

Soon the Japanese were supplementing these already ample rations from an unexpected source – the Italian prisoners in the camp. The two groups had nothing in common except for the burgundy uniforms they wore, but the Italians' joie de vivre was a source of bemusement to the Japanese. 'The Italians next to our camp', Moriki recalled,

unlike us Japanese, felt no shame or humiliation as POWs. It seemed that they were even proud of being 'honourable POWs'. Contrary to the Japanese who never contacted home, however much they were advised to do so, and who used false names and false ranks, all the Italians had contact with their homes. Therefore they lived quite comfortably as they received money and also willingly took jobs and earned an income. They gave us, who had nothing other than supplied goods, sweets, dried grapes and cigarettes.[49]

Unlike the Italians, the Japanese were not given work duty outside the camp, but as winter approached small groups were dispatched to the surrounding woodland under guard to gather firewood to fuel the braziers in the huts. Somewhat unexpectedly, the Japanese volunteered enthusiastically for this working bee – the opportunity to escape the tedium of camp life seems to have briefly overcome their innate hostility to forced labour. In addition to firewood, the Japanese brought back with them whatever 'souvenirs' they could find in the countryside – scraps of metal and small pieces of discarded farm equipment, that they fashioned into rudimentary tools. 'They became a chisel, a knife and a plane,' Moriki recalled, 'and using them we made a musical instrument, mahjong pies, *geta* (Japanese wooden thongs) and a costume box.'[50]

Camp authorities had allocated the last of the sleeping huts for recreational use, and the Japanese converted it into a theatre, complete with a stage and a somewhat sophisticated production department. Former tailors, including Moriki's close friend Lance Corporal Kinoshita, fashioned elaborate costumes, which were used in regular performances of *kabuki* dramas and *kyogen* comedies. From all accounts these were remarkably elaborate events, given the meagre facilities at the performers' disposal in the camp, and provided a highly prized distraction from the monotony of prison life. The prisoners also constructed a wrestling ring, and enjoyed watching and participating in sumo matches. The most popular pastime was baseball – camp authorities allowed the prisoners to construct a diamond and outfield, and even to string a high net behind home plate to contain foul balls. In a decision that would have serious repercussions, the Australians allocated to the Japanese a plentiful supply of baseball bats, and distributed them without keeping a tally. By mid-1944 there were dozens of bats distributed among the prisoner population, far more than were required to play the game.

Each of the Japanese prisoners had his own story, and his own demons to wrestle with. Some, like Moriki and Takahara, seem to have adapted well to camp life, and did a good job reconciling their shame at being captured with the reality of their new world.

Some prisoners decided that defiance was the best form of defence. The most dramatic example of this occurred on 9 April 1943, when a particularly obstinate Japanese officer, Second Lieutenant Maseo Naka, who had been captured at Buna by the Americans in January, earned the dubious honour of being the first Japanese prisoner to break out of the camp. He scaled the barbed-wire fences without difficulty and then spent several hours on the run. Search parties were organised, with each man armed only with a pick handle, but they succeeded in tracking Naka down and bundling him back to camp. After his recapture he was asked to demonstrate how he had scaled the fences and completed the task in two minutes, casually smoking a cigarette throughout. This gaping flaw in security arrangements at the camp apparently was disregarded by Australian authorities. For his escapade Naka received 28 days' detention, but his run-ins with authority were only just beginning. Not long after his release he was involved in a fracas with Australian guards that ended with him punching an Australian officer in the face. This time the authorities had had enough. Naka was sentenced to two years hard labour, and transferred to the detention barracks at Hay camp. In

November 1943 he attempted suicide, so he was transferred to a mental hospital in Sydney, where he remained until he was sent back to Japan in 1946.

Another Japanese officer with a talent for mischief was Ensign Ko Oikawa, a submariner who had been captured by the Americans on Guadalcanal in early 1943. Oikawa's submarine, *I-1*, had served in China, Pearl Harbor and the Dutch East Indies before a long stint in the Solomons during the Guadalcanal campaign. On 29 January *I-1* was patrolling north-west of the island as Japan was preparing to evacuate when she was spotted by two New Zealand corvettes, *Kiwi* and *Moa*. In the ensuing battle *I-1* was crippled by depth charges, gunfire and ramming, and ran aground at Kamimbo Bay. Twenty-seven of her crew were killed, but the survivors managed to swim ashore and were rescued by the Japanese. Somehow Oikawa became separated from them, and he was captured by the Americans that night, with gunshot wounds to both legs. Once at Cowra, Oikawa went out of his way to cause trouble, appearing late on parades, refusing to obey orders and being generally insolent whenever the mood took him. It was a half-hearted attempt at rebellion – Oikawa never did anything defiant enough to get in serious trouble, but he was a constant source of irritation for camp authorities.

Other prisoners, such as Toyoshima, were more enigmatic. From his earliest days at the camp Toyoshima's rank, intelligence and charisma singled him out, and he was appointed the camp leader of B Compound, overseeing the rapidly ballooning numbers of Japanese prisoners. The English skills he had picked up in Darwin and Melbourne served him well, and he acted as a conduit between the prisoners and their Australian guards. He is a difficult character to pigeonhole, however. The popular impression of him, particularly in the decades immediately after the war, was that he was a sullen and brooding extremist, the archetypal Japanese military fanatic. This is influenced no doubt by the handful of photos that exist of him as a prisoner, in which he glares defiantly at the camera, and also simply because of his role in the Breakout. But the man himself seems more complicated than that two-dimensional perception.

Sam Shallard, Toyoshima's guard in Melbourne and the Australian who spent more time with him than anyone else, spoke of Toyoshima's sensitivity and personal charm. The letters that Toyoshima wrote in captivity, to both Shallard and Lionel Bell, his young Australian fan, also suggest a more thoughtful nature than history may give him credit for. Historian David Sissons recalled an account from Group Captain Wilbur Talberg of the RAAF, who had briefly met Toyoshima in hospital soon after his capture. 'Talberg and some other young pilots thought they would like to see what a Japanese airman looked like,' Sissons wrote, 'so they went over to the hospital and said "Hello. How are you feeling?" Talberg remembered Toyoshima's face lighting up as he replied in a very open and friendly fashion "Better, Better!"'[51] Accounts from other prisoners also tend to portray Toyoshima as outgoing and likeable, and suggest he was respected by both the Japanese and the Australians. 'I liked him very much,' recalled an Australian interpreter. 'He was helpful to everyone, he cooperated with the authorities without surrendering any of his dignity. He looked good, and he had a personality to match. He tried to look after the interests of all the prisoners, not just the navy people.'[52]

But Toyoshima occasionally had a knack for causing trouble. In June 1943 he instigated a minor diplomatic stir when he complained to a representative of the Swiss consul-general, who was inspecting the camp, that books and clothes he had owned in Hay had not been transferred with him to Cowra.

A couple of telegrams between the Swiss and the Australians soon rectified the matter, and Toyoshima was reunited with his belongings, but it was an embarrassing incident for Australian authorities. In February the following year Toyoshima revealed friction among the Japanese prisoners when he complained to Australian camp leaders that he couldn't get enough prisoners to volunteer for basic work duty to clean and maintain the compound. According to an intelligence report, when it was suggested to him that he should try to convince Japanese warrant officers to do the job, '[Toyoshima], who has a fair knowledge of English, much of it of the barrack room variety, replied, "They no bloody good. Got no guts."'[53]

One of Toyoshima's comrades, who certainly could not have been accused of lacking intestinal fortitude, was Sergeant Major Ryo Kanazawa, who had been on a troopship north of New Guinea that had been sunk by American warplanes in March 1943. He had spent a week in a lifeboat and then countless days roaming the swamps and jungles on the north coast of New Guinea as part of a ragged group of stranded soldiers, before being picked up by an Australian patrol. Weak from exposure, malaria and the effects of previous war wounds (he had been wounded five times during the fighting in China, and still had two Chinese bullets in his hip and thigh), he spent months in hospital and other camps before being sent to Cowra in December 1943. In a nod to the anonymity that most of his fellow prisoners craved, he told the Australians that his name was 'Akira' Kanazawa. He had been horrified to learn that one of his comrades had already revealed Kanazawa's rank and surname to his Australian captors, but his small fabrication was enough to disguise his true identity from both the Australians and his family back in Japan.[54]

Kanazawa arrived at the camp at a difficult time. Divisions were forming between the small clique of naval airmen, who had been in captivity for nearly two years and who had acquired money and personal possessions from civilian internees in Hay, and the army troops, most of whom had endured severe privations on the battlefields of the Pacific and had only been in captivity since 1943. The army troops perceived, not without justification, that the navy fliers saw themselves as superior to the lowly infantrymen. Kanazawa, as a high-ranking army NCO, was immediately seized upon by the army troops as a leader who could restore some balance to the unsustainable political situation in the camp.

Toyoshima realised that his position as camp leader was untenable, and agreed that an election should be held as soon as possible. All members of the compound voted, and a compromise was reached – Kanazawa would become the new camp leader, with another army sergeant major, Masao Kojima, acting as his deputy. Toyoshima would form the third member of a trio of leaders, and would represent the navy faction. Superficially it seemed like a good arrangement that would ensure both groups would be well represented. But, in reality, true authority still rested with the navy men for one fundamental reason – Toyoshima could speak English, Kanazawa and Kojima could not. For the time being, however, a potentially violent conflict among the prisoners had been averted.

Although relations between prisoners seemed to be back on track, the Japanese relationship with their Australian guards was strained. On 9 November 1943, Army HQ in Sydney cabled an update to Australian army representatives in London, advising them throughout the year the Japanese had been 'truculent' but that 'by firm and careful handling they have lately become more tractable'.[55] The situation came to a head when the Japanese leaders issued a list of frivolous demands to Australian authorities that included items such as the huts only being inspected once per week, all prisoners in detention being released, Australian guards removing their boots when entering the sleeping huts and the prisoners being given time at leisure to stroll around outside the wire. When these demands were rejected, the Japanese prisoners refused to leave their huts for the morning roll call, and order was only restored when Australian guards swept through the compound armed with batons and forced the Japanese to parade. The whole incident was reminiscent of a violent incident that had occurred at Featherston camp in New Zealand early in the year, but the Australian authorities did a good job of containing a potentially deadly situation.

Throughout 1943 Australian authorities were well aware of the nervous tension bubbling away beneath the surface of Japanese souls. Prisoners who could not quite summon the courage to take their own lives hoped that Australian guards would do it for them, often resorting to the simple tactic of requesting to be shot. The situation became so bad that on 26 April 1943 the commandant of the camp issued an order (printed in both Japanese and English) reminding the Japanese that the camp was administered under Australian and British Army rules, which had 'no connection whatever with customs or practices of the nationality to which prisoners belong, except only for approved religious worship'. It then went on to include this astonishing statement:

Regulations drawn up by the Authorities for the administration of prisoners of war camps in Australia, do not include any rule or regulation which permits of any Australian Officer, NCO or private of this camp or any other PW Camp in the British Empire, giving any weapon, ammunition or implement to any PW for the purpose of his committing suicide. Further, no Australian officer, NCO or man in this Camp under any consideration will be permitted to kill any prisoner at the prisoner's own verbal request unless such prisoner is in the act of escaping custody of any guard.

In response to regular threats from the Japanese prisoners that they intended to commit ritual suicide, the commandant was dismissive, telling the Japanese that 'if any of the so-called Hari Kari experts were really sincere they have had ample time to do so before reaching this Camp'. The scepticism and complacency in these remarks are revealing – perhaps if the threats had been taken more seriously, the prisoners would not have resorted to more deadly measures.

9

'A DEAD JAP IS THE BEST JAP': THE 22ND GARRISON BATTALION

It's safe to say that being allocated guard duty at the POW camp in Cowra was not exactly considered a prime posting during the Second World War. Although the specific motivations of every man who enlisted in the armed forces were unique, the majority shared the view that their duty was on the front lines, taking on the Japanese or the Germans in a fair fight. The members of the 22nd Garrison Battalion, charged with safeguarding the camp, had basically been selected because there was nowhere else for them to go. It's saying too much to call them misfits, but they certainly didn't fit comfortably in the structure of the military. Mostly this was through no fault of their own. Many were First World War veterans whose best years in the army were behind them. Others had served already in North Africa or the Pacific and had come back too wounded or ill to return to combat. Others were simply not medically fit – prior injuries or illness made them unsuitable for the front, but army authorities were reluctant to simply turn them away. The result was that the members of the 22nd Garrison Battalion were a mixed and moody lot. Some of them enjoyed their work at the camp, seeing it as their allotted contribution to the war effort, and no doubt content not to be dealing with machine-guns and malaria in a steamy New Guinea jungle. But many of the guards at Number 12 Prisoner of War Group were none-too-thrilled to be there.

They were a curious bunch. Some, through a fluke of birth year, were uncomfortably sandwiched between two World Wars – too young for the First and too old for the Second. For many this was their second war, and they were frustrated to have been sidelined in both. First time round they had trained but never fought, and this time, instead of facing the Japanese and Germans on the front line, they were stuck in the backblocks in the middle of nowhere, guarding a bunch of recalcitrant prisoners. Even when they had time off from the camp, Cowra wasn't exactly the most diverting place for a little R&R. The town, with its population of just over 3000 and its bare scattering of pubs and shops, offered little in the way of diversions.

The Army Training Camp ensured that the town was flooded with young, bored soldiers, and the novelty of being in a country town quickly wore off for recruit and guard alike. The Army recruits, much younger and fitter than their comrades at the prison camp, and destined for combat on the battlefields of the Pacific, were lightly dismissive of the garrison battalion, calling its members the 'olds and bolds'. Much of the town's young female population had relocated to Sydney to work in war industries, so the possibility of female company for the single men, even for a casual drink or dance, was remote. Early in the war the town had bustled with khaki-clad soldiers, but on any random evening in 1944 the streets were often deserted. The men of the 22nd Garrison Battalion were as much prisoners as the inmates they guarded.

The man in charge of this eclectic assortment of soldiers was Lieutenant Colonel Montague 'Monty' Brown, a 54-year-old former dairy farmer from Dapto in New South Wales. During the First World War he had served in a creditable but undistinguished role as an officer in the Light Horse, and seemed tailor-made for admin duty. His service record reads like a catalogue of training school and headquarters secondments, with little time spent in combat roles. In 1917 he transferred to the Indian Army and spent the remainder of the war in Bombay. He served for several years in the Indian Army after the war and, on his return to Australia, was an active member of cavalry units in the militia.

At the outbreak of the Second World War, Brown was the perfect choice to head up the 22nd Garrison Battalion. It wasn't so much he was unfit for combat, he was just so *fit* for garrison duty, and the fact that he found himself in Cowra, rather than leading a battalion in the deserts of North Africa or the jungles of New Guinea, speaks volumes for the place he occupied in the army.

The operation of Cowra camp was a complicated administrative role, and there is no doubt that Monty Brown was the right man for the job. Camp commanders needed to be outstanding organisers and people managers; their skills in directing combat operations were never tested. Brown is unlucky that he is remembered by history – had he acted slightly differently, the Breakout may never have occurred, and he would have faded into comfortable obscurity like the commandants of the Hay, Tatura or Loveday camps. Although he was good with men, he was even better with horses, and he was a cavalryman through and through. When not in his office, he could usually be found enjoying a ride in the broad expanses around the camp.

Reporting directly to Brown were the four commandants of the prisoner compounds, Major Les Meagher (A Compound – Italians), Major Bob Ramsay (B Compound – Japanese), Major Ed Timms (C Compound – Italians) and Major Les Lees (D Compound – Japanese officers, Koreans and Formosans [Taiwanese]). Between the four was an impressive pedigree of combat experience and distinction on the field of battle. All had served in the First World War, and their collective battle honours included Gallipoli, France, Belgium, Egypt and Palestine, with a corresponding collection of service and gallantry awards.

Major Ramsay, as commandant of B Compound, which brimmed with troublesome Japanese soldiers, had the most important role in the camp. He had earned glory during his service in the First World War. Enlisting as a private in 1914, he had fought with the Australian Naval and Military Expedition Force in Rabaul, Australia's first action of the war. In 1915 he joined the 1st Battalion at Gallipoli as a corporal, and was commissioned in the field soon after. In August he was mentioned in despatches for a 'fine piece of bombing work executed at Lone Pine'[56] and soon after the campaign ended he was awarded the Military Cross. On the Western Front he transferred to the 53rd Battalion, and fought with distinction at Fromelles and on the Somme, again being mentioned in despatches. His front-line service ended in September 1917 when he received a shrapnel wound in the ankle at Polygon Wood during the Third Battle of Ypres, and he spent the rest of the war at a desk job in London, returning to Australia as a captain in 1919.

Although Ramsay was unquestionably brave and a born soldier, shadows clouded his return to Australia. He struggled to fit back into civilian life and had a couple of run-ins with the law for drunkenness and passing dud cheques. At the outbreak of the Second World War he was too old for an active combat command, but he was assigned to various training units and eventually to the 22nd Garrison Battalion in Cowra. In 1942 he was court-martialled for fraud in a convoluted case that centred on payments to Italian prisoners for construction work they were doing in the camp; Ramsay pleaded not guilty and was cleared of two charges and convicted of one. His sentence was a reprimand, suggesting that the whole thing was blown out of proportion, and probably never should have come before a court in the first place. In any event it didn't impact on his career – he was promoted to major soon after and given command of the unruly Japanese in B Compound, the toughest gig at the camp.

Ramsay had a son, also Robert, who served with the Australian Imperial Force (AIF) and had been captured by the Japanese during the fall of Singapore in February 1942, a fact that has intrigued students of the Cowra Breakout for decades. The implication is that Ramsay may have been unnecessarily soft on the Japanese prisoners at Cowra in the hope that the Japanese would reciprocate with Allied prisoners in their hands, and that this conciliatory attitude was a contributing factor that led to the Breakout. But it's a baseless charge – there's nothing in the records to indicate Ramsay was particularly soft on the Japanese. He fulfilled the requirements to care for them as dictated by his superiors and the military rules he was bound to follow and, if anything, was a pretty tough taskmaster at times with the Japanese he oversaw. At the end of the day, Ramsay was a dedicated soldier, and there's no evidence he treated the Japanese any differently than he otherwise would have – he certainly never mentioned the connection in any of his papers. He unquestionably must share a large portion of the blame for the Breakout, but it had nothing to do with his son's captivity. (Robert survived the perils of a Japanese prison camp and returned to Australia in 1946.)

One of most intriguing members of the guard unit was Sergeant Olag Negerevich, a Russian who had been born in Harbin in Manchuria in 1921 and was ten years old when the Japanese invaded in 1931. Life was extremely difficult for the Russian population of China under Japanese rule, and in 1939 the young Negerevich fled, arriving as a stateless refugee in Sydney by way of Java. He had learnt to speak Japanese in the years of occupation, so was mustered into the Australian forces at the outbreak of the Pacific War, and soon found himself working in Cowra as an interpreter.

Negerevich was an interesting character. His years of living with the Japanese had given him a solid understanding of their culture and mindset, but he was not a great fan of them. He particularly disliked the Koreans in the camp, although without giving a specific reason for it, stating in a letter in 1965 that he was 'prejudiced against Koreans as a race so you should accept my observations with a grain of salt'.[57] This attitude may simply have reflected the prejudice felt across Asia to Koreans before and during the war; Koreans were often viewed as inferior to the Chinese and the Japanese, and their service in the Japanese military in the war against China would have done nothing to endear them to a young Russian man living under occupation in Manchuria.

In return, Negerevich wasn't much liked by the Japanese. Marekuni Takahara considered him 'conceited, incompetent and irresponsible'. Negerevich was the only Australian Takahara singled out for criticism in his memoirs – apart from the camp dentist at Hay, who didn't believe in filling Japanese teeth and insisted on extraction.[58]

Negerevich also appeared to be somewhat of an outsider to his fellow members of the guard unit. In spite of that, he had a knack for being in the right place at the right time.

The attitude of members of the garrison battalion to the Japanese in their charge was mixed – some men got on well with the prisoners and even formed pseudo-friendships with them. Toyoshima in particular was well liked by pretty much everyone who came in contact with him. But other guards were suspicious or outright hostile to the Japanese prisoners. Fuelled by the White Australia policy, wartime propaganda and news of Japanese atrocities in Asia, Australians harboured animosity towards the Japanese in general and their soldiers in particular. For most of the guards at Cowra, these were the first Japanese people they had ever encountered, and they were wary and fearful. This was exacerbated by the frustrations they felt at being forced into the tedium of guard duty. There was a certain antagonising irony in their situation – they had much closer contact with the hated enemy soldiers than most of their comrades in combat ever would, yet they were not allowed to act on it as they would have on the battlefield. Instead of taking on the Japanese in a fair fight, they were serving them meals and tending to their bedding. This strange paradox intensified their resentment.

Private Clarrie Mead, an 18-year-old labourer from Bowral in New South Wales, was a recruit at the Army Training Camp and his attitude to the Japanese was fairly typical. 'It was not my attitude, it was the attitude that [the Australian authorities] brainwashed us to hate them,' he later said. 'They used to show us a film in the training centre called *The Rape of Nanking*. Little girls with their legs open and the bayonet straight in their you-know-what and after these sort of movies they used to brainwash us to hate the Japanese.' Nearly 50 years after the end of the war he still felt the same. When asked in a 1991 interview how his attitude had changed, his response was unambiguous. 'It has not changed at all, mate,' he said. 'I would not even feed them. One thing I would never do is shake hands with a Japanese.'[59]

Animosity for the Japanese occasionally extended beyond the guards to the general prison population. Corporal Norm Beaman had served in a cavalry unit in the Middle East and New Guinea until malaria nearly killed him. Deemed too ill to return to active service, he was transferred to Cowra and found himself driving an ambulance instead of a tank. In this capacity he had frequent contact with Korean orderlies who worked in the camp hospital. 'The Koreans absolutely hated the Japs,' he recalled.

> They despised Japan and despised the war. They had no love for the Jap whatsoever and if we pulled the ambulance up outside the hospital the Korean orderly would walk out to the ambulance and say 'what is he, Jap or Korean?'. If I would say a Jap they would just pull open the doors to the ambulance and get in behind him and kick him out. They would land him out on his backside – they just could not take them at all.[60]

Norm's work brought him closer to Japanese than most of the Australian guards and he often felt that the prisoners enjoyed intimidating him. 'It was scary anytime, to drive in there amongst all those Japanese,' he recalled. 'They had great glee in getting either side of the ambulance and just skimming a baseball across the bonnet of the ambulance. Two or three of them either side just shying the ball across quite close to the windscreen at times. It was a terrible experience ... I always thought that they were absolute animals.'[61]

It was an attitude shared by many. When asked if he would have minded if all the Japanese at Cowra had been shot, Private Henry Rankin was unabashed in his contempt. 'It wouldn't worry me,' he said. 'A dead Jap is the best Jap.'[62] For Rankin and the other members of the 22nd Garrison Battalion, they would soon get an opportunity to put that philosophy to the test.

10

'FINALLY ALL OF US CAN DIE HERE': THE MUTINY AT FEATHERSTON

It's funny how small pieces of history can sometimes align, like leaves on a fast-moving creek coming together in the current. Jack and Charlie Owen, two New Zealand brothers who served in the Pacific but were separated by thousands of miles of ocean, would both face the Japanese – one would be the victim of a massacre, the other would start one.

In October 1942, Charlie Owen sat on a bare concrete floor, thinking of home. Only 18 months ago he'd been back in Masterton, playing rugby and heading into the pubs and dancehalls of Wellington with his mates on the weekend. So much had changed since then. He'd joined the New Zealand Army in 1940, determined to do his bit against the Germans. But a looming threat in the Pacific sidelined those plans, and Charlie found himself dispatched to Fiji to guard civilian radio operators who were on the lookout for German ships. Just how he was supposed to guard them was anyone's guess – he and 20 or so other soldiers had received only the most basic training, and had been sent to Fiji without weapons. Clearly they were only here to make sure the expensive radio gear didn't get pinched by the locals, but that soon changed, and fast.

As the Japanese starting pushing their weight around in the Pacific the radio operators and their unarmed soldier mates were ordered to leave Fiji and were scattered in groups of three or four around the islands north of Fiji, to act as Coastwatchers, a kind of human trip-wire to alert the Allies to any Japanese naval or air movements in the central Pacific. Charlie and a few other blokes had been sent to Maiana Island, a scrappy coral atoll in the Gilbert Islands, just north of the equator. There wasn't much to do there, but the weather was hot, the water was cool and the locals were friendly. Charlie found one local girl, Taengeri, particularly friendly and in short order he had himself a girlfriend. When he was off duty they would explore the island and swim in the sheltered lagoon. She introduced him to her family, and taught him about her customs and traditions. For Charlie, all things considered, life was not bad.

On the morning of 8 December 1941, Charlie reported to his post at the improvised radio station. Even though it was early, it was already stinking hot, and pregnant grey clouds loomed over the lagoon. It would rain this afternoon for certain – hell, at this time of year it rained *every* afternoon. The radio operator sent his weather reports off to Fiji, and then spun the dial to tune in to the Allied military station in Hawaii, as he'd done pretty much every day since he got here. Only today, he was greeted by static. 'I can't raise Hawaii,' he told Charlie. 'Their transmitter must be on the blink. I'll try Los Angeles instead.' Spinning the dial again, he was greeted with chaos. The US west coast radio waves were thrumming with reports of attacking aircraft and burning ships. Pearl Harbor was in flames.

Charlie and his colleagues weren't initially worried – Hawaii was 2000 miles away, and the Japanese would have little interest in their speck of coral in the middle of the Pacific. They didn't know it, but the Pacific War was about to erupt, and they would be closer to the action than they could have imagined. The day after Pearl Harbor, Japanese forces landed in the northern Gilbert Islands, planning to build airfields to protect their gains in Asia and the Pacific. Two New Zealand Coastwatchers were captured, becoming some of the first Allied POWs of the Pacific War. The New Zealand government, aware it had 20 or so citizens facing imminent danger in the Gilberts, turned its back on them. The Coastwatchers were abandoned, left to fend for themselves in the face of the Japanese Pacific fleet. (After the war it was revealed that the only concession the New Zealand government made was to secretly attest the radio operators into the army, in the vain hope that if they were captured they would not be executed as civilian spies.)

For the next nine months the Coastwatchers in the Gilbert Islands lived in a disconcerting limbo – no rescue was coming from New Zealand, but the Japanese were not moving either. Charlie made the best of it, and grew closer to Taengeri – one balmy evening she told him that a baby was on the way. It was a strange time – the smallest piece of tranquillity in the middle of the mayhem of the Pacific.

In the spring of 1942 the Japanese were forced to act. At sea their navy had been smashed at Coral Sea and Midway, and on land US Marines had unexpectedly landed at Guadalcanal. The Gilbert Islands were key to holding onto their gains, and they knew that Coastwatchers were watching their every move from the southern islands. In September 1942 the Japanese swept south, taking Tarawa and Maiana, and shattering the fragile peace. Charlie and the other Coastwatchers were rounded up, torn away from friends and families on Maiana and sent north to Tarawa. At first the Japanese seemed uncertain what to do with their new captives – Charlie and 16 other Coastwatchers were tied to trees for three days, and then locked up in the asylum at the local hospital with five Australian, New Zealand and British civilians. They languished there for a month until 15 October 1942. What sparked the chain of events that took place next is unclear – local people who were there offered conflicting accounts after the war. One said that a prisoner escaped, another that an American ship shelled the island that day. The most likely scenario is that, while the prisoners were out on a working party, US planes flew over and dropped some bombs on the island. Some of the prisoners cheered; one apparently took off his shirt and waved it at the Allied planes. Regardless of the cause, the Japanese were furious at the prisoners and exacted a terrible revenge. They were lined up and their hands were tied with rope. 'They are going to kill us all!' called out Isaac Handley, one of the civilians. 'Be brave, lads!'[63] A local man called Mikaere described what happened next. 'One Japanese stepped forward to the first European in the line and cut his head off,' he said. 'Then I saw a second European have his head cut off and I could not see the third one because I fainted.'[64]

Within minutes, all 22 men had been executed. They were buried near the beach in shallow graves. When American troops invaded Tarawa a year later, the island was effectively destroyed in one of the bloodiest battles of the Pacific War. The bodies of the Coastwatchers were lost – no trace of Charlie Owen or his Coastwatcher comrades was ever found.

Six months and half a world away, Charlie's older brother Jack was also facing the Japanese, but under very different circumstances. US forces had been grappling with the Japanese on the Solomon Island of Guadalcanal since mid-1942, and in a brutal campaign on land and sea had finally gained the upper hand. As Japanese soldiers, sailors and airmen were overwhelmed, the number of prisoners needing to be secured had ballooned. Some of the US prisoners were sent to Cowra or New Caledonia, but the majority went to New Zealand, to the POW camp at Featherston near Wellington.[65]

The camp had originally been constructed in the First World War, to train New Zealand soldiers for the killing fields of Gallipoli and the Western Front. By war's end more than 60 000 troops had been through the camp, but there was little use for it in peacetime, and it was demolished in the 1920s. By September 1942 the surge in Japanese prisoner numbers led to an urgent request from the US government for New Zealand to house the bulk of the captives, and Featherston was hurriedly re-established. Within weeks the camp was accepting its first inmates and, within six months, the camp that had been designed to accommodate about 450 prisoners was home to more than 800. Although on a smaller scale, Featherston was practically a carbon copy of Cowra. Inmates were housed in four compounds and received food in both quantity and quality. In their spare time they played baseball and held sumo wrestling matches, and tended to vegetable and ornamental gardens. In the evenings they performed theatre, or sat in groups playing music on instruments supplied by their captors. If they were ill or injured, they received excellent medical care in the camp hospital. As at Cowra, the prison guard was made up of soldiers too old or too injured to see service in the front lines. One of them was Jack Owen.

As Japan's fortunes in the war changed, so too did the prisoners. The first arrivals had been labourers, many of them Koreans, who had been captured while building an airfield on Guadalcanal in the early days of the campaign. These were docile prisoners, many of whom were happy to be out of harm's way, and who were content to do work detail around the camp. They had spent most of their military career performing backbreaking labour in some of the harshest environments in the world, so the clean sheets and mild climate of the Featherston camp, far from the guns and bombs, seemed like paradise.

As the tide turned against the Japanese on Guadalcanal, however, and they suffered more defeats at the hands of US forces, the character of the camp began to change. The new batch of prisoners was predominantly combat troops, either taken during bitter land battles in the jungles and on the ridges of Guadalcanal, or navy men whose ships had been blown from under them during ferocious engagements at sea. These sons of the Empire were not grateful to be out of the war, and shared the same brutal dedication to the Field Service Code as their comrades at Cowra. They seethed with anger and self-hate, and many longed for the noble death that had eluded them on the battlefield. Like the inmates at Cowra, they were astonished at the hospitable treatment they received from the New Zealand authorities at Featherston, and saw it as a sign of weakness. In many ways they were even more militaristic and fanatical than the prisoners at Cowra, coming from a more homogenous group in the Solomon Islands forces and suffering privations on Guadalcanal that honed their sense of duty and the contempt they felt for their enemy.

Among the new arrivals were 115 sailors who had been captured when their heavy cruiser, *Furutaka*, had been sunk by American ships during the Battle of Cape Esperance in October 1942. The most senior officer in this group was Lieutenant Toshio Adachi, and he quickly became the de facto leader of the entire camp. Within a month of his arrival a dangerous rift had formed between the more moderate inmates and the fanatics who longed to purge their own tortured souls with bloodshed. The prisoners began hoarding improvised weapons, and formulated a plan to launch a violent uprising on Christmas Eve. Nervy prisoners eventually spilled the beans to camp authorities and the plan was quashed, but the desire for violence still festered in many of the prisoners.

By February the situation had deteriorated even further. On the 23rd a working party downed tools and retired to their huts, only returning to work when the furious guards forced them out at the point of the bayonet. In response the camp commandant, Lieutenant Colonel Donald Donaldson, gave the recalcitrant inmates three days to improve their behaviour. As punishment for their open display of disobedience, Donaldson ordered a doubling of the number of prisoners put to work. This was not a problem for the labour corps that had been in the camp for the best part of a year and were used to working. But the new arrivals, military men who preferred death to forced labour, were outraged. Adachi pleaded with his fellow inmates and camp authorities for cool heads to prevail – tensions in the camp were at boiling point, and he knew that bloodshed was the likely outcome.

On the morning of 25 February, the labour parties emerged from their compound as they did every day. But there was no sign of the soldiers from Number 2 Compound, who had also been assigned work duties that day. Interpreters sent to fetch them found about 250 prisoners sitting cross-legged on the ground, refusing to stand. A desperate Adachi and another officer, Sub-Lieutenant Ikunosuke Nishimura, asked for a meeting with camp authorities to try to overcome the stalemate. After two hours of intense discussion, negotiations stalled – the Japanese soldiers would not work; the New Zealanders were outraged at their flagrant insubordination. The camp's adjutant,

Lieutenant James Malcolm, ordered 47 guards to take arms and force the Japanese from the compound. One of the men in the group was Corporal Jack Owen.

It's impossible to know if news had filtered back to New Zealand about the fate of the Coastwatchers on Tarawa. The island was still in Japanese hands, and reports about the wellbeing of prisoners in Japanese captivity were rare. At the very least, Jack knew that the Japanese had captured his brother and there had been no word from him for months. At worst, Jack knew that Charlie was dead. As he took his assigned position on the roof of a building overlooking the compound, gripping his Thompson submachine gun firmly, he must have sensed that his moment of retribution was close at hand.

The guards formed an arc around the prisoners and raised their rifles. Malcolm ordered Adachi and Nishimura to force the Japanese to parade. As the officers and interpreters shouted, the prisoners rose defiantly to their feet. Adachi and Nishimura retreated into the agitated crowd. What happened next is shrouded in confusion, but it appears that the once-moderate Adachi became fired up by the crowd. 'Adachi [picked] up two large stones', a witness said, 'and took a position in the centre of the prisoners of war.'[66] Malcolm ordered Adachi and Nishimura to be arrested, and three or four guards began to advance on the prisoners to take custody of the two officers. Tempers flared and a scuffle broke out. Panicking, a guard drew a bayonet and plunged it into the thigh of a Japanese prisoner.

'The non-commissioned officer who was stabbed winced with pain, and more or less spontaneously grasped the bayonet with both hands,' Adachi recalled years later. 'The New Zealand soldier hurriedly pulled the bayonet up and out.'[67]

The blade sliced through the man's hands, severing several fingers – possibly all ten – which plopped to the ground in front of him in a pool of blood. The man screamed, and Malcolm drew a pistol in a desperate attempt to regain control.

At a later court of inquiry, he said: 'I decided upon a show of arms as my next move, there being no remaining expedient apparent to me to get over the situation.'

He fired a warning shot above Adachi's head and, when this had no effect, decided on a more direct course of action. He fired at Adachi again – and this time it was no warning shot. The bullet tore through Adachi's left arm and into the forehead of the prisoner standing behind him. The man fell dead, there was a pause as both prisoner and guard realised the gravity of what had just happened, and then all hell broke loose. The Japanese surged towards the guards, throwing rocks and sticks and anything else that came to hand. The guards, momentarily caught off guard, hesitated, but Jack didn't. His Tommy gun roared as he opened up on the men massed below him. Bullets sliced through the throng, and men fell in their dozens. The din spurred the other guards into action and everyone started shooting. Prisoners screamed as bullets cut them down in the cramped confines of the compound yard, submachine guns chattered their deafening soundtrack of death, guards fired their rifles as quickly as they could work the bolt. One guard set his submachine gun to fire in single shots, and calmly picked off one Japanese target after the next. The noise was deafening, the fire accurate and deadly.

As quickly as it had begun, the firing died off. Prisoners were rolling and groaning on the ground. Many lay still. Seaman Saito thought that was the end of it. 'When I looked around … there went up a shout, "Long reign the Emperor! The Empire of Japan forever!" from among the prisoners. I got up on my feet and cried so, too.'[68] This was apparently too much for Jack and his guardmates. 'The shots roared up again,' said Saito.

'I plunged into the guards who were firing on us, persuading myself "Finally all of us can die here ..."'

Privates Len James and Wally Pelvin were caught up in the melee, with screaming men and bullets whirling around them. 'I'm getting out!' James recalled Pelvin yelling. 'And he turned and got it in the back. It was a ricochet from a bullet.' Pelvin went down hard, and as James was kneeling to tend to him another ricochet struck him in the leg. He collapsed to the ground, and craned his neck to see where the shots had come from. 'The only person who had a chance of getting us,' he later said, 'was Corporal Owen.'

The shooting probably only went on for 30 or 40 seconds before New Zealand officers, racing along the line and bellowing for their men to cease fire, gained control. But that was more than enough time – and the result was a bloodbath. Thirty-one Japanese lay dead on the bloodstained earth of the compound. Another hundred or so were writhing in agony, their uninjured comrades desperately attempting to stem severed arteries and plug gaping wounds with shirts and blankets. Within the coming days a further 17 men would die from their wounds. Worse still, about a dozen New Zealand guards had been wounded, mostly by Japanese fists and rocks, but several, like Pelvin and James, by ricocheting bullets. Three days later, Pelvin was dead. He was 34, and left a wife and three-year-old daughter in Wellington. Jack Owen was never disciplined for his role in the massacre.

The mutiny was a disaster for New Zealand authorities. Not only had nearly 50 unarmed prisoners been gunned down, they weren't even prisoners who belonged to the New Zealanders – they had been captured by the Americans. Poor old New Zealand, which already felt isolated and sidelined in the Pacific War, was now thrust into the middle of a diplomatic storm it had little experience in or stomach for.

The first issue was how to broach the news of the mutiny to the Japanese government. New Zealand was aware that Japan had not ratified the Geneva Convention and therefore its citizens were not legally entitled to its protections. However, as in Australia, New Zealand felt it was obliged to treat Japanese prisoners under the same terms it would prisoners from other nations (this wasn't a purely altruistic decision – there were hundreds of New Zealand POWs being held by the Japanese, and New Zealand was desperate to avoid giving the irascible Japanese authorities an excuse to mistreat them).

Under advice from the British government, New Zealand announced it would investigate the mutiny via a military inquiry under the rules stipulated in the Geneva Convention, and report the results to Japan via the neutral Swiss government. Both prisoners and guards would be called as witnesses, and any charges, against Japanese prisoners or New Zealand guards, would be heard in a court martial. It was obvious that New Zealand was taking great pains with the whole process to deliver a fair and measured response, one that would hopefully appease the Japanese government – well, appease them as far as possible, given that 48 of their countrymen had just been killed.

The New Zealand government kept a tight lid on news of the mutiny. It wasn't until the first week of March that the prime minister, Peter Fraser, issued a brief and rather opaque statement to the press that was reported widely in newspapers in both New Zealand and Australia. 'The firm action on the part of the guards was necessary to quell the mutiny and to restore order,' he said in the statement. 'None of the prisoners escaped, and the camp was soon normal, and has since remained quiet. An official inquiry is being held immediately.'[69]

That court of inquiry was promptly held two weeks later, with findings distributed on 22 March. Ten Japanese prisoners were called as witnesses, including Adachi and Nishimura. As could have been expected, the court supported the actions of the New Zealand guards and laid blame for the mutiny at the feet of the Japanese prisoners. The court found that the amount of fire had not been excessive, and that the shooting of prisoners, although unfortunate, was necessary to quell a violent revolt, to protect the lives of the guards and to restore order to the camp. Somewhat surprisingly, the court findings went to some length to highlight the dangerous psychological state of the prisoners and to attempt to explain the gulf in understanding that existed between the prisoners and the guards. The court recommended that charges be laid against the ringleaders, including Adachi, but there is no evidence that he or any of the Japanese survivors were punished for their part in the mutiny.

The findings of the court were distributed to all Allied powers, and to the Japanese government via the Swiss. The Japanese were naturally outraged and, in a series of terse cablegrams, accused the New Zealand government of 'murdering' its citizens, and implied that New Zealand had now set a precedent for the treatment of POWs that Japan would be forced to mirror with Allied captives in its hands. This was an outrageous statement, given the wholesale mistreatment of Allied prisoners in Japanese captivity – thousands had already died due to overwork, malnutrition and execution; more than 30 000 Allied POWs would die in Japanese camps before the end of the war.

This diplomatic chest-thumping and wrangling continued for months, and it wasn't until October that detailed reports of the incident were widely distributed, including to the camp authorities in Cowra (although initial reports had filtered through in March and April). The similarities between the two camps were striking, and the fact that the report into the Featherston mutiny didn't raise figurative red flags all over Cowra is one of the most exasperating failures of this entire saga. As at Featherston, Cowra was populated by a mix of docile workers and hostile ex-combatants. Australian authorities were aware that the Japanese were suffering excruciating mental anguish at having been captured, and longed to do something about it. The prisoners at Cowra had repeatedly displayed the same open hostility to their captors as their comrades had in New Zealand. Featherston clearly demonstrated that Japanese prisoners were not afraid of violence; indeed, they seemed to welcome it.*

With the report from Featherston in hand, effectively a blueprint for avoiding a violent uprising among Japanese prisoners, the camp authorities at Cowra should have leapt into action: improving security, conducting more frequent and thorough searches of the Japanese compounds, interrogating more prisoners, improving the training of the guard unit, weeding out troublemakers among the prison population. Instead they were gripped by an inexplicable inertia. The disaster at Featherston didn't just ring a few alarm bells – it set off an entire carillon of them. For reasons that are still unknown, the authorities at Cowra refused to hear them.**

---

*   The mutiny at Featherston wasn't the only violent incident involving Japanese prisoners at this time. In January 1944 plans for Japanese prisoners to riot against their US captors at Camp Paita in New Caledonia were thwarted after being revealed by an informant. Twenty-two of the ringleaders committed suicide in response.

** A fascinating footnote to this whole incident is that, after the Breakout, prisoners at Cowra revealed that they had been aware of the mutiny at Featherston (probably via direct or overheard conversations with loose-lipped Australian guards) and had viewed it, at least peripherally, as a source of inspiration. If Japanese prisoners could hear about the incident at Featherston and use it to shape their future actions, it is inexcusable that the camp authorities at Cowra failed to do the same.

11

'I CONCEALED MYSELF AND EAVESDROPPED': THE KOREAN INFORMANT

By early 1944, the war was going catastrophically for the Japanese. The successes at Pearl Harbor, Singapore and Rabaul were now distant memories, as the Allies pushed relentlessly onward and drove the Japanese from the strongholds they had seized with such bloodshed only two years before. The list of Japanese defeats reads like a showreel of pain and suffering – Guadalcanal, New Georgia, Bougainville, Tarawa, Kwajalein. Dozens of other islands, atolls and peninsulas that had once been the jewels in Japan's Pacific crown now became killing fields as the sons of Tokyo, Nagoya and Sapporo were relentlessly drawn in and consumed.

On land, Allied marines and infantrymen advanced like a green wave. At sea, the once-proud Japanese Navy, the world's third-largest at the start of the war, was being smashed to oblivion, and in the sky the Japanese air and naval flying forces, once the most potent air group in the world, watched in horror as their aircraft were shot out of the sky or burned on bombed airfields. New Guinea, once the bastion of Japan's conquests in the south-west Pacific, had become a charnel house, as ridge and village fell to the irresistible Allied advance. Marine and army forces from the US and Australia pushed relentlessly along the north coast, staging amphibious landings and encircling the beleaguered Japanese garrison. For the Japanese Army troops trapped in New Guinea, there was no reinforcement, no respite, no relief.

In late 1943 Allied attention had turned to the Huon Peninsula, an isolated and rugged pimple on the north coast, and the key to breaking the back of Japanese resistance in New Guinea. Australian troops spearheaded the operation with an amphibious landing east of Lae in September, supported by the first successful airborne operation of the Pacific War, when elements from the 7th Australian Division and the US 503rd Parachute Infantry Regiment parachuted onto the airfield at Nadzab. An amphibious landing at Scarlet Beach on 22 September led to the capture of Finschhafen. The Australians then advanced along the coast and by early 1944 had pushed the Japanese back towards Madang, the final objective of the campaign. The Japanese resisted fiercely and, in spite of a lack of reinforcements and resupply, they launched several counterattacks that frustrated the Allied advance. As the Australians pushed forward, intelligence revealed that more than 6000 Japanese troops were falling back on Madang, and troops from the US 32nd Division were hurriedly landed at Saidor and smashed into the flank of the retreating Japanese. The fighting was brutal and relentless in the steamy confines of the New Guinea jungle.

One of the Japanese troops caught up in the melee was 26-year-old Takao Matsumoto, a Korean-born superior private (or lance corporal) who had enlisted in the Japanese military in 1939 from his hometown in the province of Keisho (today's Gyeongsang).[70] *Matsumoto* was, of course, a Japanese surname – like millions of his countrymen during the 35-year Japanese occupation of Korea, Matsumoto had been stripped of his Korean identity, his name changed, his hometown renamed, his native language banned and the study of his history and culture forbidden. The Japanese were cruel and merciless occupiers; the wholesale murder of civilians was commonplace, and thousands of Korean women were forced into sexual slavery as so-called 'comfort women' for the Japanese military.

If nothing else, Matsumoto was a survivor, and he kept his head down during his time in the Japanese military. Technically he had volunteered to serve in the army, but members of the local Japanese police force in his hometown had 'urged' him to enlist repeatedly until he relented – if ever there was a press-ganging, this was it. Koreans who joined the Japanese forces were typically given labour and construction roles but, unusually, Matsumoto was allowed to join a combat battalion in the 80th Infantry Regiment, which included about 100 Korean volunteers. He had a flair for military life and was quickly promoted to superior private, along with nine other members of the battalion who also became non-commissioned officers. In late 1941 the regiment was placed on a war footing, anticipating conflict with the USSR, but when this threat dissipated the regiment was sent to the south-west Pacific as part of the 20th Division. The regiment fought heavily throughout the New Guinea campaign, and was decimated by the Australians at Finschhafen in October and the Americans at Sattelberg in November. By early 1944 the regiment was caught up in the organised chaos of the Japanese retreat on Madang, and it was during this time that Matsumoto had his meeting with fate.

The Japanese forces had been cut off for months by air and sea, and were barely surviving on meagre rations and any food they could scrounge from the jungle and native gardens or pilfer from enemy soldiers. Foraging for food had become a more important pursuit than fighting, and on 25 January Matsumoto volunteered to scout around and return with breakfast for his squad. He hadn't gone far when he stumbled into a US patrol, and he was lucky he wasn't gunned down on the spot. When he saw he was surrounded, he threw his hands up. No thoughts of noble suicide or fighting to the death here – unlike the Japanese he served with, Matsumoto recognised a lost cause when he saw it.

The Americans bundled Matsumoto into a group of other Japanese prisoners and performed a rudimentary interrogation. They weren't expecting to learn much. Japanese soldiers were notoriously ill-informed about the Japanese Army and their place in it, but Matsumoto turned out to have seen lots, and had no qualms talking about it. In a series of interviews he revealed in detail the structure of his battalion, the composition of troops, the names of senior officers and information about training and deployment. He also revealed that he had come across three American airmen who had been shot down and captured near his battalion position in northern New Guinea in June 1943, and gave detailed descriptions of them.[71] One, a lieutenant, was 'emaciated so that his cheekbones were prominent', Matsumoto said. He also 'had a clean-cut face, recently shaved, and seemed gentle in nature'. Another was 'emaciated beyond description', but the third was in the worst shape of the lot, and was carried in on a stretcher with a serious leg wound. He was unshaven and filthy and was very weak. 'He kept whispering for water,' Matsuomoto told his interrogators, 'which, together with cooked rice [I gave him].' The American fliers had been starving in the jungle for days, and were delighted when Matsumoto also gave them cigarettes and bananas. After being briefly questioned by the Japanese, the Americans were taken away; Matsumoto later heard that the one on the stretcher had died and the others had been sent to a prison camp in Japan.

Through one of those administrative vagaries so common in the military, Matsumoto was not taken into custody by the Americans and shipped off to one of their POW compounds in New Zealand or New Caledonia. Instead, he was handed over to the Australians, who sent him to an interrogation camp in Brisbane, and then on to his final destination for the remainder of the war. On 12 May 1944, Takao Matsumoto, prisoner number PWJA(USA)147016, arrived in Cowra.

Matsumoto arrived at Number 12 Prisoner of War Group as part of a large draft of new prisoners. The succession of Japanese reverses across the Pacific meant a growing number of prisoners were being taken, and the camps in Australia were struggling to deal with the pace and volume of new arrivals. Earlier in the year the overcrowding had become so bad that tents were brought in to house new arrivals in Cowra. More huts had since been built, but the camp was still bursting at the seams with Japanese prisoners.

Matsumoto and a private, Terekawa, were the only Koreans in the new bunch, and they were treated with disdain by their fellow prisoners. The Japanese despised the peoples of Asia they had subjugated, and the Koreans were considered the lowest in the pile. This contempt was exacerbated by the crushing feelings of shame and self-loathing the Japanese prisoners were experiencing. It was as if through deflecting their anger towards the Koreans, they could alleviate some of their own emotional turmoil. Throughout the long journey from Sydney the two Koreans had kept their eyes lowered, as if hoping to melt into the shadows and escape the glares of hatred from the Japanese around them.

Once in the camp, the new group was ushered into B Compound and addressed in Japanese by Sergeant Olag Negerevich, the Australian interpreter. He asked if there were any Koreans in the group, and Matsumoto and Terekawa stepped forward. The two men had not known each other before being thrust together in the Brisbane camp, and they shared no bond apart from their common ancestry, but they were grateful for each other's company in the tense atmosphere. Negerevich told them that they would stay with the group until bedding and equipment were issued, and then they would be taken to a separate part of the camp. The Japanese in the group muttered among themselves as this was explained – it was clear to Matsumoto that he and his Korean comrade could do nothing right in the eyes of the Japanese, and he was eager to be away from them.

Negerevich introduced the new arrivals to Toyoshima, who, although no longer in charge of the compound, still took responsibility for the induction of new arrivals. Toyoshima's charisma and authority were instantly apparent, and several of the new prisoners bowed when he was introduced. He greeted them briefly and formally, before giving a succinct overview of the camp's routines. The group was then dismissed, and had several hours to explore the compound while equipment was issued and accommodation allocated. Matsumoto wandered around the compound, watching the Japanese playing baseball, tending gardens and chatting in groups. Matsumoto's natural survival instincts had taught him the value of information – juicy pieces of intelligence were a key tool to win favour with your captors – and he kept his eyes and ears open as he explored his new surroundings. He overheard snippets of conversation –

discussions of old comrades and battles, memories of wives and girlfriends from home, complaints that this Australian soil was too harsh to grow decent vegetables. Many of the Japanese simply sat and smoked, staring into space. The atmosphere, Matsumoto recalled, was extremely tense.

As he returned to the huts where the new arrivals had gathered, waiting for bedding to be issued, he noticed a suspicious meeting between an old hand and three of the newcomers, and he immediately spotted an opportunity to gather some useful intelligence:

> While standing there, somebody approached three of the newcomers … and called them aside. The newcomers followed him, and I, observing such a stealthy movement, sneaked along quietly, feigning indifference and unconcern and followed him to where they hid around one corner of a hut while I concealed myself around the opposite corner and eavesdropped.[72]

Matsumoto had a knack for being in the right place at the right time, and the conversation he was about to overhear set a chain of events in motion that would have serious, and immediate, consequences.

> What the old timer said to the newcomers after they had exchanged greetings is in a nutshell – here the [prisoners] have banded themselves together; and breaking out over the wire entanglements, intend to take the regiment [the nearby Australian Army Training Camp] over there by storm. We shall take arms and … pit ourselves against them. We shall devise various expedients and when we have devised them we shall break out over the wire entanglements.[73]

Matsumoto filed this astonishing piece of intelligence away, knowing that there would be an opportunity to use it to his advantage at a later date. He didn't have to wait long. That afternoon he and Terekawa were transferred under armed guard to D Compound, home to Koreans, Formosans and, somewhat perversely, Japanese officers (it had been recognised soon after the first Japanese arrived that, if the officers remained with their men, they would quickly foment dissent among the Japanese prisoners).

Eleven days after arriving at the camp, Matsumoto was working in a small unsupervised party trimming grass in No Man's Land. The adjoining A Compound was home to Italians, and Matsumoto struck up a conversation via snippets of English and hand gestures with an amiable Italian prisoner through the fence. At the suggestion of the Italian, Matsumoto and another Korean prisoner crawled under the barbed wire and spent an hour or so chatting with a group of Italians in their hut. When an Australian guard unexpectedly turned up, the other Korean bolted from the hut, wriggled under the barbed wire and made it back to his own compound without being apprehended. Matsumoto tried to hide under the bed. The sergeant dragged him out and marched him to the guardhouse. Matsumoto was given ten days of detention, and his new Italian friends were interrogated and given even tougher sentences, six of them placed on 15 days of bread and water.[74] It was a curious incident and fairly minor in the daily goings-on of a POW camp, but it resulted in some unexpected consequences. Matsumoto realised that sharing his valuable intelligence was an excellent way to curry favour with his Australian overseers.

On 3 June, he announced that he had important information to share about a dangerous rebellion brewing in the camp and, in spite of his lowly rank and separation from the bulk of the

Japanese prisoners, his claims were taken seriously enough that he was presented to an Australian officer for interrogation. Matsumoto was an experienced informant – from the earliest days of his capture he had been surprisingly astute and talkative, first with his American captors and now with the Australians – and his story of overhearing a discussion about a breakout plan was accepted without question. A flurry of official reports quickly spread the news to camp authorities.

Captain 'Poppa' Mann, who had interviewed Matsumoto, wrote an urgent report to Lieutenant Colonel Monty Brown, the commandant of the camp, which summarised the intelligence he had gleaned from the Korean:

(1) That the Japs are making a plan to escape.
(2) That they will overcome the obstacle of the wire one night by some device already planned.
(3) That they will break out all together.
(4) That they will go to the Regiment over there [the Army Training Camp]. And I presume from what I have heard that they have planned to steal arms there, and with them try to inflict as great a loss on the Australian troops as possible.[75]

In one interview, Matsumoto had provided more information about Japanese intentions to the intelligence services at Cowra than they had managed to compile in the previous 12 months. The mutiny at Featherston the previous year had sounded grim warnings about the risk of a Japanese uprising at Cowra. Now the Australians had confirmation of their suspicions – the Japanese were intending to break out of the camp, and it was going to be violent and ugly. The question was, what were they going to do about it?

12

'PROCEED TO DO THEIR MISCHIEF': PREPARING FOR A BREAKOUT

June represented a shift in both attitude and action at Cowra. For weeks rumours had been circulating around the camp and town that the Japanese were intending to riot. Korean prisoners, occasionally detailed to help unload supplies at the railyards, and no fans of their Japanese prisonmates, were particularly talkative, and the streets of Cowra positively buzzed with the news that the Japanese were up to something. Alf Bourke, a railway guard who lived only a few miles from the camp (and who would be involved in a prominent incident during a hunting trip after the Breakout) was told by a Korean worker that the Japanese were hoarding baseball bats and other improvised weapons and intended to attack the fences and break out of the camp. Such scuttlebutt was so commonplace at that time that Bourke didn't feel it necessary to report the conversation to camp authorities.

The mutiny at the Featherston camp the previous year had clearly demonstrated that the seething resentment of the Japanese and the repressive life in the camp were a fatal combination, and the toxic atmosphere at Cowra was bound to reach boiling point sooner rather than later. The optimists in the community hoped that any incident would be more like a strike than a riot, but everyone conceded that something was definitely in the air.

The only people who seemed lead-footed at this time were camp authorities. Looking back through the lens of 80 years, it seems fanciful that the camp's leaders could have any doubts about the Japanese intentions, but a strange lethargy seemed to permeate every aspect of their decision-making. That may have been justified when talk of a breakout was merely rumour, but a reliable witness had given details of a specific Japanese plan – it now seemed a matter of when, not if, the Japanese put their plan into action.

Warrant Officer Lionel Boorman, an intelligence officer who had been present when Matsumoto had spilled the beans, later recalled that when he passed on details of the conversation to Major Ramsay, the commandant of B Compound, he dismissed the suggestion as 'Balls, bloody balls'.[76] Fortunately Colonel Brown took the report more seriously, and his response, although far from comprehensive, at least took steps in the right direction. A few days after reporting the intelligence to army authorities, he attended an emergency conference in Sydney where he was asked what enhancements to his defences were required to quell any rebellion. Brown was fairly conservative in his requests – two Vickers machine-guns, plus eight submachine guns and 100 grenades for the garrison.[77] Strangely, he didn't ask for the obvious – more men to guard the camp. He did, however, state plainly that the camp was overcrowded and requested that the bulk of the prisoners should be sent to another camp, and that the population of B Compound should be reduced to between

300 and 400 prisoners. Army HQ took his requests seriously, immediately issuing the requested armaments and beginning discussions about moving prisoners away from Cowra.

On his return to camp, Brown called on his compound commandants to be vigilant, and ordered them to each put in place an emergency plan for dealing with any uprisings – again, a strange abdication of responsibility. Surely what the camp needed now was a consistent plan, so that everyone knew his role and any disturbance could be quickly quashed, not a random assortment of individual plans from each compound. Stranger still, no thorough search of B Compound was ordered. Searches following the riot at Featherston had revealed that the Japanese were hoarding improvised weapons – a similar search at Cowra would have uncovered the cache that the prisoners had been accumulating for months.

On 9 June the machine-guns and other weapons arrived in Cowra. Now that Brown had his extra defences, the question was what to do with them. The machine-guns were his most important defensive asset, but their placement was going to be tricky. Any escape attempt was obviously going to come from B Compound, but setting up machine-guns to fire directly into the camp could have deadly consequences for the occupants of the other compounds and the garrison.

The Vickers was a highly capable weapon – developed in the early years of the 20th century, it had proved its worth on the battlefields of the First World War and had been the main medium machine-gun for British and Commonwealth forces from Gallipoli to France. Some writers have suggested that the Vickers was obsolete in 1944, with the implication that the defences supplied to the garrison at Cowra were inadequate, but in truth the Vickers was the perfect weapon for the job (and in fact remained in service throughout the Second World

War, and well beyond). Vickers machine-guns were steadfastly reliable, and could be mastered with only a few hours of instruction. Their .303-calibre ammunition was fed from belts holding 250 rounds, and the barrel was cooled by water from an attached canister. The firing mechanism was automatic when the thumb trigger was pressed – as long as rounds were being fed into the gun, it would keep firing. And due to its weight and solid setup, it was also deadly accurate – once positioned to fire in an arc, it required minimal aiming from the gunner to plaster an area with bullets.

Its weight was also the Vickers' biggest drawback – it operated on a heavy tripod, and its constant appetite for ammunition and water made it impossible to move quickly. Brown had to position his Vickers guns carefully – wherever he chose to place them, they were staying. The guard towers were the obvious choice, but were soon discounted. It would be impossible to squeeze the bulky Vickers in the cramped confines of the towers, and the gun could not be traversed to the acute angles required to fire towards the ground. Even if the Vickers could be made to fit in the guard towers, there was a fairly obvious issue – there were not enough guard towers to adequately cover B Compound. The eastern side of the camp was particularly vulnerable, with lonely F Tower the only sentinel on that long stretch of fence.

The Vickers needed to be set up at ground level, and to have a wide angle of fire in the direction of any likely escape route. Machine-guns are at their most effective when firing in enfilade – firing perpendicularly into advancing troops, rather than head on – so it made sense to position the guns to fire *along* the perimeter fences, rather than directly into the compound. Escapees would then be confronted with the formidable dual obstacles of barbed wire and bullets, and large sections of the perimeter could be defended with a single gun. Colonel Brown appeared to bear this in mind with the placement of the two guns, although his options were limited by the layout of the camp. The guns needed a clear field of fire, so they could only be set up aiming into the open paddocks north and east of the camp. Number One gun was set up at the base of B Tower near the northern gates, and aimed to fire along B Compound's northern fence. Number Two gun was set up to fire along the compound's north-eastern fence, but there was a problem with this placement. In order to enable the gun to shoot in enfilade along the perimeter, the only option was to position it uncomfortably close to the B Compound fence. It was set up on a truck trailer, only 50 metres from the wire.

Brown was an experienced soldier, and well versed in the use of machine-guns. He knew that machine-guns on their own were highly vulnerable, and they needed supporting riflemen to safeguard them from attack. His plan appears to have been that Number Two gun would be supported by fire from Number One gun. This may have been the reason Number Two gun was placed so close to the wire – if it was any further back it would have been obscured from Number One gun by the B Company barracks. Brown also ordered that a party of riflemen be stationed next to the gun, but here he encountered another problem – he didn't have enough men. Instead of ordering the machine-guns and their support groups to be manned continuously, Brown instructed that the gun crews should sleep in the huts closest to their guns, and only take up their posts when an alarm was sounded. The support crew was drawn from A Company, and would have several hundred metres of ground to cover to get to its post.[78] If this seems like a complicated and risky plan, it was.

The comments from one soldier about the placement of the guns is telling. Ray 'Simmo' Simpson was one of Australia's most distinguished soldiers of the second half of the century. He would serve in four wars, and win a Victoria Cross in Vietnam in 1969, but in August 1944 he was a skinny 18-year-old recruit who had been in the army for less than six months, and was based at the Army Training Camp at Cowra. The morning after the Breakout he was part of a detachment sent to reinforce the POW camp, and was ordered to man the Number One gun while the escapees were being rounded up. 'It was a complete schemozzle,' he told journalist Harry Gordon in 1977.

> Number One gun, which looked right down across the wire fence, was wrongly sited. That's the gun I had a spell on. It should have been laying down enfilade fire from an angle inside the wire – so that the prisoners would have had to walk into a line of fire if they wanted to tackle the barbed wire. Number Two … shouldn't have been mounted at all. It should have been on the ground, firing low and flat. It was in the wrong place, too. It shouldn't have been firing into [the compound] head-on.[79]

It's hard to escape the conclusion that the machine-guns were placed in these ineffective, yet highly visible, positions partly as a deterrent. Brown was having an each-way bet – demonstrate to the prisoners that the camp defences had been beefed up, and hopefully dissuade them from trying to escape, but also have the firepower in place required to defend the camp if a breakout *did* occur. It was a strategy that seriously compromised the defences of the camp.

Throughout June a flurry of reports circulated, and meetings between commanders were held to draw up emergency plans that would be enacted in the event of a breakout. Every man, from cook to clerk, was issued a rifle and 50 rounds of ammunition, and ordered to have them close at hand at all times. To better keep an eye on the Japanese troublemakers, a tent was erected in the middle of Broadway outside the B Compound gates, and a three-man guard unit was ordered to take up a post there every night. They were armed with rifles and were connected to the D Camp guardroom by telephone, with instructions to instantly report any suspicious activity in the compound. It was an unenviable job, and nerves among the guard unit were constantly strained during the long, cold nights.

Plans extended beyond the POW camp to the nearby Army Training Camp, the military camp that Matsumoto had specifically identified as the target in the Japanese escape plans.

Located about three kilometres south of the POW camp, the Army Training Camp was a sprawling complex of huts and tents that was home to about 4000 soldiers. Of the camp's five battalions, three were made up of raw recruits, fresh from enlisting, who had been sent there to learn basic infantry skills. The majority of these recruits were in their late teens, and so green that they 'did not know what a Jap looked like', according to an officer at the camp.[80] The other two training battalions comprised more experienced men, who had completed their initial training and were now learning the skills required to fight and survive as infantrymen in the jungles of the Pacific. The camp was also home to about 100 members of the Australian Women's Army Service (AWAS), who fulfilled essential support roles such as drivers, translators, signallers, veterinarians and cipher clerks. Unsurprisingly, the AWAS personnel were stationed in separate quarters from the young male trainees.

The camp was commanded by Colonel John Mitchell, a long-term military man who had landed on Gallipoli on the first morning and taken a bullet on the first afternoon. Later in France he commanded the 8th Battalion and led his men with such dash and courage that he ended the war with a Distinguished Service Order and Bar, the Belgian Croix de Guerre, plus *five* Mentions in Despatches. During the Second World War he was a battalion commander through some of the toughest scraps in the Middle East and Greece, before returning to Australia to apply his skills to training new recruits. He was a living, breathing war hero, the archetypal Anzac legend, and was an intimidating character to the young recruits he commanded.

Mitchell was also arrogant and prickly, and his relationship with the commandants of the nearby POW camp was chequered. Much of his correspondence gives the impression that he resented having a camp full of enemy soldiers so close to his training centre, and he showed particular animosity towards the Japanese, telling a court of inquiry after the breakout that he 'personally would much prefer to kill them, all of them'.

In spite of this (or perhaps because of it), when he received word from Army Headquarters on 8 June that the Japanese were planning to break out and attack his camp, he reacted quickly. He conducted a full reconnaissance of the training camp and its surrounds, paying particular attention to the open paddocks that faced the POW camp, presumably the direction from which any Japanese assault would come. Mitchell was a good soldier, and his speculation on how a breakout would likely unfold was eerily perceptive. 'There [isn't] the slightest doubt in [my] mind', he reported to Army Headquarters,

> that these prisoners in a concerted rush, with blankets and palliasses thrown over the barb wire, would escape in some hundreds. Hundreds, of course, would be killed on the wire but one has to remember that these Japs are fanatics and to die thus removes the stigma of captivity and according to their beliefs, clears the way to their <u>heaven</u>; and to the

Comdr's mind, so long as large numbers are grouped together the danger remains, and one could reasonably expect it on a wet, drizzly, dark night, when immediately they clear the wire they become obscure and can then organise at a pre-contemplated place and proceed to do their mischief.[81]

On the night of 8 June he held a conference with the second-in-command of the POW camp, Major Charles Grace, another Great War veteran, who confirmed the details of the report from Army HQ. The following day Mitchell assembled his battalion commanders and formulated a plan to secure the camp in the event of a breakout. His plans called for one company of armed men to leave the camp and establish a defensive perimeter just south of the POW camp, with instructions to take on any Japanese they crossed paths with; the remainder of the garrison would take up arms to protect the camp, armoury and ammunition magazines. Special patrols were also ordered to protect the women's quarters. The POW camp would alert the training camp to any breakout by firing three red flares; the army camp would respond with their own yellow flares. Mitchell also ordered a supply of guns, grenades and ammunition be sent to the POW camp to beef up the defensive capabilities of the garrison. But he went a step further than that.

Starting immediately, Mitchell ordered nightly patrols of about 45 men to take up station just outside the fences of the POW camp. They would remain in place from 9 p.m. until 3.30 a.m. the following morning, lying in a frosty sheep paddock, gazing into the bright lights from Broadway and doing their best to stay warm and awake during the long night. These patrols strained the nerves in an already tense atmosphere. 'Six and a half hours,' an officer who had led a couple of the patrols later recalled, 'can be a long time and stressful.'[82] It is interesting that Mitchell felt it necessary to have his own men directly supervising the camp – his lack of faith in the POW camp garrison seems clear, and there is no evidence the POW camp authorities were ever aware that Mitchell was keeping such a close eye on them.

It is obvious from Mitchell's actions and his later testimony that he was primarily, effectively singularly, focused on protecting his camp from Japanese attack, but there was one crucial eventuality he failed to adequately plan for – the rounding up of escaped prisoners. The matter was briefly discussed, and Mitchell put forward the curious instruction that if the inexperienced army recruits were called on to assist with the recapture of prisoners, they should do so unarmed, to reduce the risk of further casualties. But that was about the extent of the planning. It was clear that the army training camp would have to play a substantial role in recapturing prisoners if a breakout occurred, so Mitchell's conspicuous failure to plan for it was a grave oversight. But in June 1944, grave oversights were de rigueur in Cowra, and back at the POW camp, complacency was about to turn to carnage.

— —

A month later on a makeshift rifle range in a paddock not far from the camp, Privates Ben Hardy and Ralph Jones were becoming reacquainted with an old friend – the Vickers machine-gun. Both men had first come across the weapon during the First World War, Hardy while serving in the 18th Battalion in Australia, and Jones in his native England, where he had enlisted at the end of the war but had been too young to see combat. Now, in another place and another war, the men were both as vintage as the gun. In 1944 Jones was 43 and

Hardy was two years older. But with their advanced years came experience – as veterans of two wars, with extensive training on the Vickers, Hardy and Jones were the natural choice for the gun crew of Number Two machine-gun, which would cover the northern boundary of the troublesome B Compound.

The two men were to become unlikely heroes. Both were committed bachelors and were shy and unassuming characters. Hardy grew up in Sydney and lived with his sister and widowed mother in the northern suburb of Willoughby. After leaving school he spent three years in the army towards the end of the First World War, but the Armistice was declared before he was sent overseas. Later he worked as a driver for Dalgety's and enjoyed fishing and shooting on the weekends. He was a sensitive man and seemed to bond more readily with animals than he did with people. 'He'd do anything for anybody,' his sister recalled more than four decades after the Cowra Breakout. 'A traveller whose car went wrong, he'd work [on it] till two o'clock in the morning and never ask for thanks, let alone money. He was that good hearted.'[83]

In September 1941 Hardy was called up as a private in the Citizen Military Forces. He was too old for active duty, but his military experience made him a valuable asset in the forces, and he was assigned to garrison duty in Australia. In February 1944 he arrived in Cowra.

Despite the age difference between Jones and Hardy, they were strikingly similar in life experience and demeanour. The two men became firm friends as soon as they met. Originally from a small town in Norfolk, Jones was a quiet and somewhat sickly child who left school at 14 to take up a motor engineering apprenticeship. He enlisted in the British military as soon as he turned 18 but was too late to see combat in the First World War. He spent a year in the occupation forces in Antwerp and on the

Rhine, before being invalided back to Britain with tuberculosis in early 1920. He emigrated to Australia in about 1926 – his girlfriend's brother had recently made the trip and sent back optimistic reports of life in the antipodes. Jones's girlfriend was supposed to follow him but, for whatever reason, she appears to have changed her mind. The reality of life in a new country was a far cry from the utopia Jones had imagined in the pubs of Norfolk, and he was forced to take whatever work he could get as the Great Depression ravaged the country. He eventually left the city and took casual jobs in the bush, finally settling in the small town of Tuena, halfway between Blayney and Crookwell in the New South Wales Lachlan Valley. Coincidentally, the town is only about 60 kilometres from Cowra, so Jones was in familiar country when he was assigned to the 22nd Garrison Battalion on his enlistment in early 1942. His career in the military was tainted by the same ill health that had plagued him all his life, and he spent several spells in hospital receiving treatment for a range of ailments. His experience on the Vickers gun from the First World War made him an obvious choice for the gun crew.

There is a fascinating footnote to the story of Ralph Jones and his life in the bush. When he had joined up, he had left the Next of Kin section of his enlistment papers blank, but sometime in the following two years he amended the document and added the name Madeleine Cook, describing her as a 'friend'. Cook was the widow of the farmer Jones had boarded with in Tuena before the war. In 1992 Marion Starr, Cook's grand-niece and a driving force behind remembrance of the Cowra Breakout, revealed in a local publication that Jones and Cook had formed a relationship after Cook's husband had died, and they intended to marry. Jones was a frequent visitor to the family farm, and he had given Cook a gold ring as a token of his commitment. Starr also revealed that, extraordinarily for the time (and today for that matter), Cook was about 20 years older than Jones and the relationship had caused a mini-scandal in the farm blocks of the Lachlan. She later revealed more about the unlikely romance:

> Our family had a farm at Tuena, about halfway between Bathurst and Goulburn, and I've always known that Ralph Jones spent the last weekend [before the Breakout] at our place. It wasn't until 1989 that my mother told me about the romance, and he had decided to marry my Aunt Madeleine. You could have floored me.[84]

It's a fascinating family tale, but in reality it's even more fascinating than the family realised. According to Cook's death certificate, she was 72 years old in 1944, which makes her nearly 30 years older than Jones. We will never know the full story of the relationship between Jones and Cook, but it's a touching postscript to the story of Ralph Jones and his ties to the district.

On the rifle range, Hardy and Jones were practising a drill they had performed many times before – getting the gun into action. They took their time mounting the gun on its tripod, securing the mounting pins, attaching the condenser tube, adjusting the traversing clamp and ensuring the gun was balanced and aiming straight down range. They didn't need to rush this part of the process – if called into action, the machine-gun would already be mounted on its trailer and set up. The important part of the rehearsal was what came next – getting the gun loaded and firing as quickly as possible.

Once the gun was set up, Hardy gave it the once-over. As the gun's 'No. 1' it was his job to ensure the gun was ready for action, and then aim and fire it. Jones was the 'No. 2', and would be in charge of feeding ammunition to the gun and performing whatever adjustments and maintenance were required to keep it in action. For the gun to function as an effective weapon, both men had to know their jobs intimately and to perform them in concert without getting in each other's way. It was a graceful ballet of death.

'Gun mounted!' shouted Hardy once he was satisfied the gun was correctly sited and set up. He was sitting on the ground behind the Vickers, with his elbows resting on his raised knees and his hands lightly gripping the gun's wooden handles. Jones was to his right, kneeling beside an open ammunition can with a canvas belt coiled inside it. Usually this belt would contain 250 rounds but today, given the haste with which this training session had been thrown together, the belt only contained 50 rounds.

'Load!' yelled Hardy. As he shouted the command, he pulled the crank handle on the right side of the gun sharply backwards, and Jones fed the metal tongue of the ammunition belt through the feed block – on firing, the feed block would strip rounds out of the belt and into the lock, the firing mechanism of the gun. Hardy grabbed the tongue on the left side of the gun, and pulled the belt further into the feed block as he released the handle. The first round stripped smoothly off the belt and into the feed block. Still guiding the belt with his left hand, he pulled the crank handle a second time, which loaded a second round and rotated the first into the chamber – the gun was now ready to fire.[85]

Jones quickly cast his eye over the gun to ensure it was correctly loaded, then slapped Hardy on the back and called out 'Fire!' Hardy pressed the thumb trigger between the two handles and the gun spat fire. At this point Hardy didn't have to do much except press the thumbpiece and aim – the gun fired automatically as each round entered the chamber. As the gun roared, Jones fed the ammunition belt smoothly out of the can and into the feed block. He paid close attention to what he was doing – if the belt twisted or caught, the gun would jam. Hardy fired in short bursts at the targets 100 yards away. They were impossible to miss – secure on its tripod, the gun could shoot accurately well beyond 2000 yards, but there would be no call for such long-range marksmanship if the Japanese attempted to break out of the camp. The range would be short, and the fire would be deadly.

Shards of timber shrapnel flew off the wooden targets as the deadly arc of lead found its mark. The Vickers fired at over 500 rounds per minute – at that rate a well-trained team could tear through 10 000 rounds every hour. Hardy pivoted the gun smoothly left to right from one target to the next. As he sighted each one, he let off a two-second burst and cut the target to pieces. Hardy had been well trained on the gun and didn't fire it in a continuous burst, the way he'd seen action heroes do it in war films at the Cowra pictures. Hardy knew that a machine-gun was most effective when it delivered a mass of well-aimed bullets into a small space – there were no long sprays of fire here. Each short burst was methodical, measured and deadly accurate.

Hardy tore through the belt in short order; 'Reload!' he shouted. At this point the command was purely symbolic – Hardy and Jones had fired their allotted 50 rounds and it was time to give the next crew a spell on the gun. It wasn't exactly a thorough training session, but it was enough to get them reacquainted with the weapon, and they felt confident they would be able to use it effectively if required. As they walked back to the truck, Hardy slapped Jones on the back. 'Good work, Ralph,' he said. 'The Japs won't be foolish enough to take that on.' Jones nodded grimly. 'I hope to God you're right, mate.' His words hung in the air for a long minute, and then the two men headed back to camp.

13

'VERY BAD BUSINESS': THE MOVE TO HAY

While the authorities in Cowra were grappling with the possibility that the Japanese might be planning an uprising, army authorities in Sydney were doing the same, and taking steps to try to mitigate the risk. They had known for some time that the camp was dangerously overcrowded. B Compound had been built to accommodate only about 500 prisoners – by mid-1944 more than 1100 were crammed in there, and the numbers were only going to swell as Japan suffered more defeats on the battlefield. Colonel Brown's failure to reinforce the garrison meant that there were only 107 Australian guards on hand to oversee the compound (out of a total of about 600 men across the entire camp). The situation was unsustainable, and had been the subject of heated discussions in the halls of Army HQ for months. The intelligence from Lance Corporal Matsumoto was the last straw, and it forced the army authorities to act.

Interestingly, it appears that just about everyone landed on the same solution at the same time – the number of Japanese prisoners at Cowra had to be reduced. In a report to Army Headquarters on 4 July, Colonel John Mitchell, commander of the Army Training Camp, spelled out the steps he was taking to safeguard his facility in the event of a Japanese breakout at the POW camp. But he added a brief footnote: 'I respectfully put forward the suggestion,' he rather gingerly wrote,

> that I am well aware of, is no business of mine and well outside the sphere of a Comdr of a Trg Centre, but one that is none the less genuinely given, that considerable dispersement of this large number of Jap prisoners be made to all other P.O.W. Camps throughout Australia and thus immediately, and believed permanently, relieve all danger of escape.[86]

Army HQ had reached the same conclusion after their meeting with Colonel Brown in June. A flurry of cables between Brown and HQ discussed a range of options, including shifting some of the more recalcitrant prisoners into a separate compound at Cowra, before dismissing those plans as unworkable. There was only one solution. Recognising that the camp was bursting at the seams and that Japanese NCOs were the source of the trouble, Army HQ determined to kill both birds with one stone. On 19 June Brown received word from Sydney that all Japanese prisoners below the rank of lance corporal would be removed from the Cowra camp and sent to the POW camp at Hay, in one fell swoop slashing the number of prisoners in B Compound by about 700 men and separating the troublesome NCOs from their men. It would take weeks to reorganise Hay camp and make it ready for the new arrivals, but Brown should get cracking with his own plans immediately.

Brown was relieved to receive the news, slipping a conspiratorial word to Major Ramsay that 'we're getting rid of a lot of your Japs'.

The relief on Ramsay's face was palpable. 'I reckon we'll both sleep a little easier after that, eh?' Brown said.[87]

News of the impending separation may have caused relief among the camp's commandants, but there was still the pressing issue of how to accomplish it. Both Brown and Ramsay had spent enough time around the Japanese prisoners to know that they would be furious at the decision. Brown in particular was a thoughtful and empathetic man, and he was well aware of the brotherly bond that existed between enlisted men and their NCOs.

Ramsay sought the counsel of Sergeant Negerevich, the interpreter, who confirmed suspicions that the Japanese enlisted men would be distressed to be separated from their NCOs. But in reality that was the point – by physically removing the men from the NCOs, they would hopefully be also removing the source of inflammatory talk, as well as the hierarchy that would be essential in any organised uprising against the guards. Break the hold of the NCOs, they reasoned, and they would break the rebellious spirit of the men.

In these assessments, the camp authorities were spot-on, which makes Brown's actions as the weeks ticked by difficult to reconcile. The transfer was eventually slated to take place on Monday, 7 August; and on 3 August, 50 guards arrived from the Hay camp to escort the 700 prisoners via truck and train on the 400-kilometre journey west to Hay. The sudden arrival of a sizeable contingent from the Hay camp should have raised suspicions among the Japanese that something was afoot. And indiscreet gossiping about the transfer among the garrison should certainly have given the game away. Once again the pubs and dancehalls of Cowra were abuzz with talk that something was going on at the camp. Curiously, the only group that seemed oblivious to this flurry of activity was the one that would be most affected by it – the Japanese prisoners.

From the earliest days of the Pacific War, Australian authorities had embraced the notion that the fate of the 23 000 Australian prisoners in Japanese hands might be tied to the way Japanese prisoners were treated in Australia. The result was that, even though Japan had not ratified the Geneva Convention, Australia would still grant its protections to Japanese prisoners of war. Prison camp commanders were frequently reminded of this decision. 'The Commander-in-Chief attaches great importance to scrupulous adherence to the provisions of the Convention,' the Adjutant-General announced in 1943, 'since any breach of these provisions is bound to react on the treatment by the enemy of Allied prisoners of war.'[88] Camp commanders generally agreed with this directive, but Brown seems to have taken the orders to extremes, and been particularly generous with the prisoners in his care. For reasons that are unclear (possibly just because he was a good bloke) Brown had decided from the earliest days of his tenure at the camp that not only would he treat the Japanese prisoners in accordance with the Geneva Convention, he would grant them the exceedingly favourable conditions stipulated in Australian instructions for *civilian internees*. This was all well and good when it came to decisions about the quality and quantity of food, providing access to sporting equipment, the provision of medical treatment and other routine aspects of the prisoners' daily lives, but Brown's generous interpretation of his obligations to the prisoners was about to have dire repercussions.

Earlier in the week Brown had asked Ramsay and Negerevich to prepare a full roll of the prisoners, organised by rank. Now, on the morning of Friday, 4 August, Brown informed Ramsay that they were obliged to give the prisoners notice of the upcoming transfer. He asked Ramsay to inform the camp leader, Sergeant

Major Ryo Kanazawa, after lunch and to schedule a meeting with the camp leaders that afternoon.

It is worth pausing here to highlight the significance of this decision and just how grave an error it was. In the Court of Inquiry after the Breakout, Brown was criticised for his decision to give the prisoners three days notice of the transfer. In his defence, he said:

> The reason for me giving [prisoners] notice of movement to another camp was in accordance with an Instruction No. SM/10127 of 12 Jun 42, which states:
> 'Para 3 – All internees will be given at least 24 hours notice of their intended transfer.'

'Although this instruction refers to internees,' he added, 'it has always been the practise [sic] at this Group to give [prisoners] at least the same notice which has been found necessary owing to Administrative requirements.'[89]

This was a disastrous misinterpretation of his obligations and gave the Japanese concessions they were simply not entitled to. As Brown admitted in his testimony, the regulation applied only to civilian internees, not POWs. Brown was under no obligation to tell the Japanese anything about the transfer, right up until the time they were marched out of their barracks and onto the trucks. It was an astonishing failure of judgement. The transfer was intended, after all, to mitigate the risk of the prisoners launching a violent uprising, as intelligence reports, information from an informant and his own eyes and ears clearly demonstrated could occur at any time. In the midst of this highly charged atmosphere, it was inconceivable that Brown would risk further inflaming tensions by giving the prisoners advance warning of the transfer. By his actions, Brown was in danger of precipitating the violence that the transfer was intended to curtail.

At 2 p.m. the camp leader, Kanazawa, plus deputy leaders Sergeant Major Masao Kojima and Sergeant Hajime Toyoshima, met with Ramsay in his office. According to Ramsay:

I had nominal rolls prepared but did not advise the Camp Leader and his staff until 1400 hrs on 4 Aug. I had called the Camp Leader [Kanazawa], Assistant Camp Leader [Kojima] and the Late Camp Leader, Sjt/Pilot [Toyoshima] (who speaks English well), [who] after looking through the list remarked that it was 'very bad business; why can't we all go?'. The Camp Leader, Sjt/Major Kanazawa, made no remarks but it appeared to me his demeanour altered.[90]

It is no surprise that the Japanese thought the arrangements were 'very bad business'. The NCOs were the backbone of discipline and morale throughout the camp. Without them, the ordeal of being a POW would be insufferable for the men.

At this point there is some confusion about what actually occurred at this meeting, and the repercussions are important.

In 1977 journalist Harry Gordon interviewed Kanazawa at his home in Japan, during which Kanazawa accused the Australian camp authorities of having pulled a swifty on the Japanese. He said that at the conference on the afternoon of Friday, 4 August, Ramsay had simply told him that there was a new batch of prisoners due to arrive and that there was insufficient space for them, and therefore some of the prisoners currently in the camp would be sent to Hay. Crucially, Kanazawa claimed that Ramsay had made no mention that the separation would be based on rank, nor showed him a list detailing which prisoners were to be moved, a 'softening-up exercise' (in Gordon's words) to get the POWs onboard with the idea of a separation, before later revealing the split would be made according to rank. Kanazawa then claimed that once the prisoners discovered the truth (within a few hours, thanks to loose-lipped Australian guards) they felt betrayed by the authorities, and this was a key factor in the Japanese decision-making. He told the Court of Inquiry, 'If the order [to separate the men from the NCOs] had been explained to us, probably there would have been some solution. Because there were no words of explanation, this incident occurred.' This account seems highly dubious.

Kanazawa himself supported Ramsay's version of events in his own evidence to the Court of Inquiry, stating that, during the conference, he was given an order informing him, 'On 7 Aug 44, NCO's and O/Rs [other ranks] will be separated, and latter will be transferred to Hay Camp. Get ready.' It was only three decades later when questioned by Gordon that his recollections changed. It should be noted that Negerevich, the only other participant in the conference still alive at the time, backed up Kanazawa's revised version of events in a subsequent interview with Gordon, and he had no incentive to implicate his Australian comrades so long after the fact. Regardless, it's difficult to escape the conclusion that Kanazawa's shifting recollection of events is the reddest of herrings. If his assertion – that the catalyst for the Breakout was the news that the prisoners were to be separated by rank – was true (as it without question was), it seems absurd that the Japanese would have been pacified simply by receiving a fuller explanation of the reasons for the transfer a few hours earlier. It was the impending segregation, not the way they were told about it, that spurred the Japanese into action.

The meeting ended at 3 p.m., and Kanazawa, Kojima and Toyoshima walked in stunned silence under guard back to

B Compound. They didn't speak, but all shared the same thought: this decision to separate the men and the NCOs was an outrage! It should not happen – could not be *allowed* to happen. Individually, they all reached the same conclusion. The time for discussion and vacillation was over. It was time to act.

14

'THE MOMENT WE HAVE WAITED FOR': THE DECISION

Following his meeting with Ryo Kanazawa and the other camp leaders, Major Ramsay attended the daily afternoon parade of Japanese prisoners in B Compound. 'On the 1630 hrs parade on the 4th,' he later said, 'I viewed the parade from the catwalk on the outside perimeter and there was nothing unusual.'[91]

Ramsay either wasn't a particularly astute observer or he didn't know his compound as well as he thought he did. Because in reality, things were happening in B Compound – *lots* of things. Throughout the afternoon the random, aimless wanderings of the prisoners ceased. Men moved with purpose from hut to hut. Small groups hurriedly gathered, conversed in low whispers and then just as quickly dispersed. Vegetable gardens were left unattended, baseball fields deserted. An unusually high proportion of men made their way to the ablutions block, where they took steaming hot showers and scrubbed their bodies thoroughly. Obviously the prisoners were up to something.

It didn't even require particularly sophisticated detective work to know what was going on: many prisoners had formed semi-friendly relations with guards, who were always eager to share camp gossip, and within hours of the meeting in Ramsay's office many of the prisoners in B Compound were aware of the impending transfer. Camp authorities were also aware of how distressed the prisoners were by the news. Again, this didn't require sophisticated intelligence gathering – the prisoners simply told them. In the late afternoon Sergeant Negerevich was approached by camp leader Kanazawa, who was desperate for more information and, with misguided optimism, to change Australian minds. When told by Negerevich that the decision was final, Kanazawa responded ominously. 'We've had a conference already about this,' he said. 'We don't like it. We'll have to have more talks. We'll have to do something.' He spoke forcefully:

> I have been watching those Vickers guns just a little while ago. The men who man them have gone off duty, and nobody has taken over. It's the same as any other night to them. That moon won't hurt us. This is their pay day. This is the night they'll drink some beer, or play cards. Tomorrow is Saturday, a rest day. If we're going to do it, tonight's the night. Saturday night or Sunday night, they might realise that it's best to man those guns. Tonight … they won't be ready to deal with it.'[92]

Negerevich was in a rush and didn't pick up on the grim portent in Kanazawa's words.

Soon after, the camp leaders – Kanazawa, Toyoshima and Kojima – met in Kanazawa's hut and for the first time openly discussed their options. It wasn't as if they needed to come up with a plan – there was already a plan in place; the prisoners had been throwing around the idea of breaking out of the camp for months. Although a loose strategy had been agreed on – break out over the wire, overcome the garrison, kill as many guards as possible and then, if things are going really well, launch an attack on the Army Training Camp – no specific tactics had been discussed. And, of course, no timeframe had been laid out, although most of the conspirators had agreed that any uprising should ideally take place on a moonless night, preferably when the weather was bad.

Decades later, Kanazawa recalled that he and the other camp leaders were fairly philosophical about the path they were heading down. Events seemed to be moving at their own pace and were beyond their control.

Each man in the trio seemed to be fulfilling a different role. Kanazawa was the politician, forming grand strategy and lobbying for every man in the camp to have input into the decision. Toyoshima was relatively neutral, stating that he thought they should only act after receiving direction from the Japanese officers in D Compound. Kojima was the pessimist. 'I don't think it will work,' he said. 'I think it will be futile.' Kanazawa turned to him angrily and demanded he explain himself. 'I know we have to do it,' Kojima responded. 'It is inevitable. But I know it will simply give us a manner of dying.' Toyoshima agreed with this statement. And there was the crux of the matter – regardless of grand plans to take over the camp, many of the Japanese prisoners saw the Breakout simply as an opportunity to continue the fight that they had begun on the battlefield and to die in the attempt.

The three men talked in hushed tones for another ten minutes, and drew up a list of the other hut leaders and prominent prisoners they wanted to bring into the discussion.

Kanazawa ordered them to regroup in 30 minutes. Shortly after 5 p.m., the men on the list filed into Kanazawa's hut. It was getting hard to disguise that something was afoot in B Compound – there were 50 names on Kanazawa's list, and a crowd this large could barely squeeze into the hut. They huddled around the brazier, rubbing their hands together for warmth, and held the first of several meetings that would determine their fate.

The conversation was hushed but passionate. Some men wanted to take a day or two to plan; some men wanted to go immediately. Argument and counter-argument swirled around the hut. One man raised concerns that the weather was forecast to be clear for several nights, and that the moon was full and bright. He was quickly shut down. Sergeant Major Yoshio Shimoyama, a 34-year-old clerk from Hiroshima, had been captured by the Americans in New Guinea in April and had only been in Cowra for eight weeks.

As had been the case for many months, the prisoners seemed to be divided into three main groups, each with a different view of the situation and desire for action. (It's difficult to determine so many years after the fact which prisoners belonged to which group – in the decades after the war, attitudes and recollections continuously shifted, as former prisoners reflected on, and tried to reconcile, their role in the Breakout. There was some disagreement between survivors about whether it was the navy or army cohort that was most in favour of breaking out.)

The first group were the hardliners, the most outspoken prisoners and the ones most committed to a strict interpretation of the Field Service Code. These tended to be the air and navy men, or the higher-ranking army NCOs – it had been easier to mould a life to an idealised warrior's code from a comfortable billet in a tent or a bunk on a ship than it had been for an infantryman who had to sleep in the mud. Kiyoshi Yamakawa, one of Marekuni Takahara's crewmates from the flying boat downed off Darwin, was particularly outspoken. 'Our comrades who died in battle are calling to us,' he said. 'Close your eyes tonight and you will hear them dimly. This is the moment we have waited for for so long.'[93]

The second group contained men who were neutral about the whole endeavour. These men weren't comfortable with their fate as POWs, but they saw no need to go charging against machine-guns to remedy the situation. These fence-sitters could have been swayed either way, but were conscious not to appear to be abandoning the military code they had sworn to honour. This wasn't just a face-saving exercise – they knew that if the hardliners prevailed, there could be serious, potentially deadly, repercussions for anyone who had spoken out against the Breakout. Warrant Officer Shichihei Matsushima was a 41-year-old mechanic who had been captured by the Americans in New Guinea in early 1943, and had a wife and young children in Yokohama. He was older than most of his comrades in the camp, and was often moody and dismissive of men of lower rank. He summed up the attitude of the neutrals when asked for his opinion. 'I don't know,' he said. 'I don't think we can accomplish much. I think we should wait, at least until we are better prepared.' Other men in this group were fatalistic, and although not particularly sold on the idea of attacking the camp, they would still do their duty. 'I have no thoughts about returning to Japan alive', one man said, 'but I don't want to die in a riot. When the time is appropriate, I shall hang myself.'[94]

The final group was made up of men who were opposed to the Breakout. Understandably, they were extremely guarded about voicing their concerns. 'I am alive,' one man tentatively offered. 'I had a narrow escape from death. Now I want to cherish my life. I want to return home and see my family. If Japan loses, this sin of being a prisoner will be cancelled out.' Realising how far he had stuck his neck out, he hastily attempted to pull it back in: 'I don't wish our defeat, though.'[95]

Discussions continued; there seemed to be as many opinions as there were men in the room. Eventually the conversation wandered off into specifics – what should they wear? What would be the signal? Should they take food? At this point Kanazawa stepped in. 'This isn't the time for all these questions,' he said. 'We still don't know if the majority will want to go. Go to your huts, talk to the men however you want, take votes. Tell them of the plan to split us up … Let's talk again here at 8 p.m.'

Just before the group departed, Flight Sergeant Hiroshi Yoshida, a pilot who had been captured when his plane was shot down north of Lae, spoke up. 'What if the majority is against it?' he said. 'Can't small groups still make their assaults? Can't some of us fight?' It was a fair question, and Kanazawa thought carefully before he answered. 'No,' he said. 'There has to be a consensus. It's all of us, or none of us. If it's to be all of us, we need to know that a majority is in favour. We'll talk later, and consider what the men have to say.'[96]

This was the first time the suggestion of all the men in the camp being involved in the decision was raised, and there has been confusion and contradiction about this crucial aspect of the Breakout ever since. Kanazawa was unequivocal – he said in evidence to the Courts of Inquiry and in later interviews that the decision to launch the Breakout was always going to be democratically made. But other survivors of the Breakout disagree. Masaru Moriki summed up the philosophical attitude

of many of the more moderate prisoners when they heard about
the move to Hay:

> Although it was sad to leave people whom we made friends
> with, it couldn't be helped. Besides, we just happened
> to come to the same camp by accidental fate, not that
> we became POWs hand in hand from the start. We had
> experienced meetings and partings many times before,
> so we were feeling rather happy to start anew in the new
> camp. However, in reality, a riot with death in mind was in
> planning by the group of hard-liners with no consideration
> to our thoughts.[97]

It's impossible to tell at this remove how many prisoners shared
Moriki's sentiments. But survivor accounts do suggest that
many men in the camp felt they were being press-ganged into
action by the hardliners. Contrary to Kanazawa's assertions that
the decision was made democratically and that it was the will
of the bulk of the prisoners to break out of the camp, it appears
there was more dissent and disagreement with the plan than
Kanazawa was willing to reveal.

Later in the evening the Japanese ate dinner in the mess
hall. Few spoke. Events were heading towards an inevitable
conclusion, and many suspected that this would be their last
meal. After dinner they filed back into their huts, where they
spoke softly and gravely about the coming night. Although
he considered himself a moderate, Moriki's hut leader spoke
passionately, and left little doubt about which way he expected
his comrades to vote. 'The separation of officers and soldiers is
a tragedy almost equal to the breakdown of the Japanese family
system,' he said. 'It was decided that we can't agree with that
order and we will fight firmly against it. The Camp leader is

having a final discussion [with the Australians] about it now, however, if our request is denied we will go ahead on attack and die in action. However, this will be decided by a vote.'[98] He then handed out pieces of toilet paper to the men gathered around him, and instructed each man to draw either a circle or a cross. 'Whether you agreed to rise for action or not', Moriki later wrote, 'the cross meant to live and the circle meant to die. Now we were made to choose.'[99] The circles won overwhelmingly. It is impossible to quantify the numbers, but a combination of survivor accounts, evidence at the courts of inquiry and accounting by historians suggests that about 80 per cent of the prisoners voted in favour of the Breakout. This number seems incongruous given how many prisoners were clearly opposed to launching the attack, or were at least ambivalent about it.

An interesting sidenote to all this is that most accounts of the Breakout claim, or at least vaguely imply, that every Japanese prisoner in B Compound participated in the Breakout to some extent, whether by charging the fences or committing suicide. But logic suggests this could hardly be the case – out of 1104 individuals, a large number of whom were not in favour of launching the attack at all, surely some of them simply chose not to participate. And there is evidence to support this. It's impossible to put an exact figure on it, but it appears that about 120 men simply remained in their huts and played no active role in the Breakout. The reasons for this varied: some men, whose injuries prevented them from rushing the fences, pledged to commit suicide but could not bring themselves to go through with it; they spent an anguished night struggling to find the courage to carry out their pledge and ultimately failing. Others were granted an exemption by sympathetic hut leaders. One of these men was Hajime Mori, a 24-year-old merchant seaman who had taken a bullet in the arm from the Americans in New

Guinea and had only been in Cowra for six days. His hut leader was 38-year-old Lance Corporal Seiji Ogi, a forestry worker from Sapporo, who had taken a shine to the young Mori. 'I think you ought to stay here,' Ogi had said. 'That right arm is useless. There'll be plenty for you to do here.' Mori accepted Ogi's gracious leave pass and remained in the compound during the Breakout. Both he and Ogi survived. And no doubt some men, reluctant to participate in the Breakout but fearful of not appearing to go along with the plan, simply held back as the attack began, and then spent a long and lonely night waiting out the carnage.

Moriki recalled that a Mr Hanaki, a naval petty officer who was kind and quiet, simply announced his decision not to participate and was prepared to face the consequences. His steadfast commitment to his principles won him favour with the other prisoners. Although some called him a coward, Moriki said, 'I never thought that. It took courage to stick to living while being pulled into death by others ... He, who decided to live as long as he could saying "I'm not going" had more dignity than those who went out attacking following the others. He had guts.'[100]

The conclusion is that it is a mistake to say that 1104 men participated in the Breakout, or that 'more than 1000' joined the charge. It was close to that – probably about 950 men were active participants – but the claim that *every* prisoner participated in the Breakout risks painting the Japanese as a homogenous group of suicidal fanatics, a stereotype that simply isn't true.

So why did the majority go along with it? Some had no choice – in at least a few huts hardline leaders simply made the decision for them. In these groups there was no vote, and no option to dissent. Other men were democratic about it –

personally they felt that breaking out was the wrong decision, but they were willing to go along with the majority decision once the votes were cast. And for many men, a decision was reached in a most Japanese fashion. Logic suggested that the hardliners had a valid argument that prisoners remained soldiers even after capture, and were therefore honour-bound to stick to the military code they had sworn to uphold. Having no viable counter-argument to this claim, many men felt that the decision had therefore been made for them – regardless of personal reservations, they were obliged to participate in the attack. Moriki summed up this sentiment.

> What was the great deciding factor to us members? It was, without saying, the paragraph from the Combatant's Code: 'One who knows the shame is strong … do not take the shame of capture in life, do not leave a disgraced name of sin in death.' This was paramount. As Japanese servicemen, we had to choose death. We couldn't keep living indefinitely with the shame of being captured. If we were going to die anyway, we should choose death as soon as possible. This [thought] was not only in the minds of the hard-liners. This was a common agony which tormented all of us.[101]

Shortly after 8 p.m. the hut leaders filed back into Kanazawa's hut to share the news. A small number of huts had voted against the Breakout, some were ambivalent, but the majority voted to proceed. In true Japanese fashion, the leaders whose huts had been opposed or undecided voiced their support for the will of the majority and their intention to go along with the plan. As far as the bulk of the prisoners were concerned, it was all or nothing. Some hardline leaders overruled the will of their hut, and simply declared that their men would participate, either by falsifying the results of the ballot or simply not having allowed them to vote at all.

Kanazawa, who later claimed that he was not particularly in favour of breaking out but felt it was his obligation to lead the men in this climactic moment, addressed the group. 'Well,' he said, 'there doesn't seem much doubt about the majority decision. We break.'[102]

He then moved on to specifics: 'Make sure everyone knows that we are moving tonight ... Start getting the weapons ready. Sharpen the knives, the saws, the chisels. Get hold of those baseball gloves ... they'll be handy on the barbed wire. So will the blankets. Start building fires under the huts, and make sure that nobody lights them.'

Someone asked about the injured, who would not be capable of storming the fences. 'Some people will have to die, of course, even before we're ready to go,' replied Kanazawa. 'Talk to those people, help them to prepare themselves. Remember that they're soldiers, just as much as we are.'

He then dismissed the group: 'We don't have a lot of time. I don't know what time we'll hit, but we can't do it until everything is ready. I'll send for you as soon as we've worked out our little campaign.' He asked Kojima and Toyoshima to remain behind to formulate a plan while the rest of the group filed out and returned, grim-faced, to their huts. There was much work to do.

And so the decision had been made. Death had been invited to this small corner of rural Australia. The only question was, how were the Japanese to meet him?

15

'FORGIVE ME FOR LEAVING BEFORE YOU': THE FINAL HOURS

Friday nights were always a time when the members of the 22nd Garrison Battalion let their close-cropped hair down, but the night of Friday, 4 August 1944 was more boisterous than most. The decision to remove the bulk of Japanese prisoners from B Compound had come as a huge relief to the strained nerves of the garrison, and the impending transfer effectively released the valve on the pressure-cooker atmosphere that had suffocated the camp for months. The men of the guard unit had received their pay that day, and intended to drink a large portion of it away in the camp canteens before daybreak. Impromptu games of cards and two-up broke out and pay packets were enhanced or diminished. The atmosphere was convivial, almost celebratory. But as the coming hours would reveal, the gaiety in Number 12 Prisoner of War Group was premature. (It also reveals much about the level of complacency at the camp that the men were free to drink and relax on the same day that the Japanese had been informed about the transfer to Hay. It appears that no camp commanders thought it prudent to increase the guard unit of B Compound or to man the machine-guns that had been set up to guard against a Japanese uprising.)

It wasn't just at the camp that men were making the most of the end of the working week. Although officially off limits to soldiers without a leave pass, the pubs of Cowra were busy with servicemen on that Friday night. Private Clarrie Mead, the 18-year-old from Bowral who was stationed at the Army Training Camp, had taken the opportunity to escape the confines of the barracks to catch up with his girlfriend in town. They and a large contingent of soldiers were drinking and dancing in the Imperial Hotel until the small hours.

Back at the camp, even as the off-duty men of the garrison drank the night away, the more astute members of the guard noticed that something was afoot in the Japanese compound. 'August 4th, 1944 had been pay day,' recalled Private Wal McKenzie in his memoirs,

> and I, and most off duty personnel, went to the canteen for a beer or two and to try our luck at two-up. I do not remember with whom I walked back to A Camp, but I do remember talking to the guard on duty and him telling us that there was a lot of activity in the Jap compound. It was a cold frosty night and I was glad to go to bed.[103]

McKenzie's informant was an astute observer – in B Compound the Japanese were preparing for battle. Now that the decision had been made, the plan was being put into effect with brutal efficiency. Some men were appointed armourers – they gathered knives from the kitchens, baseball bats from the sports shed, hoes and rakes from the gardens – anything that could be swung, jabbed or thrust in combat. Some men were appointed arsonists – they piled surplus clothing and mattresses in huge pyres in the huts, and stacked firewood around the foundations. And some men were appointed executioners – they would either assist other men to meet an early death, or greet death themselves.

As the winter's night threw a frosty blanket across the compound, men went from hut to hut passing on best wishes and saying farewells. 'The excitement was like a night before the landing on enemy territory,' Moriki recalled. 'They shook hands and they held each other.' He overheard snatches of final conversations:

'Thank you for your caring.'

'Let's do it right!'

'Let's meet again at the Yasukuni-shrine.'[104]

In the huts men sharpened knives and spoons, even the metal plates from the soles of their shoes, by rubbing them against the concrete foundations. They bashed flat the tines of forks, and hammered nails into baseball bats. Even these rudimentary weapons were beyond the reach of Moriki – he had to make do with a rough, vaguely club-shaped lump of firewood he grabbed from the pile next to the brazier. 'There was no way that we could win over the enemy with these kind of weapons,' he lamented. 'Most likely there would be no need of weapons as we would be shot before we reached the enemy's watch tower. It was O.K., and the purpose [of the attack] was to die.'

Some men did not wait for death to come to them. In Hut 11 three men, Kawai, Yamada and Kamiya, were considered too infirm to take part in the attack. The oldest, Kawai, stepped onto a bed and looped a rope around a rafter. He tied the rope around his neck, turned to the small crowd gathered around him and said, 'Forgive me for leaving before you,' then stepped into space. Once he was dead, his comrades removed his body and laid it out in a corner of the hut. Yamada and Kamiya then both followed his example. 'Mr Kawai died easily,' a witness recalled, 'but the younger Mr Yamada and Mr Kamiya had some troubles, so the assistants pulled their legs from below and let them die'.[105] It was a ritual repeated by about a dozen men in huts throughout the compound.

Soon after, 29-year-old Lance Corporal Keishin Tsuno came running up to his friend, Masaru Moriki, who, like him, came from Tosa province. 'Have you heard the news?' he asked breathlessly. 'What are we going to do?' Moriki didn't know what to say. He wasn't in favour of the Breakout, but didn't want to appear cowardly. After a pause, Moriki said the only thing he could think of: 'Let's act like true Tosa-persons of the South-Sea Force.' Moriki thought the answer was ambiguous, but Tsuno took it to heart. 'He must have understood it to be "Let's die in honor",' Moriki later recalled.

> He didn't participate in the attack and walked alone to the empty hut. It was only a short distance but that walk must have been a long depressing walk for him. Mr Tsuno hung a rope over a beam and died alone. In the moments before, he must have been thinking of his parents, his wife and his children who lived in the rural area of Tosa, and said farewell to them.[106]

Moriki never forgave himself for uttering those words. 'I am still tormented by those thoughtless words of mine till this day,' he wrote more than 50 years later. 'If I hadn't said that, maybe he wouldn't have chosen death. "Keishin Tsuno": For as long as I live, I can and will not forget this name.'

It's a sad tale, made sadder by the realisation that Moriki was mistaken about his friend's death. Tsuno did not meet a lonely end hanging from the rafter in a hut. He participated in the Cowra Breakout, and was shot and killed after breaking through the wire. The result is the same, but perhaps had Moriki known the true story, the guilt that he carried for more than five decades could have been assuaged.

In other huts men sat quietly; some sang soft songs, others chatted in small groups. There was a feeling of sombre expectation – most were anxious to just get on with it. Cups of homemade sake were passed around and imbibed eagerly, but few prisoners became drunk. Many men simply sat alone with their thoughts.

One man who was a particularly deep thinker was Warrant Officer Shichihei Matsushima, and he had struggled with his thoughts ever since the decision to break out had been made. As he had implied during the meeting of the hut leaders, he was looking forward to seeing his family after the war was over, and felt that this mass suicide would do little to help Japan's war effort, and was simply unnecessary. He also felt that the decision to die had been made by the young, single men in the camp, and did not take into account the feelings of older men, such as himself, who had wives and children to return to in Japan. He struggled with his thoughts during the long, torturous hours, taking time to write a poem expressing his anguish. Eventually he could stand it no longer. He had to act.

There was only one solution – he had to inform the Australian authorities about the Breakout. But how was he to do it? Any attempt to warn the guards would surely be observed by the other prisoners, and the reaction would be swift and deadly. After more hours of troubled thought, he settled on a plan: if he could be taken into custody by the Australians, he would be separated from the rest of the prisoners and could speak freely without fear of retribution.

His plan was sound but his execution of it was comically inept. Had the stakes not been so high, nor the consequences of failure so deadly, Matsushima's ham-fisted attempts at espionage would be a source of mirth. He determined that the best way of ensuring his separation from the other prisoners was to write an anonymous note that incriminated him to such an extent that camp authorities wouldn't hesitate to haul him away and interrogate him. He would then be free to spill the beans away from the prying eyes, and sharpened blades, of his fellow inmates.

He took a strip of toilet paper and wrote his own name and prison number, and then composed a conspiratorial missive in Japanese. 'He has an assumed name,' he wrote.

> He is a great extremist and against the peace of the camp. The majority of the camp are anxious to have him removed. I have spoken to the officers, but they don't take any action. The man should be interrogated and transferred elsewhere, otherwise something will occur which will cause inconvenience to those in charge of B camp and also the commander. We hope that the peace which now prevails in the camp will continue.

Matsushima then tied the note to a stick and threw it over the fence into Broadway. He had signed the letter 'Y.S.', which he later said he chose at random, but which caused confusion in the days after the Breakout – those were the initials of Yoshio Shimoyama, one of the toughest hardliners in the camp, and hardly a man who was likely to dob in a fellow extremist. In the end it was a moot point – the note was not discovered until days after the Breakout, by which stage the compound was already a smouldering ruin and Shimoyama was dead.[107]

Some time after he had delivered his first note via stickmail into a ditch beside Broadway, Matsushima decided that a more direct course of action was required. Fearing that the translation of his note would eat up valuable time, he decided to pen another note in English, this time addressed directly to the compound commander, but still pushing the ruse that Matsushima was a troublemaker who should be detained and interrogated. This was easier said than done – Matsushima's grasp of the language was not extensive. This time he wrote: 'No. 145431. He bad man. Him inspect Cnmande. You this see. Spek tell Cnmande B Camp.' Again he signed the note 'Y.S.', creating yet another wild goose for Australian intelligence officers to chase as they attempted to untangle the plot in the days after the Breakout. Again he lobbed his note over the fence into Broadway. Again it was not discovered until after the Breakout.

As the hours crawled by and no armed guard appeared to arrest him, Matsushima became increasingly desperate. He wrote a third note, this one in even worse English than his previous effort. 'B Camp No. 145431. he bad man. Him inspect cnmand. You this is see. Speak tell cnmander B Cnp. – Y.S.' But time was running out and he felt it was too risky to throw it over the fence that evening. He stuffed it into his pocket, where it would remain unread until long after it was too late to be of any use.*

---

* Ironically, all Matsushima's note-writing did result in him being detained and interrogated, but only after the Breakout had occurred and far too late to prevent the bloodshed. It did, however, give Australian authorities a chance to speak to a man who had valuable insights into the running of the camp and the events that led to the Breakout, an opportunity they might otherwise have overlooked. Matsushima's opinion was that the apparent organisers of the riot, particularly Kanazawa and Kojima, were moderates, and that any objections to the plan to break out had been consistently overruled by the hardliners. He also added that plans to launch an attack on the camp had been discussed nightly for months.[108]

As the hour for action drew near, the compound leaders agreed on a tactical plan for the attack and spread the word to the hut leaders. The plan was simple but ambitious, and while the Japanese knew that by morning many of them would be dead, they didn't intend to throw away their lives cheaply. The Cowra Breakout wasn't a quest for freedom, but it wasn't a straightforward suicide charge either. The Japanese were warriors, and they wanted to take the battle to the Australians as they had done in the jungles of New Guinea, in the skies over Milne Bay and in the waters of the Coral and Arafura seas. And before they met the glorious death they had long been seeking, they were going to take as many Australian soldiers with them as they could.

The Japanese planners divided the huts into four groups, based on their location in the compound. The north-eastern group (Huts 3, 4, 7, 8, 11, 12, 15 and 20) would form the main thrust of the assault. This group of about 200 men would cover 100 metres of ground to the perimeter fences on the northern side of the compound and scale them as quickly as possible. Their goal was another 50 metres beyond the third line of barbed wire: Number Two machine-gun set up on its trailer. Sharp Japanese eyes had observed that the gun was only ever manned in daylight hours, and a courageous expedition to the wire earlier in the evening had confirmed that the trailer was deserted. Once they had seized the gun, the Japanese would turn it against the Australians in B Company barracks, and use the confusion and slaughter as a springboard to take over the whole camp.

A second group comprising the 12 huts in the south-eastern block (Huts 23, 24, 27, 28, 31, 32, 35, 36, 37, 38, 39 and 40) would charge across 100 metres of open ground and tackle the perimeter fences north of F Tower. This group of about 300 men had probably the easiest job of any group, as this stretch of perimeter was poorly defended and was flanked by open fields. Once through the fence, the plan was for this group to attack the POW camp from behind, and to lead an assault on the Army Training Camp once the POW camp had been captured.

A third group was formed by the huts in the south-west (Huts 21, 22, 25, 26, 29, 30, 33 and 34). This group of about 200 men would charge the gates that opened onto Broadway at the southern end of B Compound and, once through, they would turn left into Broadway, break into D Compound and free the Japanese officers, before launching an assault on the southern gates of Broadway.

A final group, made up of about 300 men from the north-western huts (Huts 1, 2, 5, 6, 9, 10, 13, 14, 16, 17, 18 and 19) would break through the perimeter fence leading onto Broadway and turn right, charging through the northern gates and attacking B Company barracks as it was coming under fire from the machine-gun captured in the first charge.

(There is some confusion about which huts were allocated to each group. The above description is based on a highly detailed map produced during the Court of Inquiry, compiled from witness testimony. It includes details as specific as the location where each Australian and Japanese body was found and the number of blankets recovered from each section of the wire, so would seem to be an authoritative source. Its allocation of huts to each group is also simple and logical – the four objectives would be attacked by those huts closest to them. However, Sergeant Major Hiroshi Yoshida, who briefly took over as camp leader after the Breakout, gave evidence that the huts were allocated to each group numerically – Huts 1 to 10 would attack south on Broadway, 11 to 20 would charge the Vickers gun, 21 to 30 would attack north on Broadway and 31 to 40 would attack the fence near F Tower. While this system makes sense on paper, the staggered layout of the huts would make it difficult to implement in practice. Given the complexities of organising an attack of nearly 1000 men at short notice, in the dark, it seems more likely that the plan outlined on the map was the one put into action. Yoshida's plan would also have tasked Toyoshima and his comrades in Hut 13 with attacking the Vickers gun, when in reality they attacked Broadway.)

The signal to launch this organised chaos would be a bugle call from Toyoshima at 2 a.m. Like so many men who had gone to their deaths in wars over the previous century, the Japanese at Cowra would attack to a soundtrack of military music. The camp leaders were adamant that every man understood, and was honour-bound to obey, a key tenet of the plan: the attack was to be made only against men in uniform. Under no circumstances were civilians to be harmed.

As the long, cold night drew on, the activity in the compound slowed down. By now blades had been sharpened, fires prepared and parting words spoken. Many men dozed, some simply sat and waited. In the theatre at the southern end of the compound, 24-year-old Toshiro Uchino, a merchant seaman from Fukushima who had been a prisoner for nearly two years, sat alone on the floor. He contemplated for a long moment, and then drove a carving knife into his stomach, completing the *seppuku* ritual by drawing it across his abdomen and finally upwards. He collapsed to the floor as the blood pooled around him, and died slowly and in agony.[109]

Not far away, Moriki and Juichi Kinoshita, the two friends who had shared adjacent beds in a Brisbane military hospital and had travelled to Goulburn and Cowra together, stood in the cold night air, talking in soft voices. Kinoshita had put his needlework skills to good use in Cowra, making intricate costumes for the traditional plays that the prisoners regularly performed in their makeshift theatre. Kinoshita farewelled his friend and made his way to the theatre, where he carefully laid out the costumes he had lovingly crafted over many months. Uchino's body lay in the corner. 'Mr Kinoshita hung himself surrounded by the costumes he created,' Moriki later said. 'I wonder why he didn't go with the others [to attack]. Instead, he died alone in the entertainment club room. I think he had a love of costumes and wanted to die surrounded by them. Although it was his fate, his death was especially sad since he had a wife and children.'[110]

And so another figure was added to the ghastly ledger of death. Kawai, Yamada, Kamiya, Uchino and many others had already added their names to the tally. Within hours, hundreds more would join them.

16

'ALL HELL BROKE LOOSE': THE ATTACK ON BROADWAY

Private Alf Rolls lit a cigarette and tried to shake off the cold that pierced him to his bones. He had really drawn the short straw tonight – guard duty was tedious and uncomfortable at the best of times, but to be allocated guard duty in the tent in the middle of Broadway, right outside the Japanese compound, in the small hours of an icy winter's night, was really something to gripe about. As he walked his beat along Broadway, he thought back to many a chilly night he'd spent working the family farm at Grenfell – coincidentally, only 50 kilometres down the road from where he now stood. He wondered how the family were doing without him – he had recently put in an application to be transferred out of the army and back to the farm as an essential worker, so hopefully his nights of frosty patrols would soon be over. God knew there was more to life than being a soldier in this lonely outpost. When he'd been called up two years earlier at age 38, he assumed he'd have bugger-all likelihood of actually serving. If his relatively advanced years didn't count against him, the near-total deafness in his right ear, a hangover from an old farming accident, surely would. But the army works in mysterious ways, and so he found himself here, babysitting a bunch of troublesome Japanese.

And they certainly appeared to need babysitting tonight. They were restless and furtive. Lights-out was supposed to be at 9 p.m., but Rolls could still see the faint glow of braziers burning in several of the huts, and he'd heard talking for most of his time on duty. Once or twice he saw a prisoner scurrying between huts, and had considered firing two shots in the air, the warning signal that would bring the whole camp to alert, but held his fire. Many of the prisoners were fresh from the jungles of New Guinea and Bougainville, and had stomach complaints that made hurried nocturnal dashes to the latrines a fairly common occurrence. But tonight seemed different – there seemed purpose to the Japanese movements. The atmosphere was – well, *heavy*. Rolls thought he saw something in the shadows and gripped his rifle tighter, peering into the inky darkness that pooled outside the glare of the searchlights.

There! Movement! A shadowy figure was creeping cautiously but purposefully along the near wall of the closest hut. Suddenly the figure turned towards Rolls and started sprinting across the open ground between the huts and the twin set of gates that opened onto Broadway. Rolls stepped forward, holding his rifle at the ready. He glanced at his watch – it was just after 1.45 a.m.

As the Japanese prisoner reached the first set of gates, he began waving his arms and shouting frantically. It was a weird kind of noise he was making – he appeared to be both yelling and attempting to keep his voice low – but he was extremely agitated, and kept gesturing wildly towards the Japanese compound. Rolls couldn't understand what he was saying – the prisoner appeared to be talking in a mix of broken English and panicky Japanese, but when he began to climb the inner gate, Rolls had had enough. He held the muzzle of his rifle high, and fired a shot in the air. Working the bolt quickly, he fired a second round – the two-shot warning signal.

The Japanese prisoner froze at the sound of the shots, unsure what he should do. He stood impotently between the two gates, and didn't attempt to climb the second set. 'The phone rang from B Company, and I answered it,' Rolls later said. He explained the situation to the guardhouse and 'they said they were sending a private and a corporal down to take [the prisoner] over.'[111]

The Australians didn't know it but, like Shichihei Matsushima, the determined note-writer, this Japanese prisoner had decided he didn't want any part in the Breakout. And, like Matsushima, he felt his only course of action was to inform the Australians about what was afoot. But his methods were rather less subtle than his older comrade's, although just as ineffective.

Within minutes the guard officer from D Company, Lieutenant Tom Aisbett, arrived on the scene. Aisbett was a 34-year-old former schoolteacher from Sydney who had trained as an antitank gunner earlier in the war before joining the garrison in Cowra. Only an hour or so earlier he had climbed into bed fully clothed – technically he was on duty and he wanted to be ready in case the Japanese were up to something. At the sound of the shots he sprang out of bed and strode with purpose to the guard post. There he was confronted by a nervous Australian soldier and a Japanese prisoner who was hysterical and muttering indecipherably in Japanese. The prisoner was clutching a blanket and kept waving his arms in the direction of the Japanese huts. When he saw Aisbett approaching, his hysteria went up a notch. 'The PW Japanese between the gates had his hands up and kept shivering and crying,' Aisbett said. 'He was endeavouring to tell me something, but I did not understand Japanese.'

By now the prisoner knew he was nearly out of time – surely someone in the Japanese compound had seen his frantic interaction with the Australian guards, and any minute now they would come for him. In desperation he switched from Japanese to the few words of English he knew. The only word he could muster that seemed to come close to describing a planned mass attack on the camp was one he'd heard the guards bandying around whenever a Japanese prisoner had refused to work. 'Strike!' he called out. '*Strike!*' And then, perhaps in a final, desperate attempt to get the Australians to take him into custody and protect him from the violence he knew was coming, he called out a word he had heard the Italians using to describe the detention centre: 'Calaboose!'[112]

Unsurprisingly, Aisbett had no idea what the prisoner was trying to tell him. Before he had a chance to figure it out, two men from B Company arrived to escort the prisoner back to their barracks. 'Hullo,' said one of the men to Rolls. 'What have you got here for me?' Before Rolls could answer, all hell broke loose.

The Japanese prisoner had been right to be fearful – several other prisoners had witnessed his dash to the gates and had rushed to tell Hajime Toyoshima. Realising they had been betrayed and that the whole plan was at risk of coming undone, Toyoshima knew there was only one option – the attack had to be launched immediately. He stepped out of Hut 13 onto the frozen parade ground, raised the bugle to his lips and issued a long, piercing note.

The sound was startling, completely unexpected, in the still, cold air. Aisbett, Rolls and the other guards momentarily froze, unsure where the sound had come from or what it meant. Then it came again: a long, mournful note piercing the night.

And then suddenly, chillingly, the sound was replaced by another – and this time the Australians knew exactly where it was coming from and what it meant. At the bugle signal, nearly 1000 Japanese prisoners spilled from their huts and roared with ferocious fervour as they charged towards the wire. At the same time prisoners knocked over the blazing braziers in their huts, and ignited the clothes and mattresses that had been piled on the floors. Within minutes most of the huts were ablaze. A large group of burgundy-clad figures came charging straight towards Aisbett and his small party at the gates. The Japanese informant saw them coming and hurled himself over the gate and into Broadway.

Aisbett didn't hesitate. 'Run for your lives!' he shouted, and the Australian guards turned and sprinted for the southern gates of Broadway, about 350 metres away. As they ran they heard the chorus of screams swell behind them, and a frightful commotion as the burgundy wave surged against the B Compound gates. The timber frames couldn't possibly resist the weight of this human wave, and the locks shattered. Aisbett dared a glance over his shoulder as he ran – the Japanese informant was on his heels, wide-eyed and terrified. Behind him, Broadway was a mass of furious, charging men. They waved clubs and knives as they came on, intent on running down the Australians. Aisbett had never been in combat, but he knew deadly intent when he saw it – the Japanese were after blood. There was no option but to get out of Broadway.

The Japanese prisoner panicked and swerved into the ditch at the side of Broadway. Whether he was trying to get away or simply hide is unclear, but in seconds the Japanese wave engulfed him. He was clubbed and stabbed to death.* Although his effort to warn the Australians had not been understood, his intervention brought the camp to alert probably ten minutes earlier than it otherwise would have, and those ten minutes were crucial in dealing with the Breakout. Decades later, Aisbett said about him, 'By his warning the prisoner saved many lives and, in my opinion, the whole garrison.'[113]

Aisbett and his men were now close to the southern end of Broadway. The guards there had opened the gates and were calling furiously to the Australians to hurry up. Aisbett didn't look back again, but he could tell from the frantic look of the guards who were calling to him and the roar coming from behind him that the Japanese must be close. Very close.

The whole camp was awake by now – no one could have slept through the din of the Japanese charge – but curiously there was no shooting. The Vickers gun crews had not yet reached their guns, and the general order to open fire had not been given. Aisbett shot a withering look up at B Tower. He knew there was a crew with a Bren light machine-gun up there – by now they should have been raking the ground behind him with fire, cutting down the Japanese waves. But the tower was eerily silent.

The Australians reached the gates and charged through. As the guards struggled to close the gates behind them, the first Japanese prisoners reached them. The Australians didn't hesitate – they opened fire with their rifles through the slats of the gates at point-blank range. The first five Japanese went down in a bloody heap. Behind them, the burgundy wave kept coming.

---

* The identity of this prisoner has never been established, but based on the report into the cause of death of the prisoners in the Breakout, it was likely he was one of this group: Hakuzu Marukami, Wataru Ueno, Takio Ichimura, Yoshio Sukita, Ichiro Izumida or Uchiro Watanabe.

Aisbett ran headlong into his commanding officer, Major Les Lees. Originally from New Zealand, Lees was a former police officer who had fought in the Great War in Gallipoli and France. He was a tough operator who knew a battle when he saw one. 'Find out what's wrong with the tower!' he barked at Aisbett, who was already running for the stairs. He bounded up them two at a time, and found two panic-stricken soldiers at the top struggling to clear a jam in the Bren gun. Aisbett shoved the soldiers aside, quickly cleared the jam and got the gun in action. He opened fire on the mass of Japanese below him.

Aisbett was an expert marksman and he did deadly work with the gun. 'He could write his name with a Bren,' one of his comrades later recalled, 'and down below him in the choked lane leading to the officers' quarters the line of dead and dying bore his personal signature.'[114] Aisbett poured fire into the mass of burgundy below him, and men fell in their dozens. A group of brave souls turned right and charged the gates of D Compound, breaking the padlock and forcing their way in. Aisbett followed them with fire from the Bren gun, and bodies were soon scattered around the D Compound gates. The Japanese still in Broadway took cover in the only shelter available to them, the stormwater ditches on both sides of the road.

Marekuni Takahara, the navy flying boat gunner who had been shot down near Darwin in February 1942, was part of the group that charged the gates. Decades later, the horror of those minutes stayed with him:

> The guards in the towers, although confused by the emergency, turned their searchlights on us and showered us with intense machine-gun fire illuminated with red, blue and yellow tracer. People all around me went down like ninepins. I could hear groans everywhere. As it was

impossible to move down the centre of the road, we crawled along the drains on either side, climbing over the dead in the hail of bullets. Finally we reached a heap of corpses near the officers' gate.[115]

Masaru Moriki was in the same attack group as Takahara, though there is nothing to indicate the two men knew each other. Moriki's leg had not healed well from the bullet he had taken in New Guinea, and he was forced to walk with the aid of a stick. This was obviously a great hindrance during the charge to the wire, and he fell several times trying to keep up with his comrades. He finally reached the fence long after the shooting had started.

I reached the barbed wire fence panting and climbed like mad. Tracer bullets flew continuously by my ears. A cloud of dust rose eerily on the ground before me. People who were killed by the first shots were hanging on the barbed wire fence. Somehow I went over the fence even though my clothes were snagged by the barbed wire … The shooting got more intense and the cloud of dust rose near my feet non stop. It was said that the bullets that come to your feet were the most dangerous on the battlefield. [Because] It was proof that the enemy was aiming precisely.[116]

(This account is interesting because it suggests a departure from the plan worked out by the Japanese leaders. Moriki appears to have been in the group allocated to turn right into Broadway and attack the guards at the northern end. But instead, he and his comrades turned left, and charged alongside Takahara's group towards the officers' compound at the *southern* end. It is entirely understandable that men in the heat of battle may forget their instructions or choose to ignore them, but it's also an excellent reminder that we shouldn't place too much faith in the Japanese plans as a reliable indicator of how the attack unfolded. At the end of the day, the Cowra Breakout involved lightly armed men charging against machine-guns, and each of those men chose his own course of action once the shooting started.)

As Moriki limped forward, comrades fell all around him. 'The spirited ones who got out first fell upon each other outside the gate,' he said. 'I heard moans from ones who had been injured and were not quite dead, and I saw in the night the blood run from the seven or eight motionless bodies making dark stains on the asphalt.'[117]

In the ditch on the side of Broadway, Takahara lay next to his friend and former crewmate Kiyoshi Yamakawa. As a sweep of machine-gun fire spat dirt into their faces, Yamakawa cried out in pain. 'They've got me in the leg!' he shouted, and almost reflexively raised the knife he held in his hand and plunged it into his chest. 'It must have missed his heart,' Takahara recalled. 'He was in a bad way but could understand me if I spoke to him. Whether it was good luck or bad luck, I don't know; but I was by his side. I decided to stay and look after him until he was dead. I said "I'll stay with you, Yamakawa. Don't die!"'

About 50 prisoners had managed to break into D Compound, where the Japanese officers were held. There had always been a plan to free the officers, but this charge was more likely simply a desperate attempt for the Japanese to escape the hail of bullets coming down Broadway. Regardless, Lees ordered the Australians to open fire on anyone moving in D Compound but, as the compound also contained Koreans and Formosans who appeared to be taking no part in the

Breakout, to not hit any of the buildings. The Japanese who made it into D Compound huddled behind the huts, with Aisbett and the Australian riflemen picking off any who exposed themselves.

There were only 12 Japanese officers in the compound. There had not been time in the hours before the Breakout to alert the officers to the impending attack, but they quickly realised what was happening. Ensign Ko Oikawa, the submariner who had been captured at Guadalcanal, was thrilled that the moment of action had finally arrived. He was determined to join his comrades in the attack, but other officers, noting the machine-gun fire tearing into the ground outside the huts, held him back. Finally he could stand it no longer. 'I'm going,' he said to the small group of officers. 'This is our only chance – who's with me?' Only one man was, Second Lieutenant Ichiro Fujita, a doctor from Gifu prefecture who had been captured in New Guinea in early 1943 and had celebrated his 25th birthday the previous day. The two men raced from the safety of the hut and across the open ground at the front of the compound. Their intention wasn't clear – perhaps they wanted to link up with the men in Broadway and lead a final charge, perhaps they simply couldn't stand the suspense any more and had to join the fighting – but the result was the same. As soon as they cleared the hut they attracted a volley of fire. Fujita went down first, with bullets in both legs. He lay moaning on the frosty earth. Oikawa caught a bullet in the thigh, and was able to drag himself back towards the hut. His comrades reefed him back into safety, where a young medical officer, Probationary Officer Masanomi Aoki, treated his wounds. Fujita was too far from the hut to be reached. The officers called to him, hoping he could crawl towards them, but he was too badly wounded. He bled to death soon after. Fujita was the only Japanese officer to be killed in the Cowra Breakout.[*]

While all this drama was playing out in D Compound, Takahara, Moriki and hundreds of other men were desperately trying to avoid getting hit as they lay in the drainage ditches on Broadway. It was the only thing they could do – there was not a scrap of cover anywhere along the roadway, and any attempt to move was a death sentence. But as the ditches ran straight along Broadway, directly towards the Australian positions, they offered only slight protection, and the bodies began to pile up as men were hit where they lay. Suddenly, all was darkness – a stray bullet had cut the power to the camp. But the full moon and burning huts still provided plenty of light for the Australians to aim by.

As Takahara lay in the ditch, desperately trying to press himself even further into the frozen ground, he felt a searing pain in his left buttock. 'I thought that I had been hit,' he said. 'I felt with my hand and found that I was all right.' Takahara had only been grazed by a bullet, but the same shot had then smacked into the body of Private Kinta Toki, who was sheltering behind Takahara, killing him instantly. 'Eventually amid a pile of corpses Yamakawa and I were the only ones alive,' Takahara recalled. 'Lying there motionless, one was conscious only of the cold and the danger of being hit.'

This attack on the southern end of Broadway was really over soon after it had begun. The Japanese were hemmed in to a barbed-wire pen – they couldn't get through the gates leading to the Australian barracks, and the weight of fire from the

---

[*] Curiously, Fujita's military record identifies his cause of death as not only the wounds to his legs, but also a self-inflicted wound. There is nothing in witness accounts or the official cause of death ledger to indicate that Fujita committed suicide after being wounded.

guard towers above and the riflemen below meant that they couldn't move without being hit. As Takahara lay in the ditch, he saw a brave or suicidal Japanese prisoner occasionally rise and confront the guards. 'Long live the Emperor!' they would cry, before being met by a hail of bullets. The initial excitement of the charge and the courage provided by the homemade wine had now faded, and the cold reality of the situation now began to sink in, figuratively and literally. 'We have a saying "A full moon in winter means good but cold weather,"' Takahara said. 'Whether it applies to Australia, I don't know; but it certainly applied to Cowra that night. As we lay there face downward feigning death, the cold ate into us. One couldn't help urinating. Initially that felt warm, but very soon it, too, was as cold as ice.'

At the other end of Broadway, almost exactly the same scene had played out. In B Tower, Private William Turner had fired two warning shots as he saw the mass of prisoners breaking into Broadway. The group that had charged right and attacked the northern gates had been met by a similar volley of fire from the guard towers, and the rifles and submachine guns of the garrison. Bodies littered the ground, and wounded and terrified men huddled in the ditches on either side of the road. No prisoner who broke into Broadway managed to escape from it.

During all this commotion, the guards in B Company barracks had been hurriedly dragging themselves from bed and rushing to their posts. One of them was Private Charles Shepherd, a 31-year-old labourer from Sydney, who had been rejected from active service due to poor eyesight. As he rushed down the steps of the B Company guardroom, he was confronted by a Japanese prisoner, who presumably had scaled the fence in another part of the compound and doubled back to the Australian positions. The two men froze face-to-face for an instant, before the Japanese plunged a knife into Shepherd's heart. The prisoner ran on, and Shepherd sank to the ground, where he died alone at the foot of the steps.

Major Bob Ramsay, the commandant of B Compound, was wiping sleep from his eyes as he emerged from the B Company barracks in civilian clothes and sandshoes and into scenes of chaos. He saw prisoners charging in all directions, grabbed a Verey flare gun from the guardroom and fired three red flares into the dark sky – the prearranged signal to alert the Army Training Camp to a breakout. Within seconds three distant yellow flares arced skyward in reply – the Army Training Camp was now on full alert.

Private Alf Flynn, the C Company butcher, had not been in bed long when the Breakout began. 'It was a cold bright moonlight [sic] morning,' he recalled decades later.

> I took off my overcoat and boots and went to bed fully clothed to keep warm [unlike the Japanese prisoners, the Australian guards had no braziers to warm their sleeping quarters]. We had three blankets, a groundsheet and a bag of straw in a fold up bed. I was dozing off when I heard two shots from a rifle which was a warning of a breakout. We had heard rumours but I thought there is no way that the Japanese are going to get out. I scrambled out of bed and at the time it was funny. The cook had been to the canteen so I suppose he was not too good on his feet at that hour of the morning. Dancing around on one leg putting on his trousers like a yo-yo going up and down. All I had to do was pull on my boots.[118]

Flynn grabbed his rifle and ran outside, where he was greeted by pandemonium. 'All hell broke loose,' he said. 'Firing of machine-guns rattling away mixed with rifle fire and bullets flying through the air like bees, screaming Japs yelling and the huts were burning and lighting up the sky. The smoke from the firing of guns and the burning of huts was lying all over the compound. It was an eerie feeling.'

There were so many bullets flying around, particularly down the length of Broadway, that there was a real danger of getting hit. Several Australians were in fact wounded by friendly fire during the Breakout, including Private Reg McDonald, who was shot in the chest; Lance Corporal Roy Mills, who took two bullets in the thigh and stomach; and Private Keith McGuiness, who was hit in the foot. It was a miracle that no one was killed. '[The shooting] was far too confused,' recalled McGuiness decades later. 'I fired two or three slugs from my position by the main gate. People were blazing away everywhere, and the Japanese seemed to be just crazy. I felt a sting in my foot, and suddenly I was being bundled into the RAP [Regimental Aid Post].'[119] 'It was as bad as a day in action in any part of warfare,' recalled Corporal Norm Beaman, who was in charge of driving an ambulance from the camp hospital.

> There were bullets flying and ricocheting everywhere. It was a strange sight to see the Japs going around the huts with old knives and goodness knows what and the next thing you would see an officer appear with a rifle or a revolver and having a shot and it was hell on earth for a while. There must have been several of our blokes that must have been hit. Some not very seriously. They would land in the ambulances and we would run them into Cowra Hospital.[120]

Wal McKenzie had pulled his coat on over his pyjamas as soon as he heard the warning shots and raced to the northern gates of Broadway. 'It was very bright moonlight,' he said, 'and the glow from the fires lit the whole area ... There was a lot of noise, probably more from exploding fibro and crackling Cyprus pine than from all the shooting.'

As he watched the carnage, a couple of Japanese prisoners scaled the gates. One went down as soon as he hit the ground, either from an Australian bullet or a broken leg, but the other

landed on his feet and kept running, weaving from side to side towards five or six of our guardsmen who fired several shots each before he fell a few yards in front of them. He had a knife in his hands and no doubt I was pleased to see him fall. I remember the feeling of adoration of such a brave young man.[121]

The commotion was so loud that even the people in the town knew that something was going on. At the Imperial Hotel, Clarrie Mead had retired for the night with his girlfriend.

I was in the Imperial Hotel with a sheila at 2am in the morning and the alarm went. I didn't hear the alarm and she woke me up and as soon as I heard it I knew it was on. I got dressed and I guarantee that it was the fastest three miles that you have ever seen anybody run. It was out on the Sydney Road up to the army camp. I grabbed my rifle and bayonet and when I walked up the hill the officer said to me 'where have you been Private Mead?', and I said I had a little bit of gastric and I was on the toilet![122]

Back at the camp, there was chaos within the Japanese compound as well as outside it. An Australian orderly in the B Compound hospital was preparing for an influx of wounded he surely knew would not be far away, when a Japanese prisoner kicked in the door and came at him with a knife. A Korean orderly, Tairisu Miyamoto, stepped between the prisoner and the Australian. 'All Korean orderlies set upon the Jap,' a report later described, 'and ejected him from the hospital whence he made in the direction of the perimeter fence but he was shot dead in the hospital yard.'[123]

All around the camp similar small dramas were playing out, insignificant in the grand scheme of things, but meaning everything for the participants. Death was everywhere. Some lives ended with a bang, others with a whimper. Major Ramsay was heading towards Broadway when a Japanese prisoner came at him with a knife. 'As soon as he saw me,' Ramsay said, 'he veered off round the Quartermaster's Store. I called on one of my orderly room clerks who was standing by with a rifle to shoot him. This he did.'[124]

For the time being the situation in Broadway was relatively under control. Sometime before 3 a.m. Major Lees ordered that the Australians at the southern end should cease fire, unless a prisoner attacked the gates – which they occasionally did. Takahara recognised the camp's wrestling champion, Lance Corporal Kanjiro Naruta (whose skills were so extensive he had once fractured another prisoner's skull during a 'friendly' wrestling match), rise up from the ditch where he had been sheltering in Broadway. 'Shoot! Shoot!' he cried out in Japanese. 'A shot rang out followed by a groan,' Takahara recalled in his memoirs. 'He did this several times, always with the same result. Although he received ten bullet wounds he is, I am glad to say, alive and fit amongst us today.'[125] (Naruta's wounds, although ghastly, weren't quite as extensive as Takahara remembered. A report after the Breakout indicated he had been hit four times – in the chest, shoulder and both thighs.)

All in all, the attack on Broadway had been a colossal, frightening, bloody failure. The Japanese achieved little more than to hem themselves in to a long, rectangular cage, where the Australians cut them down with barely a pause. The dead lay in grotesque piles near the gates and in the road, and the wounded and survivors sought whatever shelter they could find in the muddy ditches. Although the bulk of the Australian shooting appears to have been a reasonable response to the Japanese attack, there is evidence that, for some Australians, the breakout into Broadway provided an opportunity to settle old scores with the Japanese, or to vent animosities that had been building up for months, even years. Negerevich, the interpreter, said that he saw Australians shooting Japanese prisoners well into the following morning, long after the ceasefire order had been given, and even when ordered not to. Wal McKenzie recalled a concerning incident: 'The yelling of the prisoners had already died down but over all the other noise I could hear Jacky Currie yelling and laughing from the tower when he was manning the machine-gun. "Got that bastard! Yippee have a go at this one! Look at all those deadies, ha ha ha".' McKenzie said that Currie's behaviour was so erratic that many assumed him to be drunk, and he was later removed from duty. As Moriki lay in the ditch, desperately trying to avoid getting shot, he heard Australian guards goading the prisoners into offering them better targets. 'Come on, Jap!' one yelled. 'Bloody idiots!' called another.[126] One Australian officer later reported with undisguised relish that 'during the height of the break the flames from the huts gave extremely good light for shooting',[127] as if referring to an evening rabbit hunt on a country estate.

At about 3 a.m. Major Ramsay contacted the Army Training Camp to request reinforcements for his stretched garrison. A heavily armed group of 149 soldiers arrived about an hour later, and for the first time all night Ramsay was able to strengthen his posts with an adequate complement of men. (Private Ray

'Simmo' Simpson, the future Victoria Cross winner, was one of the soldiers in this group, which is how he came to be manning Number One machine-gun as described in Chapter 12.)

Back on Broadway, in the ditch near D Compound, one of the wounded was Hajime Toyoshima. He had taken a bullet in the chest during the charge to the officers' quarters and had either crawled or been dragged into the ditch. He lay on his back looking up into the star-filled sky, feeling the icy air draw into his lungs with each laboured breath. He calmly lit a cigarette and took a few half-hearted puffs. And then he took the sharpened dinner knife he had been carrying and drew the blade across his own throat. For the Zero pilot, who had soared through the skies over Pearl Harbor and Darwin, who had befriended an Australian guard in Melbourne and replied to fan mail from a small boy, who had won friends, both Japanese and Australian, as camp leader, and who had blown the bugle call that had started the carnage, the war was finally over.

17

'THEY GOT US':
THE VICKERS GUN

Ben Hardy sprang out of his cot as soon as he heard the warning shots ring out. Ralph Jones came running up to him, wiping sleep from his eyes and looking a less-than-intimidating figure in his army-issue flannel pyjamas. 'What the hell is going on, Ben?' he said. 'It's on,' Hardy replied simply. 'We need to move.' Both men grabbed their uniforms and were just beginning to change when the night was suddenly torn by a mass of screams and shouts. 'Bloody hell,' said Hardy as the chorus of screams grew louder. 'There's no time! We have to get on the gun!' The two men slipped on their army boots and didn't waste time tying the laces. They grabbed their heavy woollen great coats and slid them over their pyjamas as they stumbled down the steps of the barracks. The cold night air greeted them like a slap.

Hardy and Jones couldn't believe what they were seeing. A wave of burgundy figures was surging across B Compound, accompanied by a terrifying soundtrack of screaming. There was no shooting yet – the only sound was the roar of the charging men. The crest of the wave broke against the first wire fence, and the burgundy-clad figures began throwing blankets over the wire barricade. There was no question where they were heading – the trailer and its Vickers machine-gun stood lonely and exposed in the sharp glare of the searchlights.

The two men sprinted towards the trailer. They only had about 100 metres to cover, but that seemed to take all the time in the world as the prisoners began scaling the first wire obstacle. The Japanese spotted the two Australians running towards the gun, and the screams grew louder, the scrambling through the wire more frantic; the noise was ferocious, all-consuming.

At the first wire fence, Lance Corporal Kiishi Ishii, a 26-year-old tailor from Tokyo who only two months earlier had still been fighting in New Guinea, threw a blanket and coat over the wire. He wore a baseball glove on his left hand, and used it to hold down the wire as he desperately tried to scramble over. In his right hand he held a baseball bat, into which he had hurriedly driven half a dozen nails in the hours before the Breakout. The wire caught at his clothes and the angry barbs tore into his skin. He was amazed he hadn't come under fire by now; the trailer and its machine-gun, the objective of the men charging across the compound, still stood empty.[128] Although that meant they were safe from its fire, it presented a problem. The Japanese had no knowledge of the operation of an Australian machine-gun. If they got to it first, they might not be able to make it work.

He didn't have to worry. As Ishii was struggling to get through the first fence, Hardy and Jones reached the gun. They scrambled onto the trailer, and into the positions they had rehearsed. 'Load!' Jones threw open an ammo can, and swiftly loaded the belt. Hardy pulled back the crank handle twice. Jones slapped Hardy on the back: 'FIRE!' Hardy pressed the thumb trigger and the gun spat fire.

At first Hardy directed the fire at his designated target zone, along the north-eastern perimeter fence. He could see prisoners breaching the wire near F Tower, and his first burst killed five of them and wounded several more. But suddenly he recognised the main threat – Number One gun was not yet firing, and without its covering fire Hardy and Jones were on their own. And hundreds of Japanese prisoners were surging towards them. Hardy abandoned his fire zone along the fence and swung the gun around to meet the threat immediately in front of him. He took aim at the mass of burgundy figures and let rip. At less than 75 metres range, he couldn't miss. The slugs tore into the burgundy wave, cutting men down as they desperately tried to free themselves from the deadly embrace of the wire. Screams of triumph turned to agony as bullets sliced through the throng, and men fell in their dozens. Ishii was finally cresting the first fence when his close friend, Lance Corporal Michinosuke Sawada, was hit in the leg. As Ishii tried desperately to free him from the wire, another round caught Sawada in the abdomen. Sawada died hanging on the wire. Ishii carried on, racing towards the second fence and throwing himself onto the frozen ground as bullets arced towards him. (Ishii was still there when dawn broke – his close shave with death was enough for him, and he decided that he wanted to live.)

On the gun, Hardy and Jones were performing their task with grim determination. These were the first shots either of them had fired in anger, but it didn't show. Hardy was sweeping the gun left and right, picking off targets with short bursts, but the burgundy wave kept coming. The Japanese were spreading out now, putting more distance between each man as they launched against the second fence and presenting Hardy with smaller targets. The machine-gun roared, and more men

B Compound before the Breakout. Above, a view of the ground crossed by the Japanese as they charged the fences; below, the view from A Tower overlooking Broadway, showing the three rows of barbed wire fences that surrounded the camp.

Zero pilot Hajime Toyoshima (L) on Bathurst Island, shortly after his capture, with Sergeant Les Powell who is brandishing Toyoshima's pistol.

Recruits at the Army Training Camp in Cowra receive instruction on rifle shooting. In spite of their commanders' concerns, a large proportion of the trainees were well versed in the safe handling of rifles.

Italian prisoners in the woodworking shop at the camp.

Japanese prisoners playing baseball on the ground that would become a killing field.

Aftermath: above, bodies and blankets tangled in the barbed wire surrounding B Compound; below, the remains of Japanese sleeping huts that were burned to the ground during the Breakout.

AWM P02567.005

AWM P02567.004

An assortment of improvised weapons carried by the Japanese prisoners as they charged the fences. Among the baseball bats are axe handles, tree branches, hoes, and even the neck of a guitar.

Four of the Australian men killed during the Breakout, clockwise from top left: Lieutenant Harry Doncaster, Private Ben Hardy, Private Ralph Jones, and Private Charles Shepherd.

The funeral service for Privates Hardy, Jones and Shepherd was attended by hundreds of local people from Cowra.

Japanese prisoners being buried at Cowra cemetery a few days after the Breakout.

Japanese relatives of men who died during the Breakout, in a civilian internment camp and in an air battle over Darwin attend a service at Cowra Japanese War Cemetery in 1965.

fell. At about the same time Privates Harry Yum and Alf Fickel reached Number One gun, and began firing in enfilade at the Japanese breaking through the wire in front of Hardy and Jones. This created a murderous crossfire and, for the prisoners struggling to get through the wire, it was a deathtrap.

The shooting from both machine-guns left 23 corpses draped grotesquely on the wire, and another 50 or so men writhing on the ground with horrendous wounds. But still the Japanese kept coming. The second fence with its tangle of concertina wire was the most formidable obstacle, but the Japanese found they could lift it and crawl under. Another six men died as a sweep of the machine-guns caught them at the second fence. Sergeant Major Shonai Kichiro, who had been plucked from a life raft by an American destroyer after his troopship had been sunk north of Biak, took a round to the head. He paused momentarily, as if dazed by a punch, and then plunged a knife into his heart. Shigeo Taira, a 23-year-old forestry worker from Okinawa, had his occupation listed in his capture documents as a 'military coolie'; as a non-combatant labourer he was unlucky to be in the Cowra camp in the first place. As he grappled with the second fence a bullet tore through his right foot. He called out to a friend to finish him off; that friend obligingly stabbed him in the chest, but the wound failed to kill him. Taira's friend apologised profusely, and left Taira sobbing in frustration at his failure to die. (Taira's meeting with death was merely postponed – he was picked up the following morning and taken to the camp hospital, where he languished for seven weeks before succumbing to his injuries on 23 September, one of the last casualties of the Breakout.)

More men went down in the tangle of wire between the second and third fences, but their objective was in sight, and there were now bodies as well as blankets to protect them from the wire. At the third fence the fire added 15 more Japanese to the grim ledger of death, and the cries of the wounded soon replaced the shouts of the survivors.

At this point Hardy and Jones would have been forgiven for retreating to safety – they had killed and wounded a dozen prisoners, and their fire had disrupted the key Japanese thrust of the Breakout. But they knew what damage the machine-gun would cause if it fell into Japanese hands. They stayed at the gun, and kept firing.

By this stage the 100 or so uninjured prisoners had cleared the third fence and were surging towards the trailer, screaming and waving baseball bats and knives as they covered the last 50 metres. Hardy lowered the muzzle of the gun as the Japanese charged, and his fire cut down more men at the base of the trailer. But it was hopeless – there were too many prisoners, and Hardy and Jones were on their own. It was at this moment, right when the fighting was most desperate, that the power went out in the camp, bathing the trailer in darkness. With little light to see by and the buildings in B Company barracks creeping dangerously into the field of fire, Number One gun stopped shooting.

It's impossible to know what happened next – as the Japanese converged from all directions, it appears Jones made a frantic leap from the trailer, across the heads of the Japanese. The prisoners pulled him to the ground, and stabbed and bashed him. Incredibly, he managed to break free and crawled away from the truck. A small group of Australian guards under Captain John Small was rushing to reinforce the gun and discovered him near the trailer. 'They got us,' he said, before passing out.[129] He died soon after.

On the trailer, Hardy kept firing until he was overcome. His last desperate act was to attempt to dismantle the gun so that the Japanese couldn't use it against the garrison. The burgundy wave swept over the trailer, and Hardy was swallowed by it.

Soon after, Small reached the trailer with two men. 'I noticed 6 or 8 Japanese scrambling under the gun trailer,' he later said, 'and ordered a volley to be fired into them … I also noticed the body of one of our men who appeared to be smashed to a pulp, lying in front of the truck. It looked as though he was thrown out of the truck after he was killed. I subsequently found out that this was Pte Hardy.'[130]

One of the men with Small was Lance Corporal Harry Rankin. As he approached the truck he noticed 'a bit of a movement and a Japanese came round the end of the truck with a knife in his hand and I shot him'.[131]

Alongside Rankin was Private Les Thomas. As he jumped onto the trailer he heard movement in the darkness. 'I had my rifle alongside me and I jumped up and shot a Japanese who was making towards the end of the truck.' What Thomas did next clears up one of the great mysteries of the Cowra Breakout. The enduring legend in the story of the Breakout is that, just before he was overcome, Hardy had removed the lock (the firing mechanism) from the machine-gun, and therefore prevented the Japanese from turning the gun on the Australians. It has even been suggested that the supposedly missing lock was found in Hardy's pocket after he was killed. It's a stirring tale, and one that began doing the rounds of the POW camp as soon as the shooting had stopped. The Court of Inquiry held after the Breakout was certainly intrigued by it, and asked both Rankin and Thomas about the state of the gun when they reached the trailer. 'On inspecting [the gun] I found that the feed block had been removed and dropped to the side of the gun with a belt that was partly used,' Thomas told the court. 'Where was the lock of the gun when you got there?' the president of the court asked him. 'It would be in the gun,' he replied, and alluded to the rumours that the lock was found on Hardy's body. 'It would be a spare lock if he had one in his possession. If it had been removed I could not have fired that gun.'

Both Thomas and Rankin testified that Thomas had the gun back in action in under a minute, and fired a short burst to make sure it was operating correctly. 'In the shortest possible space of time I got the gun ready for action,' he told the court.

This testimony clarifies what happened on the trailer in the moments immediately before and after the Japanese captured the gun. There's little doubt Hardy attempted to disable the gun before he was overwhelmed but, as an experienced machine-gunner, he didn't waste time with the fiddly procedure of removing the lock. The feed block was just as important as the lock in keeping the gun operating, and it was far more accessible. When he realised his position was hopeless, it appears Hardy opened the top cover of the Vickers and removed the feed block, dropping it to the side of the gun where it hung suspended on the partly used ammunition belt (the court concluded that Hardy had only managed to fire about 85 rounds before he was overcome). The first prisoners to reach the trailer murdered Hardy, flung his body to the ground and then attempted to bring the machine-gun into action against the Australian garrison. Thanks to Hardy, it wouldn't fire, and the Japanese had no knowledge of the workings of the weapon. Even if they had known how to reinsert the feed block, they likely didn't see it hanging beside the gun in the dark. As far as the Japanese were concerned, the gun was out of action. Within seconds the first shots from Small's group started to smack into the trailer, and so the prisoners took one last step before retreating. In a bid to prevent the gun being used to mow down even more of his comrades, one of the prisoners swung the gun away from the compound and locked it in position with the muzzle pointing skywards. When Thomas climbed onto the trailer 'the gun was elevated to the limit ... and pointing to the paddock', he told the court. 'The traversing clamp was locked as hard as possible, I had a job to release it.'

It's unclear where the story of the missing lock came from. It's possible that Hardy's courageous actions in the final moments of his life were simply misunderstood by soldiers unfamiliar with the workings of a Vickers gun. Or perhaps someone who heard the story decided it needed an extra dash of adventure to make it a better yarn. Regardless of how he did it, the result is the same – by disabling the Vickers gun, Hardy prevented the Japanese from turning it on the Australians, and thwarted the key objective of the Japanese plan. With no weapons to use against the garrison, the Japanese were now at a loss. With nothing else to do, they scarpered into the bush.

18

'LIKE A MOB OF STAMPEDING BULLOCKS': BREACHING THE WIRE

The 300 or so prisoners tasked with storming the wire on the eastern side of the camp had by far the easiest task of the night. There were no Vickers machine-guns on trailers here, or guard towers and sentry boxes spitting fire with Bren guns and rifles. The only defence along this entire perimeter – all 650 metres of it, overlooking two prisoner compounds – was F Tower, which stood isolated and alone like a lighthouse on a rocky outcrop in an angry sea. To make matters worse, on the night of the Breakout the tower was manned by only one soldier, Private Kevin Mancer, a 24-year-old former bus driver from Liverpool in New South Wales who had originally enlisted in the air force but had been discharged for unspecified medical reasons. Now he found himself alone in F Tower, the loneliest man in the already lonely outpost of Cowra. To complete the farce, he had only been equipped with the most meagre of armaments – his personal rifle, an Owen submachine gun and a handful of grenades, which had been hurriedly distributed with minimal training after 22nd Garrison Battalion commander Colonel Brown's conference with Army HQ back in June.

The Owen gun was a curious weapon. Invented in 1938 by Evelyn Owen, a self-taught tinkerer in a suburban home in Wollongong, the Owen was cheap to produce and ruggedly reliable. Wartime propaganda films show the Owen being completely submerged in a puddle of ooze then fired without being cleaned. This made it perfect for jungle warfare, and the weapon was highly regarded by Australian soldiers doing battle with the Japanese in the cloying jungles of New Guinea. But its 9 mm ammunition was feeble compared to other submachine guns, and it lacked punch even at close range. It was an odd and completely impractical choice for a soldier in a guard tower, particularly one who had to cover as much ground as Mancer did.

Just before 2 a.m., Mancer heard the two warning shots and saw mayhem unfolding from the huts below him.

All of a sudden somebody gave a yell in the compound, and there was a concerted rush for the fence. They came out of the back end of the huts, and they came over the fence in the bottom corner, right near my tower. All I had was an Owen gun, and I had five clips of cartridges, I think, and only my rifle left. I ran out of ammunition for the rifle and rang up and told them [company headquarters]. They could not get any through, and they told me to stand by and wait until such time as they could get through. I had hand grenades, but I couldn't use them. For one thing, the Japanese were too far away from the tower. And another thing, the tower does not give you any chance to use a grenade except at terribly close quarters. You can't even swing your arms to throw a grenade. There isn't enough space.[132]

Needless to say, the decision to man the tower with only one solider, equipped with a completely insufficient cache of weapons, was an oversight that is difficult to comprehend. Time and time again, it seems the Australian camp commanders would not – *could* not – comprehend the gravity of the threat that loomed in front of them. Mancer fired off all of the pitiful supply of ammunition he had with him, likely hitting no one (it would have been a very unlucky prisoner indeed to be felled by an Owen gun at such long range) and then watched impotently as nearly 300 prisoners scaled the perimeter fence and disappeared into the night.

The only other Australians anywhere near F Tower that night were Privates Hilton Keegan and Joe Roberts. Keegan was a burly 24-year-old miner from Lithgow in New South Wales – 'one of the youngest, fittest and best-trained soldiers in B Camp', according to a comrade.[133] Roberts was 42 and hailed from Boorowa, New South Wales. He had only recently joined the 22nd Garrison Battalion and, although he had been issued with an Owen gun, he barely knew how to use it.

Keegan and Roberts were on duty in sentry boxes outside the perimeter wire. A high berm known as the 'catwalk' ringed the camp, and provided a good vantage point for guards to keep an eye on B Compound. Keegan's sentry box was at the northern end of the compound, not far from the Number Two machine-gun manned by Ben Hardy and Ralph Jones. Roberts's sentry box was near F Tower – the two men would walk a beat towards each other, meet in the middle and then patrol back to their sentry boxes. They were the only two Australians between F Tower and Number Two machine-gun. Soon they would be confronted by not one but two waves of the Breakout.

Shortly before 2 a.m. they met on what they assumed would be their final patrol before being relieved. From their vantage point they could see lights in many of the hut windows and saw movement in the shadows of the searchlights. 'There's something going on in there,' said Keegan. 'I have a mind to fire warning shots.' His words were still hanging in the air when the two warning shots fired by Rolls pierced the night sky. Soon after, the bugle call rang out and Keegan and Roberts saw a mass of burgundy figures surging towards them. 'The prisoners came out of their huts screaming "Banzai! Banzai!"' Roberts recalled decades later. 'They charged the fences like a mob of stampeding bullocks. You've seen crows rise up off a dead sheep when you fire a shot at them, well that's how they came up and over those fences.'[134]

Keegan fired two shots into the air as a warning to the other guards, and then let rip with his Owen gun on the human wave descending on him and Roberts.* Roberts raised his own Owen gun and pulled the trigger – but nothing happened. In the excitement he had forgotten to release the safety catch. He handed the weapon to Keegan, who quickly got it into action (it's not recorded what Keegan said as he handed the gun back, but we can assume it was terse), and Roberts sprayed bullets at the Japanese. 'Then as Keegan was out of bullets,' Roberts recalled, 'I loaded the guns and Keegan did all the shooting as he was so much more competent than me.'

The ammunition soon ran out, and Keegan and Roberts realised they were in a perilous position. Japanese prisoners were all around them, scrambling through the wire to both the right and left, Number Two machine-gun was roaring as Hardy

---

*   This brings to at least three the number of Australian guards who fired warning shots – as all fired their shots at slightly different times, it is impossible to form a cohesive timeline of the opening minutes of the Breakout. When a witness claimed they 'heard warning shots', it's impossible to determine whether it was the rounds fired by Rolls, Turner or Keegan they heard.

and Jones did their deadly work, and Mancer was blasting away with his Owen gun and rifle in F Tower. B Compound was an inferno as the huts burnt, and the guards in B Company were stirring to life and beginning to take pot shots at the Japanese they could see fleeing across the compound. 'Bullets were whistling all around us,' said Roberts,

> so when one threw up dirt at our feet we decided to shelter in the ditch beside the cat walk. We could hear Japanese not far away coming up the trenches towards us. Keegan told me to take the gun off my shoulder and be prepared to fight. The enemy must have heard us talking as they did not approach further.[135]

Keegan and Roberts spent a terrifying 20 minutes with their heads down behind the catwalk, not game to raise them in case they got shot, and expecting the Japanese to descend on them at any minute. 'We were finally relieved by an officer and three men who came along the catwalk firing sporadic shots,' Roberts said. 'Keegan and I could hardly believe our luck that we were still alive.' (It's unclear who this officer was, but it could well have been Captain Small and his small group of men who patrolled the area after discovering the body of Ben Hardy.) Roberts later said that when the officer found them sheltering in the ditch, he threatened to charge them with cowardice, a completely unwarranted accusation. When he recounted the story nearly 50 years later, Roberts was still stung by the claim.

One of the Japanese prisoners charging across the compound was Leading Seaman Ichijiro Do, a former mechanic from Yokohama who had been wounded in the right knee by a round from a tank at Buna in early 1943, and captured by the Americans. Do was a hut leader and, as such, intended to lead his men into battle, but his injury slowed him down and he arrived at the wire long after his men. By this stage the guards had reinforced Mancer's position in F Tower with a Lewis light machine-gun, and were raking the perimeter with fire. After clearing the first fence, Do went to ground in a shallow ditch while waiting for a break in the fire. Two of his men lay wounded nearby, so he crawled over to tend their wounds. As he took shelter a third man, Private Negawa, grabbed him around the waist and begged him not to continue the charge. 'Mr Do, watch out!' he cried out. 'Don't move now! You'll be shot if you move now!' Negawa was terrified and obviously had no intention of running into the hail of fire. Do later confided that he was confused and troubled by Negawa's actions – Negawa had always been a hardliner, and now that the moment the hardliners had long agitated for had arrived, Negawa was afraid to die. On reflection, Do realised that all of the prisoners were defined by contradictions, and Negawa was no different. As for Do, he had never been particularly in favour of the Breakout, and was content with the limited role he had played in it. Do and Negawa greeted the morning still lying in their ditch.[136]

Nearby, another hardliner was involved in a dramatic incident that would have fatal consequences. Lance Corporal Sahei Matsumura was running for the wire near F Tower when he took a bullet in the right hip and hit the ground. Running alongside him was Sergeant Major Yoshio Shimoyama, one of the men who had lobbied hardest for the Breakout to occur. Shimoyama saw Matsumura go down and knelt beside him. As several witnesses watched, Shimoyama took out a knife and plunged it into Matsumura's throat, before carrying on. In a strange nuance of Japanese behaviour, this was seen as a grave betrayal. Had Matsumura asked to be killed, Shimoyama's actions would have been entirely justifiable. But to finish off a wounded man and to remain alive yourself, especially after having been such a vocal advocate for death, was unforgivable. Shimoyama was now a marked man.

In the compound behind him, 18 of the 20 sleeping huts were burning fiercely. The pine and fibro construction, aided by the clothing and straw-filled palliasses that had been heaped on the floors, provided the perfect fuel for the inferno, and the prisoners had not had difficulty setting them aflame. On their way to the wire the escapees had also torched random utility buildings in the compound, including the combined orderly room/canteen and the tailor/barber's shop. (The barber himself, Lance Corporal Senichi Izumida, a 25-year-old from Hiroshima, would never again trim hair or beards, regardless of the state of his shop. He had taken a bullet to the head in the charge on Number Two machine-gun and was now lying dead in the grass outside the wire.[137]) All in all, the fires engulfed 21 of the 30 buildings in the compound.

In front of one of only two sleeping huts not on fire, Sergeant Major Kanazawa anxiously watched the assault on Number Two machine-gun and the fence near F Tower. He saw large numbers of prisoners breaching the wire at both sites, but beyond that could not tell what was going on. He would have much preferred to join the fight but had elected to stay behind with Masao Kojima to form a sort of loose HQ for the uprising. In the event that the prisoners successfully took over the camp, someone would have to take charge, and Kanazawa was the obvious choice. Occasionally a prisoner would scurry up to him with progress reports, but the news was unrevealing and unsurprising – the prisoners were through the wire and still fighting. Many were dead.

Finally Kanazawa could stand it no longer. Leaving Kojima in charge, he limped across the corpse-strewn parade ground as quickly as his war-wounded legs would carry him. As he approached the fence at Number Two gun, he could see burgundy-clad figures scrambling all over the trailer, but the gun was disconcertingly quiet. Clearly the attempt to take over the weapon, the key objective of the whole attack, had not gone to plan. He scrambled under the wire, doing his best to avoid the bodies (and parts of bodies) tangled grotesquely in the wire. When he finally made it to the trailer, a breathless private told him the gun was out of action, before running off into the night. Kanazawa was now at a loss – realistically his place was back in the compound, overseeing the closing stages of the battle and whatever came after. But he couldn't face trying to cross the wire a second time, and breaking back *into* the camp seemed ludicrous now that he was out. He bent down and grabbed a baseball bat from the hand of a dead man lying in the frosty grass beside the trailer, and then limped off towards the dark hills on the horizon, unsure of what he was seeking or what he would find.[138]

About an hour later, Kojima entered the southernmost of B Compound's two kitchens and locked the door behind him. Technically he was in charge of the compound now that Kanazawa had disappeared, but he had seen that the assaults had failed and that there was no chance the prisoners would take over the camp. Even the shooting had died down. Soon the Australian guards would sweep through the compound and the attack would be over. The end had come. He climbed onto a butter box, looped a length of heavy cord around his neck, stepped into space and died slowly.

As the dawn approached, the fires that had engulfed the huts slowly burnt out without fanfare. The blue-grey smoke from burning buildings and cordite dissipated in the chill night air, and stillness settled over the camp like a blanket. The power had not been fully restored, but emergency generators had been fired up, and an eerie yellow half-light bathed the whole ghastly scene. There was no longer anything to shoot at, but the Australian guards remained at their posts. There was nothing to do now but talk in low voices and wait for the dawn. Many were grateful that the lights were out. They'd seen enough already, and God only knew what horrors daylight would reveal.

19

'AN AIR OF ELECTRIC UNREST': RESTORING ORDER

It was going to take a brave man to throw open the gates and step into Broadway the morning after the Breakout, given what had happened there the previous night. At about 7 a.m. on 5 August that man stepped forward – he was a lieutenant in B Company and the deputy compound commander, with the delightfully unheroic name of Vincent Herbert Powis Patis. Originally from England, 35-year-old Patis had emigrated to Australia as a young man and had served in the military since 1938. He was an unassuming figure, described by his commanding officer somewhat equivocally as having a 'pleasing personality' and 'very fair regimental bearing'.[139] He was also rather slight, weighing only 63 kilograms at the time of enlistment.

But what he lacked in physical presence he made up for in decisive thinking. On the night of the Breakout, Patis had just returned to the camp after attending a wedding in town when he heard the warning shots. He rushed to wake up his boss, Major Bob Ramsay. 'By the time I had reached the door,' he said, 'I heard a roar coming from B Compound and I shook him awake and told him there was a riot in B Compound.'[140] He then quickly weighed up the situation and correctly concluded, mostly from the sounds of gunfire, that Hardy and Jones were at their post at Number Two machine-gun, but that the Hotchkiss light machine-gun in B Tower was not firing. Racing to the tower, he took command of the gun and discovered that the firing mechanism was jammed and it would only fire in single shots. He spent the next five hours at the gun, laying down covering fire and picking off Japanese who stormed the northern gates.

Sunrise revealed ghastly scenes in the POW camp. Most of the members of the 22nd Garrison Battalion had never been in combat, but they now knew what a war zone looked like as they surveyed the smouldering ruins and mangled bodies. Just before 7 a.m. Ramsay ordered Patis to gather a party of men and round up any Japanese survivors. Broadway was eerily silent. Bodies were strewn across the roadway and piled up in front of the northern gates, obviously dead, but down both sides of the road burgundy bundles were crammed into the ditches like rags in a drawer. It was impossible to tell if these men were alive or dead, or what their reaction would be when confronted by Australian guards.

Patis assembled about a dozen men, unlocked the gates, and stepped into the unknown. Courageously, Ramsay was by his side, and the two men edged warily along the roadway, flanked by nervous sentries with fingers on triggers. An interpreter shouted for any surviving Japanese to throw down their weapons. One of those survivors was Masaru Moriki. 'We who failed to die and [were] desperately lost were ready to take any fate,' he recalled. 'The group of Australian soldiers with an interpreter in the middle came closer to us.'

Illustrating just how feeble the arsenal assembled by the Japanese really was, the interpreter's instructions would not have been out of place if asking a group of kindergarteners to pack up after a picnic: 'Please put the forks, spoons, knives and other things such as sticks down in front of you,' he said. The prisoners obliged, and slowly rose from among their dead and wounded comrades with raised hands. The Australians watched for any sign of treachery. They didn't need to worry – the surviving Japanese prisoners were spent. After months of fantasising about launching an attack on the camp, they had finally done it, and had witnessed hundreds of their mates earning the heroic death they had been denied on the battlefield. For the survivors, the dawn brought the odd realisation that they had now been defeated in battle and taken prisoner by their enemy for the second time in this war. Curiously, this seems not to have affected the bulk of the prisoners too severely. Like the man who attempts suicide and fails, and then does not feel the need to try again, once the Cowra Breakout was over, the Japanese appear to have gotten the immediate desire for violence out of their systems. Once the shooting died down and the sun came up, they were finished.

There were more Japanese still alive in Broadway than the Australians had expected – hundreds more. It seemed impossible that *anyone* could have survived the storm of fire in that cramped space, but once the Japanese were lined up in rows and counted, the Australians were astonished to discover that they were facing 431 very much alive and unwounded prisoners. A count of the bodies still clumped along Broadway revealed that only 78 men had been killed there, a surprisingly small number given the ferocity of the fighting.

Ramsay ordered that the survivors be corralled into Broadway, then set a small group of guards under Captain

Small the unenviable task of searching the smoking ruins of B Compound for survivors. Accompanying Small was Captain Edward Jordan, an interpreter, who had spent most of the pre-dawn hours coaxing random shivering escapees into being taken back into custody. The two men entered B Compound with a nervous guard unit and began searching under buildings and along the perimeter fences for survivors. Once again, they found many more alive than expected, most of whom came forward meekly with heads bowed and hands raised. They also discovered a dozen or so incinerated bodies in the burnt-out huts, who they assumed had perished in the flames. 'I noticed several bodies in the ashes,' Small reported, 'which were too hot to get near.'[141] (In spite of some Australian reports after the Breakout that these men had been dissenters who were opposed to the attack, and had been lashed to the beds by their fanatical comrades, there is no evidence of this in Japanese sources, or indeed of any prisoner being wilfully murdered for failing to agree to break out. Almost certainly these men had committed suicide, either before the huts were burnt or in the flames themselves.)

Small sent Jordan with an armed escort to search the hospital buildings, which the Korean orderlies had bravely defended only a few hours before. The desperation of the Japanese to avoid recapture bordered on the comical. 'Some four or five escapees were found hiding under various buildings in the hospital enclosure,' Jordan reported. 'On going through the wards, two escapees were found to have taken refuge under the blankets of unoccupied beds.' A few prods of the bayonet encouraged them to join their comrades outside.

Negerevich had also joined the search, and Small sent him to explore the southern buildings of the compound accompanied by an armed private. 'We went to the kitchen and tried to open the doors but they were locked,' he said. 'I looked through the window and saw one body suspended on a rope; I recognised him as PW Kojima.'[142]

On inspecting one of the two sleeping huts still standing (Hut 7/8), Negerevich noted three more bodies swinging from rafters, but didn't stop to identify them. As he escorted a batch of survivors from the compound he saw 'two incinerated remains with flowers around them, lying [in] what used to be the orderly room'.

The search party herded the survivors back into Broadway. In total they had found 118 prisoners alive and unwounded in the compound. Meanwhile another 73 prisoners who had been collected in random batches wandering around the countryside were added to the mix, meaning that there were now more than 600 prisoners locked in the makeshift holding cage that was Broadway. Ironically, the perimeter fences and towers of Broadway that had been designed to keep prisoners out were now being used to keep them in. Camp authorities had no choice – until they got a clearer idea of just what they were dealing with, they needed to keep the Japanese contained and under close guard.

Meanwhile Ramsay ordered two trucks to enter Broadway to convey the most seriously wounded to the camp hospital, while walking wounded were instructed to form an orderly queue and 'wait their turn' for treatment. (Australian wounded had been conveyed by ambulance to the hospital in town, and the bodies of Hardy, Jones and Shepherd were already in the town morgue, transported there by ambulance drivers from the Australian Women's Army Service, a distressing assignment for the servicewomen.) Somewhat controversially, Ramsay also detailed 15 prisoners under armed guard for the unpalatable job of collecting the bodies of the Japanese dead, and conveying them in trucks to a designated holding area outside the perimeter, not far from where Hardy and Jones had been killed on the Vickers gun. Given the severe injuries that high-velocity rifle and machine-gun fire can inflict on human flesh at close range, this was a ghastly assignment for the prisoners. (Parts of it also proved impossible – the bodies in front of Number Two machine-gun and near F Tower were so entangled in the wire that they could not be removed.) It was the first of several distasteful, but probably unavoidable, decisions the Australians made in the coming days.

Just when Lieutenant Colonel Brown thought he had enough on his plate, the reliably unhinged Japanese officers in D Compound, never reluctant to cause a ruckus, delivered Brown a letter stating that they were responsible for the Breakout and requesting that they promptly be executed by firing squad. This was clearly ridiculous – the Japanese officers patently had no knowledge of the uprising before it burst into violent life in front of them and, apart from Oikawa's and Fujita's ill-conceived dash into machine-gun fire, they had not participated in it. Brown did exactly the right thing in response to the letter – nothing.

At about 4.30 p.m. Ramsay suggested to Brown that the prisoners be shifted back into whatever buildings in B Compound were still standing. 'I asked for Capt Jordan and Capt Esdale to come down to "B" Compound gate with me,' he said, giving evidence to the Court of Inquiry, 'and in batches of 20 to 25, explain to [the prisoners] that they were going back into the Compound, and that the Compound had been declared a detention barracks; warning them that they were not to move from the mess huts except only towards the latrines and ablution blocks'. The prisoners were also warned to go nowhere near the perimeter fences or the parade ground – Australian guards were all too ready to open fire on anyone who tested the rules. As the prisoners returned to the compound that they had so violently fled 14 hours earlier, they were issued with two blankets each and told to make themselves as comfortable as they could on the floor of the mess hall. Ramsay also ordered the first three groups of prisoners into the compound to recover all the blankets that had been draped over the perimeter fences at the three points where there had been a breakout, a gruesome task given the number of their comrades whose bloated corpses were still ensnared in the wire. Within a couple of hours, the prisoners were safely, if not particularly comfortably, accommodated in the mess hall, which was at least warm and well stocked with food.

Once back in the compound, Moriki summed up the attitude of many of the prisoners – he was astounded that they were being fed and clothed after having tried to destroy the camp and kill the guards only hours before. 'It was unexpected that the Australian force's treatment of us would be so lenient even after we had created trouble as serious as we had,' he said. 'All our clothes were burnt so we had no change of clothes. A truck full of blankets were brought in, bread was delivered and somehow daily necessities were also arranged. The topics we talked about were mainly about the attack and we heard about the last moments of each squad's dead.'

Throughout the day (and for much of the following week) the job of searching for escapees continued. Initially it was conducted by small groups of guards from the POW camp, who scoured the surrounding paddocks and found dozens of cold and hungry prisoners, who were usually only too happy to be taken into custody with the promise of a hot meal and a warm bed. The local police were called in from Cowra and the surrounding towns and search aircraft buzzed over the scrub- and rock-strewn hills.

Meanwhile Patis was everywhere, doing everything. While the Japanese were being counted, Patis took charge of a party to scour the paddocks outside the camp to recover and treat wounded prisoners who had made it through the wire – and there were dozens of those. Ramsay had absolute faith in Patis's organisational skills and discretion, so tasked him over the next couple of days with the toughest assignments, including the removal of bodies from the barbed wire and the identification of the dead. Patis took to the grim task with the same focus he applied to all aspects of his life. 'The following day,' he said, 'I was in charge of twenty Japanese whom I took down to the wire where the first break was, about opposite the No. 2 machine-gun post and a couple of engineers cut the wire and I supervised the taking of the bodies out of the wire.' It's worth pausing to contemplate what a ghastly job this would have been – yet another example of Australian authorities enlisting the help of prisoners with the duties related to the recovery of bodies. But in reality, it's highly unlikely these decisions were made punitively. It was essential for the camp to be restored to order as quickly as possible, and there were too few Australian guards with too many responsibilities as it was. It would have been unthinkable to enlist the Korean or Italian prisoners to assist with the gory clean-up, and there was no compelling reason to excuse the Japanese from doing work that was a direct result of their own actions, no how matter distasteful it was.

Thanks to Cowra's icy winter weather, the task was not as bleak as it might otherwise have been. 'Severe frosts every night,' recalled a long-time war graves man, 'froze the bodies as stiff as sides of beef in a butcher's freezer. Consequently the rate of deterioration was much slower than any of us had expected.'[143]

The man who made this pragmatic statement was Sergeant Jack Leemon, a 34-year-old from Sydney who had enlisted in 1942 but was declared 'unfit for marching' and assigned to the Graves Registration Unit. For the next decade Leemon was involved in fascinating but somewhat disquieting work dealing with war dead on battlefields across the world. In his memoirs, *War Graves Digger*, he pulls few punches, and describes plying his gruesome trade from the jungles of New Guinea to the Thai–Burma Railway to post-war Japan with remarkable detachment – this wasn't a man who was squeamish. He went about his job with a kind of grim stoicism, even adding a wooden cross to the head of his camp stretcher emblazoned with 'RIP'. On 5 August 1944 he received urgent instructions to head to Cowra, with only vague descriptions about what he might find there. In short order he and a small group of other graves workers boarded an army truck for the long drive, a trip he describes as a 'nightmare' due to the speed at which they lurched down the rough country roads. As the truck approached Cowra it had to pass through several heavily manned roadblocks. 'At one of them,' Leemon said, 'a souvenir fiend was displaying with pride a baseball bat which had been used to bring an untimely end to an Australian guard, bits of human tissue plainly evident.' (This seems an unlikely tale, but is not beyond the realm of possibility.)

Soon they arrived at their destination. 'The camp was an astounding site,' Leemon said, 'with bodies scattered in all directions. A lot of them were hooked in the barbed wire fences, while inside the compound, Japanese wearing the distinctive burgundy-red POW uniforms, milled restlessly. An air of electric unrest was pervasive.' There to greet them was their boss, Director of War Graves Services Lieutenant Colonel Athol Brown, who had flown in from Melbourne to supervise the recovery and interment of bodies. 'You will be responsible for the identification of the dead,' he told Leemon. 'I don't know how you will do it, nor do I care. It's up to you. If you want anything, ask for it but get going, they won't keep forever.'

Over the next two days, Leemon worked alongside Patis and his party of Japanese to collect and lay out the mangled bodies of the dead prisoners. 'To everybody's surprise,' Leemon said, '[the Japanese] gave no trouble, going to a lot of bother to patch up bodies that had been mangled by gunfire. Not only that, they "weighed in" to help with identification also.' This last statement is important – Australian authorities have attracted criticism for their decision to force Japanese prisoners to help identify their dead comrades, a potentially traumatic and unnecessary burden to place on the already exhausted survivors. But if Leemon's recollection is accurate (and there's no reason to think it isn't), the Japanese were not formally tasked with helping to identify the dead, but simply volunteered to help when the Australians were stumped. 'I was thumbing through a box of basic documents,' Leemon said, 'vainly trying to locate a photograph that looked like one of the dead near me. One of the Japanese took a quick look, broke into a torrent of Japanese and in a moment I had a self-elected identification committee.' Certainly there is nothing in the official documents that contradicts Leemon's claim – the key report into the identification of the bodies says only that the prisoners provided 'assistance' and that 'other Japanese were used for the purpose of recognition'.[144]

Once this process was complete, Leemon's men fitted identification tags to the wrists of each man, stacked the bodies in rows and covered them with tarpaulins awaiting further examination. Soon after, Wal McKenzie observed a disturbing incident involving the pile of corpses. 'On the Sunday,' he said,

some people came up from the town and I saw three boys; they were walking around what looked like a big heap covered by a tarpaulin … they finally sneaked up to the corner of the tarpaulin and lifted the corner up and they all turned away. One was retching and the other two ran … I had seen the [dead] men stacked there – what a sight to see.[145]

Over the next few days a thorough examination of the bodies was carried out by the government medical officer, Dr Jim Garner, who, accompanied by Lieutenant Colonel Athol Brown and a local police officer, confirmed the identifications to the best of his ability and compiled a report indicating the nature of the wounds on each body, which still makes for grim reading eight decades later. After vacillating about how to document the range of injuries he observed, Garner finally settled on two broad categories to describe the cause of death: gunshot wounds (GSW) and self-inflicted wounds (SIW). Several of the bodies, including Toyoshima's, showed evidence of suicide after having received gunshot wounds that Garner considered would have been fatal. In an interview with author Harry Gordon in 1977, Garner revealed two interesting observations he'd made as he went about his gruesome task:

Most of the bodies carried previous gunshot wounds, which indicated that the Japanese had not surrendered voluntarily; and those who killed themselves showed a considerable knowledge of anatomy, even to the extent of tying belts around chins rather than throats – so that they would die fast of a broken neck, rather than slowly by strangulation.[146]

While this macabre accountancy was taking place, Korean labourers from the camp were busy preparing a large burial plot at the local Cowra cemetery (which was located, as chance would have it, within sight of the camp). In sensitivity to the townsfolk, many of whom would be none-too-thrilled to learn that the hated enemy was being buried alongside Great-Aunt Ethel, the plot was placed well away from the civilian graves. Bulldozers were brought in to dig long trenches, in preparation for the arrival of the more than 200 bodies.

That night back in the camp, Monty Brown was in his office doing maths by lamplight. He double-checked his figures, then triple-checked them. He compared nominal rolls to prisoner lists to reports from his officers, and compiled a tally in a thick ledger. He was being fussily precise – he had to be. Having just overseen one of the largest prison breakouts in history, it would be a disaster if even a single escapee was not accounted for. His numbers made for bleak reading. The total number of Japanese in B Compound on the night of the Breakout had been 1104. Of those, 138 remained in the compound during the uprising (20 or so committing suicide and the rest simply not participating) and 588 prisoners broke into Broadway, where they were either killed or recaptured. He put pen to paper and wrote a line he never imagined he would ever have to: *Total Number of Escaped Prisoners.* He did some quick calculations and angrily scratched a figure on the tally sheet: *378.* Good Lord. Nearly 380 prisoners had breached the wire and fled into the countryside. A small number of those had since been recaptured, but there were still more than 300 Japanese unaccounted for. And that meant they were out there, roaming among the civilians of Cowra. Brown's eye fell to the window, where not far away he could see the the skeletons of the burnt-out huts standing starkly against the backdrop of bare hills. He closed the ledger. It had been a long day – the next one could prove to be even longer.

20

'SHADOWS IN THE DARK': THE GREAT ROUND-UP

By mid-morning on 5 August, things were pretty much under control at the POW camp. The burning huts had been extinguished (or, more accurately, had extinguished themselves when they had burnt to the ground); prisoners sheltering in ditches in Broadway had been rounded up; bodies had been collected from within and without the camp and were lying in grotesque rows outside the wire; wounded men, both Japanese and Australian, had been transported to hospitals in the camp and in the town, and groups of nervy guards roamed the camp grounds, heavily armed and with twitchy fingers resting on triggers. They secured broken gates, repaired breaks in the wire, occasionally uncovered an exhausted and shivering prisoner and prodded him back to the compound at the point of the bayonet, and generally dissuaded the Japanese from causing any more trouble.

In the hospitals in A and B Compounds, two surgical teams began the vital work of operating on the wounded prisoners.

Over the next two days, 126 prisoners were treated, most willingly, some unwillingly – the desire for death was still strong in some prisoners, and the treatment of their wounds was yet another sting to their honour they found difficult to endure.

The most pressing consideration for Colonel Brown was to determine how many prisoners had escaped from the camp, and where the hell they had gone. There were more than 300 still unaccounted for. Where they were and what they were doing was anyone's guess. Reports from the Army Training Camp had made it clear that the planned Japanese assault on that camp had not eventuated, so the assumption was that random groups of prisoners had scattered all over the countryside, and were probably trying to get as far away from Cowra as fast as their weary legs would carry them.

In the town itself nerves were strained. Everyone knew that the Japanese had finally broken out, and farmers near the camp reported that lots – maybe hundreds – had made it out of the camp and were now roaming the countryside. With little official information to go on, the rumour mill went into overdrive on the streets and in the shops and homes of Cowra. Everyone had an opinion, and a lack of solid information, or even basic logic, was not an impediment to sharing it. Someone heard that 50 Australian guards had been killed. Another gave the opinion that the Japanese would soon be raiding farmhouses in search of food and weapons. In probably the most farcical claim, a rumour spread that the prisoners were heading north because Japan was in that direction, and they didn't realise how far from home they actually were (this was an anecdote my grandparents were still passing on to me as a young boy when I grew up in the district in the 1980s).

In this atmosphere it was little wonder that the wives and families of the Australian soldiers who lived in town were anxious. Major Vern Northwood was a 34-year-old officer at the Army Training Camp, who had originally hailed from Perth. His pregnant wife lived in town, and he described a novel system for informing the families that their husbands were okay:

> A number of the officers and NCO's in my Battalion had wives living in Cowra. We knew they would all be worried as you could hear the machine-gun fire and see the flames from the burning huts as the break-out occurred and many Cowra people also saw the carnage on the wire the next morning. All leave was cancelled but in my Battalion I allowed everyone who had a wife or fiancé in Cowra to write a brief note saying he was OK. We wrapped the notes around stones and as we drove around patrolling the streets our drivers would give a couple of toots outside the appropriate address to attract attention and the note would be thrown on the lawn.[147]

Families who lived on farms near the camp had spent one of the longest nights of their lives listening to the carnage unfolding not far away. Twenty-four-year-old Rita Reid lived with her fiancé, Cecil, and his young son from a previous marriage. She liked the Italian prisoners who occasionally called in to chop wood for the camp, and engaged in friendly conversations with them with a mixture of simple English and hand gestures. One day when the Italians came to the house to fill their water bottles, one of them asked Reid to give him her hand, and he delicately measured the width of her finger with a piece of string. The following week he returned to the farm and presented her with a ring he had fashioned from a belt buckle. 'He could have been a jeweller ... before he was taken prisoner,' she recalled decades later. 'They seemed so friendly and wanted to talk.'[148]

The Japanese were another matter altogether. Like many of the townspeople of Cowra, Reid had heard stories of Japanese barbarity and had been relentlessly exposed to the propaganda pieces that spoke of the Japanese peril on Australia's doorstep. Reid was terrified of the Japanese, and said there was always a different 'atmosphere' around them. One day she was riding her bike near the camp and came across a group of Japanese being marched along the road by a couple of Australian guards. The prisoners stepped aside for her to pass, but she panicked and lost control of the bike in the loose gravel. As she fell a few of the prisoners made to help her, but she rebuffed them sternly and the guards rushed up to make sure she was not hurt. The whole incident seems fairly innocuous (and in fact the prisoners appear to have been acting with kindness in their efforts to assist her when she fell), but Reid was greatly alarmed by her close encounter with the Japanese. 'I was only too happy to get on the bike and take off,' she said. When it was time to come home, she took a longer route lest she should run into the group again.

On the night of the Breakout, the Reids were woken by the warning shots, and clearly heard the bugle call and the screams of the charging men. They were concerned but not surprised – rumours had been swirling around town for weeks that the Japanese were planning to break out of the camp. They stood on their veranda in the pre-dawn light and watched as shadows from the burning huts in B Compound flickered and danced across the camp. When the shooting intensified, Reid had had enough. 'We'd better get in the car and go,' she said to her fiancé. 'Don't worry,' he replied. 'There's enough shooting up there that we'll be all right.'

The family reluctantly returned to bed, and Reid was roused less than an hour later when Cecil's son came into their bedroom. 'Dad,' he said in a small voice. 'The Japs are here.'

Cecil grabbed his shotgun and ran to the front window. Reid could see shadowy figures creeping through the garden, and picked up snippets of frantic conversation in Japanese. As the family huddled in the living room a bullet, an over-shoot from an Australian rifle at the camp, smacked into the doorpost not far from Reid's head. Other bullets began spattering into the weatherboard walls and tin roof like deadly hail. (Reid's fiancé prised one of out the laundry wall the next morning and kept it as a souvenir for the rest of his life.)

Soon after, the power went out – the house was on the same grid as the camp – and the family spent an anxious few hours huddled in front of the fireplace. By 4 a.m. the firing had died down, and then a couple of hours later a neighbour knocked on their door. 'Are you there, Cecil?' he sang out. 'I've got a couple of Japs.' While Reid rang the camp, her fiancé and the neighbour forced the two cold and terrified Japanese prisoners into the chook pen. One of the Japanese poked some cigarettes through the wire as a peace offering, but Cecil wouldn't take them. A short time later a truck arrived from the camp and whisked the prisoners away.

As groups of soldiers from the camp and police from the nearby towns scoured the countryside, they were accompanied by George Folster, a war correspondent from NBC in America, who had spent most of the war reporting from battlefields in the Pacific and had raced to Cowra from Sydney as soon as he had heard about the Breakout. On arrival he instantly knew he was in the middle of a big story, and energetically set about piecing it together as best he could. Over several days he travelled far and wide, speaking to police, soldiers and flighty locals as he produced a series of somewhat breathless (if not always accurate) reports, most of which didn't make it past the watchful eye of the military censor. 'Crisscrossing the tense countryside in a small English car,' he wrote, 'and afoot and with mounted villagers, I saw evidence and was told stories of how the Japanese had terrorized the district and had taken their own lives in horrible exhibitionist ways.' Folster was obviously a great communicator as well as a talented writer, and the people of Cowra seem to have opened up to him without suspicion. Even after 80 years, it's a delight to read his neat, typewritten pages and to learn of the adventures of a bemused newspaper man from Boston and his encounters with the endearingly unworldly citizens of Cowra.

> Districts I covered were like armed camps with armed civilians marching through streets of small towns. Other groups combed the rugged countryside on horseback and armed police stopped and checked NBC car on rutted country road. No one slept much that week. Farmers built fires nightly and kept their families around them to prevent attacks whilst they slept, and kept loaded guns never more than a few inches out of their hands.[149]

Folster had an eye for a good story, and recounted several engaging incidents, including the story of George Price, a local farmer who set a booby trap of empty kerosene cans, hoping to snare any Japanese prisoners who crept into his yard. The plan came undone when his dog chased a cat into the contraption, 'the clatter arousing George, who raced around the shanty swinging an axe over his head'.

In spite of the concerns of the locals, Folster instinctively picked up on a crucial element of Japanese intentions: that civilians were not to be harmed. 'There is no evidence of the slightest violence to any civilian,' he wrote, 'and the Japs kept the battle between themselves and the guards.'

For the Japanese prisoners who had made it out of the camp, there was indecision, fear, hunger and, above all, cold. The plan to break out had been finalised so quickly that no Japanese appears to have contemplated what would happen if large numbers of men had earned their freedom but the camp (and all its stores) had not been captured. Now there were hundreds of men aimlessly roaming the countryside, and each man had to decide what he would do. For many, the answer was simply to sit and wait. They were shocked to find themselves alive after witnessing so much violence, and had no desire to participate in more bloodshed. They banded together in small groups, tried to make themselves as comfortable as possible, and spent a long and cold night waiting for the Australian guards to round them up.

In some instances these groups of prisoners could be unexpectedly large. When Captain Lord Kane, the camp's intelligence officer, led a party to round up a group of prisoners who had been spotted heading towards the town, 73 men gave themselves up and were marched back to the camp. Another group of Australian guards rounded up 18 prisoners within a few minutes. Some prisoners were not given the opportunity to hand themselves in, even if they wanted to. Moriki described a group of prisoners who had sheltered in a cave. The men were discovered by an Australian search party and ordered to show themselves. They were unsurprisingly nervous, so one man volunteered to act as chief negotiator. 'I will talk to them,' he said, and left the cave, waving a handkerchief in surrender. 'As soon as he got to the mouth of the cave', Moriki reported, 'machine-guns fired at him. His body was covered with bullet holes like honey comb, and he rolled once and fell.' The rest of the group was taken into custody terrified but unharmed.

Roy Treasure (who would later find fame as a boxer) was a 17-year-old living on the family farm at Cowra on the night of the Breakout. He was woken by the gunfire, and spent a long and frightening night at the window of the farmhouse, gripping a .22 rifle. 'We saw all these shadows in the dark heading around the house,' he recalled years later. 'They never actually came in close ... They were like sheep going around the house.'[150]

The following morning Treasure cautiously emerged and headed to the cowsheds for milking. 'I noticed these five Japanese walking within I suppose less than a quarter mile ... they were wandering around looking for a spot to hide and I noticed them get under these big bushes or a fallen limb from where a big box tree had fallen over.' Soon after, an army search party arrived on the property. Treasure pointed them in the direction of the five prisoners, who were still sitting idly in the shade. The Australians approached the Japanese, and opened fire. 'They just killed the lot of them,' Treasure said. 'It's a memory that's stayed with me always. They didn't look a dangerous bunch, the Japanese. I frankly don't think they'd have hurt a fly. But I don't blame the soldiers. There was a lot of propaganda about, a lot of stories about how desperate the Japanese were.'[151]

For other Japanese, the dilemma about whether to live or die could only be solved by action. If the Australian guards had failed to take their lives, they would take matters into their own hands. Private Jim Webb was a young recruit at the Army Training Camp and had been ordered to patrol a paddock near the camp on the morning of the Breakout. His patrol group came across a Japanese prisoner, and Webb was put in charge of him. The man was kneeling on the ground, bending forward with his hands obscured. 'I picked him up by the scruff of the neck because I wanted to see what was going on,' Webb recalled, and as that happened his guts dropped out. He had a homemade knife in his hand under his tunic and he had cut himself right open. So you can imagine the shock I got and, of course, they carted him off somewhere, perhaps to the hospital, perhaps back to the main camp. That was a rather traumatic event for me to see.[152]

Some Japanese concluded that the only noble way out was in a hail of bullets, and there are a small number of examples of Japanese prisoners attacking Australian soldiers during the manhunt. Lieutenant Durrant Langley, part of the guard unit of A Compound, was leading a 16-man patrol north of the camp when they encountered a large group of prisoners moving stealthily through the long grass. Langley called for the prisoners to halt and, when they showed no sign of surrendering, the guards opened fire. In the melee that followed, about a dozen Japanese were killed and an Australian soldier, Private Joe Phillips, received a stab wound in the neck after a prisoner leapt from a tree to attack him. Langley's men chased the prisoner into the scrub and found him about an hour later suffering from grievous self-inflicted wounds. He had tried to disembowel himself and cut his own throat – neither wound successfully ended his life that day, but he died in hospital the next.

Throughout the day the great round-up continued, and prisoners were found in every conceivable hiding place. They were found cringing in creekbeds, shivering in sheds, cowering in caves, even hiding out in haystacks. Lance Sergeant John Schaefer, a 36-year-old former painter and truck driver from Sydney, was the D Company compound sergeant and had spent the hours of the Breakout taking pot shots at the Japanese from the southern gates of Broadway. The next morning he was tasked with rounding up escapees south-east of the camp. Over the next couple of hours he and his men came across several groups of prisoners, some dead, most alive, and began loading them onto trucks for return to the camp. A couple of the dead bodies had ropes or towels around their necks, which the men had used to hang themselves, but one body had injuries that suggest some foul play had taken place.

'We came across another dead prisoner of war,' Schaefer told the Court of Inquiry, 'and he had a towel around his neck, I think about 6 feet of towelling. This man had his brains half out of his head and there was a stick about 4 feet beside him.' It's not clear exactly what Schaefer is getting at with this description – he seems to be implying that the man hanged himself with the towel – but that wouldn't account for the man's brains being 'half out of his head'. The body was discovered hundreds of metres from the camp, too far for the man to have been hit by rifle or machine-gun fire during the Breakout, and it's inconceivable that he travelled that far with a head wound as grievous as Schaefer described. So the question remains, who clubbed or shot the prisoner in this lonely corner of a Cowra paddock? The Court of Inquiry certainly wasn't interested in finding out, asking no follow-up questions after Schaefer made his provocative statement. It's a mystery that can't be solved.

Another mystery that confounded authorities in the days after the Breakout concerned reports that at least one Japanese prisoner had managed to flee to Sydney. The report makes for curious reading, and probably says more about hysteria associated with the Breakout than it does about the actions of Japanese prisoners. Early on the morning of 9 August, a passenger on the mail train from Cowra reported that he had seen a Japanese prisoner jumping from the train as it pulled into Granville station in western Sydney. In spite of the fact that by this time all of the escaped prisoners had been loosely accounted for, and that the dress, demeanour and actions of the suspect suggested that he was unlikely to even be Japanese, let alone an escaped prisoner, authorities swung into action to apprehend him. The witness reported that a shadowy young man of Asian appearance and dressed in a dark suit and woollen overcoat had absconded from the train and run across the tracks as the train pulled into Granville. A railway employee who had questioned the suspect reported that he had asked to buy a ticket to Kirribilli and, when told there was no train station there, had instead purchased a ticket to Wynyard with money he produced from his shoe. After interviewing dozens of people, conducting a thorough search of every station between Granville and Wynyard, and combing through Japanese records, authorities announced that they could find no evidence that suggested the man was an escaped Japanese prisoner. They did, however, discover that a Philippine ship currently moored at Kirribilli was missing several of its crew, some fairly strong circumstantial evidence that suggested the origins of the suspect. Authorities were nothing if not dogged, however – their three-page report ends with the statement, 'Police officials and Passport Guard are maintaining unceasing vigilance'.[153]

An even more dramatic train-related incident (and one that unquestionably involved Japanese prisoners) occurred on Sunday morning on the line between Cowra and Blayney. The early morning mail train was approaching Cowra when the driver, Sylvester Nolan, saw two figures lurking by the tracks in the murky morning light. Two prisoners, Labourer Kiyoshi Tanaka and Lance Corporal Masanobu Kaigi, had determined to end their lives in the most dramatic and gory way possible. They hid in bushes beside the railway line as the train approached and then, at the last minute, lay down on the tracks with their necks stretched across the rail. Nolan had no chance to stop. Immediately after impact, he brought the train to a screeching halt, and clambered down to confirm it really was two men he had just run over.

Nauseated and near hysterical, he ran to the passenger car shouting for military men to come and help him. One of the passengers was a warrant officer from the POW camp, Richard Wetherwick, who came to his aid. Wetherwick agreed to collect the gruesome detritus from the railway track and wait for it to be collected as the train rumbled on its way to Cowra.

Not all encounters with escapees were this violent. Alf Chambers lived on a farm with his wife, Marj, who was expecting their first child. Even though they lived about 20 kilometres from the camp, they had spotted Japanese prisoners walking across their paddocks throughout the day on Saturday. Shortly after dusk the following night, the barking of Chambers's dogs warned him that someone was approaching the farmhouse. Chambers stepped onto the back porch and confronted two prisoners, who he could barely make out in the dim evening light. He ordered the men to halt and, by the light of a kerosene lamp, ushered them onto the porch. Noting the sorry state of the prisoners, his wife appeared with cups of milk, buttered bread and cold lamb chops from last night's dinner. She retreated inside to call the camp, while Chambers kept a wary eye on the prisoners as they wolfed down the meal with their bare hands. They made no attempt to escape, and even engaged Chambers in stilted conversation in broken English. 'The big Jap took his hands off the table,' Chambers said,

and started fiddling with his belt. I warned him to put his hands back on the table. He then offered me his belt, saying he had made it himself in the camp. He asked for a piece of string to hold up his pants, and gave me his belt for a souvenir … Meanwhile the smaller Jap kept his hands on the table, cushioning his head in his arms and went to sleep. He had picked up a nasty bullet wound in the back of his neck, which was badly festered.[154]

The prisoners remained at the table for another 45 minutes, until a truck arrived to take them back to the camp.

At Cowra Cemetery, the first 100 or so identified Japanese bodies were ready to be interred by Monday evening. Under a cloak of secrecy they were taken from the ghastly pile beside the camp, wrapped in blankets and transported by military truck on the 1.5-kilometre drive to the cemetery. Folster, the NBC correspondent, continued his knack of being in the right place at the right time, and was there to witness the interment (to the consternation of Australian authorities). He described the dramatic scene in a report:

In Cowra Cemetery I saw a Bulldozer opening graves in the hard winter ground for the Japanese, and about fifty Australian soldiers and a number of Italian prisoners helped to construct the graves, each being about sixty five feet long and eight feet wide. The Japanese burials began on Tuesday night [sic], and before I was thrown out of the cemetery by an Australian officer and guards, two of whom politely escorted me to the gate with bayonets, I saw with what apparently orderly, workmanlike and considerate handling this Japanese interment was. In an attempt to deny the citizens of Cowra this macabre sight and experience, the burials took place at night, and the only indication of activities in the cemetery was the posted guards and distant flickering flares lighting up the immediate area of the graves.[155]

Second Lieutenant Fujita, the only Japanese officer to die in the Breakout, was buried in a coffin in an individual grave. Two of his officer comrades attended and four Japanese privates acted as pallbearers.

Back in the camp, yet another violent and intensely personal drama played out in the days following the Breakout. Early on the morning of Wednesday, 9 August, Australian guards saw a group of Japanese prisoners depositing a bundle beside the wire next to Broadway. The bundle turned out to be the body of Sergeant Major Yoshio Shimoyama, the hardliner who had killed a comrade during the charge to the fence. His fellow prisoners considered his actions an unforgiveable crime, especially since Shimoyama had survived the Breakout after advocating so hard for death. It seems that the survivors needed an outlet for their frustrations and sadness, and Shimoyama was the obvious target.

'Everybody blamed him,' said Leading Seaman Ichijiro Do decades later. 'If he had not come back, we would never have blamed him for what he did to a wounded man. But the proper thing would have been to take his own life while he was out. When he came back to the camp, he was a dead man.'[156] What happened to Shimoyama is unclear. Do claimed a lynching party grabbed him and strung him up in the canteen, spitting at him, 'You should have done this yourself.' Moriki claims, however, that Shimoyama realised he was in an untenable position and took his own life to restore his honour. (Interestingly, one Australian authority vaguely implied that murder was the cause of Shimoyama's death. Lieutenant Colonel Athol Brown, the Director of War Graves Services, typed a list of Japanese casualties in the days after the Breakout. As the last of the casualties he examined, Shimoyama is the last name on his list. Next to his name he typed the cause of death as 'SIW [self-inflicted wound], Strangulation'. At a later date Brown returned to the document and made various amendments in black pen. Next to Shimoyama's name, he has crossed out the letters 'SIW'.) Regardless of how it happened, the result was the same – yet another tally was added to the bleak ledger of death.

21

'GET BACK, YOU BASTARDS!': THE BAD DEATH OF HARRY DONCASTER

At the Army Training Camp, the priority since the first shots had been heard was to secure the camp, as per Colonel John Mitchell's instructions in the conference of 9 June. Keen-eyed observers had suspected the Japanese were breaking out when they heard the distant crackle of gunfire – the three red flares arcing into the night sky like dying stars confirmed it. Within minutes the whole camp was on alert, and if the gunfire in the distance hadn't been enough to wake the young recruits, the alarm signal certainly was. 'It was arranged,' recalled Major Vern Northwood, 'that when the break-out occurred the alarm was to be given by the camp pickets running around the corrugated iron huts with a pick handle to rouse the troops inside. You can imagine the racket that made.'[157]

Men rushed from their barracks, hastily fastening tunics and wiping sleep from weary eyes. They were issued with unloaded rifles and bayonets, and set to work putting into practice the drills they had rehearsed so many times before. Despite their lack of training, the young soldiers performed their duties admirably, and there was never any real concern that the camp was under threat from the Japanese. Patrols scoured the countryside and even rounded up a few escapees, who no doubt had simply blundered in their direction after finding themselves free of the POW camp.

Officers from the training camp had been liaising with the commanders of the POW camp in person and by telephone since the warning flares had gone up, and by mid-morning an army field officer, Captain Alec Dysart, had been appointed a permanent liaison to report back to the army camp about the situation at the POW camp. In spite of all this activity, there was a sense of procrastination in the army camp about the largest of elephants in the room – the rounding-up of escaped prisoners.

It should have been plainly obvious to Colonel Mitchell and his staff that the army camp would be called on to help in the search for escapees. With more than 300 POWs roaming the countryside the army camp was the only resource anywhere in the area that could gainfully contribute to the search. And yet there was a strange lethargy in the army camp to put any plans into effect, and an even stranger lethargy from the POW camp to ask them to. It wasn't until 4 p.m. – 14 hours after the first prisoners had breached the wire, and less than an hour before dusk – that the army camp brigade major, Major Rupert Rattray, headed over to the POW camp to discuss the matter. This inexcusable delay has never adequately been explained.

After consultation with Brown and Ramsay, Rattray phoned the army camp with instructions to organise about 500 men into parties to help search for prisoners. Rattray spoke to Staff Captain Frank Morris, who immediately began organising officers to round up men for the search parties, and trucks to transport them into the countryside.

By this stage the army camp commanders were well aware that hundreds of Japanese had been mown down in the escape attempt, and that at least two Australian guards had been killed. For all they knew the men who had murdered the Australians were among the escaped prisoners, so they were acutely aware of the dangerous nature of the mission they were being asked to perform. Yet, inexplicably, they put into action the plan that Mitchell had briefly outlined at the 9 June conference, back when a breakout from the camp was simply a theory. Now that the breakout was a bloody reality, this decision is incomprehensible. Twenty-three groups of 20 to 30 recruits each would form the search parties, armed only with bayonets in scabbards. The officers who would lead them would not be armed at all. It's no exaggeration to say that the prisoners they would be confronting, with their knives and baseball bats, would be more heavily armed than the soldiers. Even if the camp commanders believed the recruits were too inexperienced to carry loaded weapons, they should have at least been issued with unloaded rifles (as, indeed, the troops tasked with defending the army camp were). A bayonet attached to the end of a rifle is a far more formidable weapon than a bayonet carried in the hand, and the prisoners they were likely to encounter would not have known that the rifles levelled at them were unloaded. Officers should have been carrying loaded pistols – they were, after all, predominantly combat veterans who were highly experienced with firearms.

To make matters even worse, darkness was rapidly falling by the time the decision to organise search parties was made. It wasn't until 4 p.m. that the first serious discussions about it were even held, and well after 4.15 by the time officers had begun rounding up men for the search. Given that sunset on 5 August was due at 5.19 p.m., this was an astonishing decision. By the time men were scrambling into trucks that would take them on their mission, the army camp was already cloaked in a disconcerting gloom. Sending lightly armed men out on a search mission against an armed and fanatical enemy, men who had nothing to lose and who were intent on killing as many Australians in uniform as they could, would have been a dangerous task in full daylight. To attempt it in darkness was insanity. (This was tacitly acknowledged by the officers organising the search, who issued instructions that the parties were to end the search at dark. Given that there was less than an hour of daylight left, and that during this time the search parties had to organise and equip themselves, drive 15 kilometres, disembark from the trucks and then conduct a search on foot, this order was already impossible to comply with the moment it was issued.)

Into this chaotic scenario stepped Lieutenant Harry Doncaster, a 38-year-old stonemason from Ballarat in Victoria. Doncaster was tall and athletic, and was well known in Ballarat for his sporting achievements. He was a particularly good runner, and had won several trophies for the middle-distance events as a member of the Ballarat YMCA Harriers Club (one of Australia's oldest sporting clubs, which still exists). By the time the Second World War began he already had nearly two decades service in cadets and the militia, in addition to the regular army. He was a veteran of the Middle East, and had served under Mitchell in the 2/8th Battalion before being reassigned to training duties back in Australia. His wife, Jessie, and seven-year-old son, John, waited for him back in Ballarat.[158]

Doncaster had not been in the training camp during the Breakout – he had been granted compassionate leave, and only returned at 10 a.m. on 5 August. Records don't reveal what family or personal incident prompted the leave, but it's safe to say that Doncaster was already in a troubled state of mind when he was recalled to the camp. When he received orders to immediately assemble 25 of his men to join a search for Japanese escapees, and that he would be leading them completely unarmed, he was 'very upset'.[159] Weeks earlier, he and his mate Lieutenant Stan Platz, a veteran of the 1942 Battle of Milne Bay, had agreed that if they were ever called on to help deal with the Japanese prisoners, they would take their revolvers. Bugger what Old Man Mitchell had to say – both Doncaster and Platz had been in combat and knew that going up against a determined enemy armed only with your fists and wishful thinking was bloody insanity. But on 5 August, when the orders came they came in a rush, and there was no time to return to their barracks to grab their sidearms – within minutes men were scurrying onto truckbeds and sergeants were barking orders. 'I don't like this, Platzie,' Doncaster said. 'We should be given our revolvers.'[160]

Doncaster and Platz joined 21 other officers, each leading about 20 or 25 men, and supervised as the young soldiers scrambled aboard a fleet of three-ton trucks. In charge of the patrol was 28-year-old Captain Raymond Roberts, and in a hurried conference outside the canteen at the army camp he gave an overview of a vague plan. The trucks would head about 15 kilometres north along the Cowra–Canowindra Road, in the direction that most of the prisoners still on the run were believed to have headed. Each search party would be dropped off at one-mile intervals, and would fan out and walk south on foot, hoping to ensnare the escapees in a giant human net. 'Can you show us the area on the map, sir?' Doncaster asked. 'I'm afraid not, Harry,' Roberts replied. 'We don't have a map that covers that ground. But it's all pretty easy country. Just form a line and head south. Round up any Japs you come across and load them onto the trucks.'

Doncaster and Platz were uneasy as they joined their men on the trucks. It was disconcertingly dark – by the time they got out on the Canowindra Road it was hard to make out much in the gloom. Platz's sergeant pointed out to him a large rock-strewn hill that loomed in a paddock up ahead. 'Looks like we'll cop that, sir,' he said with dismay. Platz made a rough calculation. 'I think we will just miss it,' he said. 'That will be in Lieutenant Doncaster's search area.'[161] Platz was right. As their truck sped past the hill, he saw Doncaster leading his men up its rocky slopes. He raised a hand to his old friend, but Doncaster didn't see it in the gathering shadows. It was the last time Platz saw Doncaster alive.

As Doncaster advanced through the gathering twilight, he was extremely uneasy. He barely knew the men – boys, really – in his patrol group, and he only had one NCO with him, 23-year-old Sergeant Henry Warway, to help hold the patrol together. He didn't know the ground either – with no maps to guide them, his truck had taken a wrong turn on the way out of town, costing them precious minutes of daylight – and his group had certainly drawn the short straw when they were allocated this rocky hill as their search area. He told the men to unsheathe their bayonets, and to extend in a line with a few yards in between each man. He would have preferred to move in an arrowhead formation, like he had done on patrol in the Middle East, which would have enabled him to keep better control of his nervy young soldiers, but there was too much ground to cover, and too few men. And besides, an arrowhead formation was going to make bugger-all difference if they came across any Japanese – they weren't carrying anything to shoot with. Hopefully the Japanese would be wounded or worn out from their busy day and would give themselves up without a fight. The patrol began to move uphill. *So much for the easy country*, Doncaster thought. This hill was steep. It was rocky too, and dotted with dark clumps of scrub. *If I was on the run*, Doncaster thought, *this is where I'd hide.*

For the next 15 minutes, the small group edged forward up the slope. In the distance Doncaster could make out other groups of soldiers moving cautiously forward in line, but he still felt isolated and exposed and, without a weapon, didn't even know what to do with his hands. He bent down and picked up a jagged rock, about the size of a cricket ball, one of thousands strewn on the slope around him. He knew it wouldn't do him much good in a fight, but he felt better to be holding something – anything – he could use to defend himself.

They were near the top of the hill now, and a group of large, scattered boulders loomed on the crest. Doncaster ordered the nearest couple of privates to veer right around the first boulder. Doncaster went left. He saw movement up ahead. 'Over here!' he called to his men as a Japanese prisoner stepped out of the inky shadows. He caught movement to his left, and saw another Japanese on top of a boulder. 'Get back, you bastards!' he shouted, and raised the rock in his right hand. There were more Japanese now, and they were moving towards him. He pelted the rock at the first man, who ducked out of the way. Another Japanese came at him, and fast. Doncaster had done his fair share of boxing, and he let the man close to within arm's length, before launching a jab with his powerful right arm. He caught the Japanese squarely on the jaw, and the man went down hard. Doncaster sensed movement behind him and started to turn, but he was too late. A prisoner leapt onto his back, and Doncaster hit the ground. He let loose with another fist and landed a glancing blow on a Japanese shoulder. He shouted and kicked, and yelled furiously. His boot connected solidly with someone, but it wasn't enough to slow him down. The Japanese swarmed onto him.

— —

Private Jim Battiscombe, an 18-year-old from Melbourne, was the closest man to Doncaster as they neared the top of the hill. He moved to the right around the boulders with his mate, Private Fred Hannah, who hailed from Sydney and was a week shy of his 19th birthday. Both gripped their bayonets with white knuckles. *What are we doing out here?* he thought. *It's nearly dark, the Japanese are all over the place, and all I'm carrying is a bloody bayonet.* As he and Hannah rounded the boulder he heard Doncaster yell, and the two men rushed forward. There was a Japanese man standing on top of the nearest boulder. In the gloom they could just make out their lieutenant as he threw a rock at another man who had just appeared. And then the Japanese charged. Battiscombe saw Doncaster flatten one of them with a punch, before a burgundy-clad figure launched himself onto Doncaster's back. Battiscombe thought he saw a knife, but it was hard to tell in the low light. But what he saw next was unmistakable. As Doncaster writhed on the ground, with Japanese all over him, a man, unusually tall for a Japanese, stepped forward. He held a club, or possibly a baseball bat. He raised it, and then brought it down on Doncaster's head.

— —

Hannah was standing near Battiscombe as the Japanese attacked, and he later gave a lurid account to the Court of Inquiry.

When Lieut. Doncaster called out, 'Over here' Pte Battiscombe and myself went over immediately and we saw a Japanese standing on a rock with a knife. He was apparently a decoy because as we closed others seemed to jump out from all over the place. A couple of them were on Lieut. Doncaster and they all seemed to concentrate on him and there was one Jap standing between Mr. Doncaster and myself. I went over and struck at him with the bayonet and he just snarled and struck with the club he was holding which would be about six feet long and struck me across the knuckles.

As Hannah recoiled from the blow he lost his balance and went down.

I rolled down the hill approximately 15 yards and I when I looked around there were about three Japanese just about on top of me. Two were armed with clubs and the other one had a knife. Then I was chased down the bottom of the hill.

It should be said that Private Hannah was not the most reliable of witnesses. He claims the Japanese were on his heels for a full two hours, and only gave up the chase after five miles, a suggestion that the court interviewer found incredulous. 'I doubt whether you could run five miles,' he said. 'I could, Sir,' came the defiant reply. Regardless, there is no doubt that the privates were outnumbered by the Japanese, who came at them with violent intent in near darkness. The young soldiers were armed only with bayonets, they were alone and scared, and they had just seen their officer beaten to a pulp. Unsurprisingly, they scarpered.

Private Dick Scoffield, yet another 18-year-old trainee, was slightly behind Doncaster during this melee, and didn't see his lieutenant attacked. What he did see was a Japanese prisoner coming straight at him. 'Two or three more came out towards me,' he said. 'That is when I lost my nerve. They had knives the ones that came towards me.' The fear in these words is palpable; little wonder that he lost his nerve. He panicked, and pegged his bayonet at the nearest prisoner before bounding down the hill, calling out hysterically to the rest of his platoon as he went. He reached his mate, Private John Perry, who read the scene instantly and joined Scoffield in his charge down the hill. Scoffield was later grilled about why he had discarded his bayonet – there was genuine concern that the Japanese had picked it up and used it on Doncaster.

Scoffield, Perry and Battiscombe barrelled down the hill until they ran headlong into their platoon sergeant, Henry Warway, who struggled to make sense of the story the privates were hysterically relaying. After sending a couple of men off to make contact with the other search parties, Warway headed up the hill alone to survey the situation. He told the Court of Inquiry that when he got to the top of the hill he 'could hear Japanese talking, but I could not hear Lt Doncaster'. He then made an extraordinary statement. 'As I could not hear Lt Doncaster, I assumed that he had been killed.' He returned to his platoon and told them, 'I had heard Japanese voices, and that there was no sense in trying to take the position. I said that the Japs had rocks and knives and clubs and that there was no sense in attacking uphill. It was now pitch dark.' This was an astonishing position to take, and it was clear the court took a dim view on his lack of action (although officially it didn't reprimand him). Even if Warway had moved on the Japanese, though, it was too late for Harry Doncaster. He was already dead.

Back down on the road, Platz was sitting with his men after having completed their patrol. They had covered about

12 kilometres across country that Doncaster's men would have dreamed of. It was flat and open, and the only obstacles that held them up were farm fences and the occasional small dry gully (referred to as a 'donga' by Platz, a South African term that had first been picked up by Australians during the Boer War). They were waiting for a truck to come and pick them up when Platz saw a young soldier sprinting towards him down the road. (It's not clear who this soldier was, but he was most likely one of the privates sent to get help by Sergeant Warway.) Platz went forward to meet him.

> He was distressed and hardly able to talk. Then he said 'Sir, the Japs are in that hill and I think they have captured our Officer and one of the boys.' When I asked him how many Japs and how were they armed, he answered 'about 6–7 Japs carrying baseball bats and knives.'[162]

Platz flagged down a passing truck and ordered its men to disembark. He then sent the truck back to the camp with instructions to urgently report the emergency to Captain Roberts and to ask him to return with an armed patrol. More trucks had arrived carrying soldiers back to camp after the search. Platz stopped all of them, got the men off and set up a cordon around the base of the hill in the hope of cutting off the escape of the Japanese who had attacked Doncaster. 'One truck was carrying back 3 re-captured Japs, one of which spoke very good English,' Platz later said. 'I took this P.O.W. to the base of the feature and told him to call his mates to come off the hill and surrender themselves. They answered him clearly so that meant we still had the Japs contained.' By now it was approaching 10 p.m. – it had been more than two hours since Platz had sent the truck back to camp and asked for an armed patrol to be urgently sent out. As it turned out, Captain Roberts had not been back to the camp, and had been out in the field all evening organising trucks to take captured groups of prisoners back to the POW camp. The sergeant who had been sent back to raise an armed patrol couldn't locate Roberts, and it took several hours for him to convey the story to officers at the camp and for the men to be armed and transported back to the Canowindra Road.

Some time after 10 p.m. Roberts arrived on the scene, at about the same time that the armed patrol finally turned up. The patrol consisted of about 30 men armed with rifles, Owen submachine guns and Bren light machine-guns, as well as torches and flares. As Platz was the only man on the scene with any knowledge of the ground they were to search, Roberts asked him to lead the patrol. 'Yes,' Platz replied. 'But you accompany us also.'

The patrol fanned out and set off up the hill, shining torches and firing the occasional flare to light their way; shadows jerked and danced from trees and boulders as the flares lazily drifted to earth under parachutes. As the patrol neared the crest, one of the men called to Platz, 'Here's your officer.' Platz approached and saw the body of Harry Doncaster in the moonlight.

I found him lying face downward with his two arms underneath him, and down towards his crutch, the head turned to the side, and he appeared to be badly battered. We approached it very warily, because the feature towards the summit was very rocky and lent itself to anyone hiding behind the rocks. It was fairly light, the moon was well up, and we had flares. We didn't touch the body in case anything was underneath it, and I took hold of Mr Doncaster's left leg by the toe, and eased the leg backwards and allowed it to fall to the ground. His movement was very free and there was no stiffness or anything like that, and one lad commented that he was fairly warm and it appeared he hadn't been dead very long. He definitely appeared dead.[163]

Doncaster's shirt was torn and covered in blood, but Platz couldn't tell if he had been stabbed as well as bashed. The shocking image of his murdered friend stayed with him for the rest of his life. 'His face and head were beyond recognition,' he recalled years later. 'He had been "pulped" by being slashed with a sharp object and bludgeoned by the baseball bats.'[164]

The group didn't linger; there was nothing they could do for Doncaster, and the men who had killed him were still out there. They pushed on along the crest, weapons cocked and ready. As they rounded a boulder, they spotted a figure standing beneath a tree in the shadows up ahead. 'Look out, sir!' shouted a jumpy lance corporal. 'Japs up ahead!' He raised his Owen gun ready to fire. 'Calm down, son,' replied Platz. 'That Jap won't cause us any trouble.' He shone his torch at the figure – the man was hanging from a tree branch, his feet moving in small circles as his body swayed in the cool winter breeze. Passing him, Platz entered a clearing where he found the bodies of half a dozen more Japanese. 'They had climbed up on top of the boulders,' he said, 'made a noose from their belts etc and pushed themselves into a hanging position. A more eerie sight you could not observe.'[165]

As Platz and his men surveyed the ghastly scene, a couple of members of the patrol appeared with a live Japanese prisoner, who they had found crouched among the boulders. 'He was shaking with fear,' Platz said, 'and I would say with no wish to die.'[166] The patrol collected Doncaster's body and brought it down off the hill, along with the Japanese prisoner. Back at the trucks, a sergeant approached Platz and asked if he could personally escort the prisoner back to camp. Smelling a rat, Platz replied, 'He will be OK, Sergeant. He will come back to the compound in the truck with us.' The sergeant, it was later revealed, had been Doncaster's platoon sergeant in the Middle East. The sergeant was insistent that the prisoner should be handed over to him. Platz told him to take up his request with Captain Roberts, the senior officer on the scene. Soon afterwards, the Japanese prisoner was removed from Platz's custody, and Platz didn't hear of him again. 'I do not know the outcome,' he later said, with just a touch of evasiveness, 'nor did I discuss it with Captain Roberts.'[167] The fate of the prisoner remains unknown. The Australian patrols climbed aboard their trucks and returned to the camp. Few spoke during the journey.

At about 11.30 p.m. another armed patrol, this time 100 men strong and personally accompanied by Mitchell, the commandant of the training camp, returned to the hill and thoroughly combed it for weapons, evidence or Japanese. They found the bodies of about ten prisoners who had hanged themselves, but apart from that returned to the camp empty-handed and without firing a shot.

A few hours later, Lieutenant Durrant Langley (the man who had already led a small battle with escaped prisoners soon after the Breakout) was put in charge of a group of soldiers from the army camp contingent, with instructions to cover the road north of the POW camp and to apprehend any Japanese who came his way. He was sceptical that any prisoners would go to the trouble of breaking out and scarpering into the countryside, only to return to the camp the following morning, so he was astonished to see at about 4.30 a.m. a group of six burgundy-clad figures descending the hill towards the camp. They were armed with 'baseball bats, an axe handle, and I should say what appeared to be large lumps of wood from broken trees'.[168] Langley fired a warning shot at the feet of the Japanese, and they immediately went to ground. Langley ordered them to stand and drop their weapons, which they did reluctantly, before slowly edging towards the Australians. They climbed through the fence beside the road as the Australians covered them with raised rifles.

It was then that one of the soldiers noticed the Australian-pattern bayonet. It had been discarded by the Japanese among the other weapons, so Langley couldn't tell which Japanese had been carrying it, but the bayonet, like the axe handle and one of the lumps of wood, was stained with dried blood. Langley knew nothing of the attack on Doncaster, of course, and so he simply noted the unusual condition of the weapons and put them in storage. At the later Court of Inquiry, the court representatives made much of the discovery of the bayonet – in a case with few witnesses and little evidence, they were desperate to find a murder weapon and link it to a specific Japanese prisoner. They confirmed that the bayonet was the one thrown at the Japanese by Scoffield, and suggested that the bloodstains indicated it had been used to finish off Doncaster. They pressed Langley on the physical characteristics of the Japanese he had captured, and were particularly keen to find out if one of them had been unusually tall (a description the privates had used when detailing the assault on Doncaster). They even asked Langley outright if he thought the men in this group were the same ones who had attacked Doncaster. Unsurprisingly, Langley had no answers to questions about an incident that he hadn't witnessed, and the line of questioning was quickly abandoned. The attempt to tie Langley's Japanese to Doncaster's murder was purely circumstantial. Japanese prisoners had been roaming the countryside all night and picking up whatever weapons they came across. The court found that the small group of men apprehended by Langley had probably come across the discarded weapons near the hill where Doncaster had been killed, and were unlikely to have been involved in his murder. No charges were laid against the men Langley had apprehended, or indeed against any other Japanese prisoner.

Early in the morning of 6 August, Doncaster's body was transferred to the civilian morgue in Cowra. The bodies of Hardy, Jones and Shepherd were already there. An autopsy revealed that Doncaster had died of a fractured skull, caused by the force of a blunt instrument such as a club or heavy piece of wood. His face and head had also been slashed by a knife or other sharp instrument. Although his shirt had a small tear in the back, he had not been stabbed, and his body displayed no other injuries. He was buried in the local Cowra cemetery, alongside the other three Australians who had been killed in the Breakout.

The Court of Inquiry to examine the circumstances of the death of Harry Doncaster was convened a few weeks later. In its findings it confirmed that Doncaster had been killed while on duty, and cleared him of any wrongdoing, stating that he carried out his duties in 'the best tradition of the service'.[169] It laid the blame for his death squarely at the feet of the Japanese who assaulted him, and concluded that he 'died from the effects of injuries feloniously and maliciously inflicted on him by some person or persons, such persons being escaped Japanese prisoners'.[170]

The court was, however, critical of the actions of many of the Australians involved in the saga, including Colonel Mitchell, Major Rattray, Sergeant Warway, and Privates Battiscombe, Hannah, Scoffield and Perry. It stopped short of formally reprimanding them, but deferred back to the army 'for any action which may be deemed necessary'.[171] The court was especially critical (in its highly conservative fashion) of Mitchell, particularly his decision to stick to his original plan of sending unarmed men out to search for prisoners when he knew that the Japanese were armed and had already killed at least two Australians. They referred to this, in unabashed understatement, as an 'error of judgement'. No doubt the infantrymen forced to comb the hills armed only with bayonets, and their officers armed only with their fists, would have used far more colourful language than this to describe the situation.

When the court posed the reasonable question to Mitchell of why he was happy to send out armed patrols later in the evening when he had been so reluctant to in the afternoon, his response was that the situation had changed – with Doncaster's death, he now knew there was a 'killer' among the escaped prisoners. That position was completely untenable: Mitchell already knew there were killers among the Japanese when he ordered the search parties sent out – the bodies of Hardy, Jones and Shepherd had been lying in the morgue for 15 hours by this time, and the camp had been informed of the deaths at 7 a.m. Indeed, it held little water with the court, which dismissed his claims and stated in its official findings that Mitchell should have armed every party he sent out – he had both the knowledge of the situation and the manpower to do so.

In the end, no Australian was ever formerly reprimanded for his role in the death of Harry Doncaster, and no Japanese was ever convicted of it, although Mitchell's reputation was so tarnished he soon moved on from his role at the training camp and was placed on the reserve list in November 1944. He never held a command position again. It was curious that Australian authorities were not more dogged in their determination to find Doncaster's killer. There was a strange lethargy to follow up on witness statements that may have exposed the identity of the murderer. Perhaps the authorities reached the conclusion that the man who killed Doncaster was one of the Japanese who had been found hanged on the hillside later that night. We will never know for certain.

Back in Ballarat, in a small whitewashed cottage on Doveton Street, Jessie Doncaster hugged little John close, and wept silently, waiting for the end of a long winter's night that would never really come.

22

'SHOOT FIRST AND TALK AFTERWARDS': THE HUNTING TRIP

On Sunday, 6 August, something occurred that could easily have turned the Cowra Breakout from a serious incident to a fully fledged international disaster. Alf Bourke, the local railway guard who lived not far from the camp, had been expecting the Breakout for weeks, like so many of Cowra's townsfolk. It was the talk of the town at pubs and dances, and it seems it was only the military authorities who doubted the veracity of the rumours.

Early on the morning of 5 August, Bourke was awakened by the thunder of gunfire and, shaking awake his wife, told her, 'It's on over at the camp.' He stayed awake for a couple of hours and then went back to bed, taking his loaded shotgun with him.

The next day, the town was humming with rumours about the Breakout – it was hard to separate fact from fiction, but it was pretty clear that large numbers of Japanese had escaped and were roaming the countryside. Bourke was warned by a mate from the garrison that the prisoners were desperate and to keep his guard up – 'If you run into any of them,' he said, 'be prepared to shoot first and talk afterwards.'

Early Sunday afternoon, Bourke told his 13-year-old son, Ray, to load his .22 rifle, and Bourke grabbed his shotgun. In a straight-faced report he made to an inquiry months later, he stated that his plan was to take his son on a hunting trip for rabbits to feed his dogs, but he later admitted that this was the most exciting thing that had happened in sleepy Cowra for a long time – maybe ever – and he was keen to be part of the action.[172]

Bourke and Ray left the homestead and walked west across the paddocks towards the camp. Bourke expected (and probably hoped) they would come across some escapees, and he was not disappointed. They had walked about two kilometres when they spotted a burgundy-clad figure loitering near some rocks and timber at the top of a hill about a kilometre away.

Bourke and his son approached cautiously and circled the hill, but the Japanese had disappeared. Ray rounded a bluff of rocks and suddenly called out, 'Look out, there are six of them, Dad!' Bourke raced to Ray's side and was confronted by a startled group of prisoners.

I could then see six Japanese, three in one little basin, and three in another basin about four of five feet away. I would be about fifteen to eighteen feet away from them. They all stood up when they saw us, and one of them spoke sharply to the rest, and made a circular motion with his hand to the others at the same time walking in the opposite direction. By his actions and orders which I thought he had given to the others I thought he meant to surround us. The one who had given the orders and who I took to be the leader, began to move towards us in a circular direction.[173]

Fearing the Japanese was about to attack, Bourke raised his shotgun and fired, catching the man in the chest at short range. The Japanese fell dead, and another ran towards a pile of stones that had apparently been collected as an arsenal. Bourke fired again, hitting the second Japanese in the head and killing him instantly. Bourke called out to Ray to run to the nearest farmhouse and summon help from the camp.

Bourke kept the shotgun levelled at the surviving Japanese until his son returned, accompanied by farmer Clarrie Wright, his son and another man called Harper – all three carried rifles. They had put a call in to the authorities, who sent a party of men under Warrant Officer Fred Martin with a truck to convey the surviving prisoners (and the bodies) back to the camp. What happened next is confused, and it's almost certain the participants were muddying the truth when they later recounted the event. At one stage one of the prisoners produced a length of heavy twine and attempted to strangle himself. He failed, but this unsurprisingly put the Australians on edge. When the Japanese failed to respond to instructions to get into the truck, Martin fired a warning shot over their heads, which had little effect. Harper attempted to manhandle one of the Japanese into the truck, and a scuffle broke out – in the melee Martin shot one of the prisoners. Curiously, it's unclear whether the man was killed or simply wounded, but the descriptions of the incident are vague. The Japanese were eventually forced into the truck, and they and the bodies of their dead comrades were taken back to the camp. The fate of the man Martin had shot was not recorded.

It's impossible to overstate the significance of the Bourke incident. It was one thing for Australian guards to open fire on Japanese prisoners who were armed and attempting to attack them. It was an entirely different matter for civilians to be shooting unarmed Japanese POWs. Australian authorities were already grappling with the dilemma of what and how to tell the Japanese about the Breakout – how were they possibly going to explain Bourke's rabbiting misadventure? The perception that armed groups of vigilantes were roaming the Australian countryside and murdering Japanese non-combatants could have had dire repercussions for the 23 000 Australian POWs in Japanese hands. Little wonder the authorities were keen to sweep the whole saga under the rug. Bourke was not called to give evidence after his rudimentary statement. Moreover, Dr Jim Garner, the medical officer who examined the bodies of all the Japanese killed in the breakout, was encouraged in no uncertain terms to turn a blind eye to evidence that Japanese prisoners had been shot by any weapons apart from rifles and machine-guns in the camp. During the coronial inquiry he said, 'Those who I found died as result of gunshot or rifle wounds they could have been caused by garrison guards firing on the escaping prisoners; and by the weapons used by those men.' His intention is clear here: to specifically state that the gunshot wounds he inspected were caused only by weapons employed by camp guards during the Breakout. To drive the point home, the sergeant assisting the coroner asked him to categorically state that all the wounds he examined were caused by rifles or machine-guns. Recalling the pellet wounds he had seen in one of Bourke's victims, Garner replied, 'All except one.' He was greeted with silence from the bench, which prompted the nervous and telling response, 'Did I say the wrong thing?' Clearly he had. He amended his response: 'All right then. They were all consistent with rifle and machine-gun fire.'[174]

Thanks to Bourke and his quest to score a few rabbits, the story of the Cowra Breakout was quickly spiralling out of control.

23

'WHERE ARE YOU HIT?':
THE FORGOTTEN AUSTRALIAN

Read any book or article on the Cowra Breakout, or even the information panels at the old POW camp site or in the Cowra tourist information office, and they will all tell you the same thing: four Australians were killed during the Breakout and in the days that followed. Their stories are familiar by now – Privates Ben Hardy and Ralph Jones overcome by marauding prisoners during their defiant last stand on the Vickers machine-gun, Private Charles Shepherd stabbed in the heart as he rushed to his post, and Lieutenant Harry Doncaster valiantly fighting with rocks, and eventually his bare hands, as escaped prisoners swarmed around him.

But there was a fifth Australian soldier in the days after the Breakout who also pulled on a uniform, who rushed from his warm bed on a cold winter's night, who carried a rifle and was prepared to use it, and who paid for his dedication with his life. He was Sergeant Tom Hancock and, for reasons unknown, his story has been forgotten.

Tom Hancock was a farmer at Kings Plains, a pinprick on the map 75 kilometres north-east of Cowra, near the dusty township of Blayney. The Hancocks had lived in the region for as long as anyone could remember (and indeed, they still do – Hancock's grandson, Paul, still works the same farm his grandfather and great-grandfather did before him). Hancock's father, William, had moved to the district as a young man in the early 1870s, and had taken up a plot of good farmland at Kings Plains. He married a local girl and had a daughter and five sons, with Tom coming along second last in December 1890.

Life moved pretty slowly on the farms around Kings Plains. A quick scan of the local paper, the *Leader*, reveals that articles of interest in this era included a punch-up between a cricketer and a cyclist whose bicycle wheel was damaged by a hearty six over square leg, the temporary closure of the local school after its only teacher, a Mr Gardiner, came down with a severe bout of 'erysipelas of the face', and the stirring tale of a small boy, Albert Death, who managed to avoid the fate seemingly foretold by his surname when he escaped the horns of an angry bull by hiding under a tree stump.

Hancock didn't serve in the Great War, possibly because agriculture was considered an essential industry and the recent death of his father had left the farm in Hancock's hands. He married a local girl, Hattie Willis, in 1920, and they settled on the farm at Kings Plains, where they had a daughter, Coral, and two boys, William and John. Life was tough but good, and the family was happy. When the Second World War broke out, Hancock was keen to do his bit, in spite of his advanced years. When he enlisted in March 1942 Hancock was 51, far too old to be considered for active service. He was even too old to be considered for garrison duty at the POW camp, so he enrolled in the only military force that he was eligible for – the Volunteer Defence Corps (VDC).

The VDC had been formed in 1940 by the Returned Sailors and Soldiers Imperial League of Australia (today's Returned Services League) and was modelled on the British Home Guard. First World War veterans, too old for active service, joined the unit to provide essential military services within Australia. First World War hero Sir Henry Chauvel was brought out of mothballs and took the role of Inspector General of the VDC, a post he held until his death in 1945. The earliest incarnation of the VDC made for quite a sight, as the bespectacled veterans of 1914–18 launched sedately paced charges at each other armed with broomsticks and cricket bats, plinked away at paper targets with .22s borrowed from local farmers, and marched and drilled as much as their weary bones would allow. The VDC was never particularly well equipped at any stage during the war, but in its early years it had to make do with whatever bits and pieces it could lay its hands on. Hundreds of German machine-guns, captured during the Great War and brought home as war trophies, were pressed into service with the VDC. New recruits marched in civilian suits, and grenade practice involved filling a jam tin with kerosene, lighting a fuse and hastily lobbing the thing at the nearest tree before it set fire to your sleeve.

In 1941 the army took control of the VDC and, as the risk of invasion swelled, so too did the ranks of the unit. By the time Hancock recited his oath to the King and signed his attestation papers, nearly 100 000 men had likewise answered the call. This new version of the VDC was predominantly focused on guerrilla tactics to be employed in the event of a Japanese invasion. The VDC would effectively be Australia's last line of defence, and ensured that a sizeable proportion of the population would be armed and trained should they be required for combat on the streets of Sydney or Brisbane.

Each VDC battalion operated in the area in which it was raised – this made sense, given that the bulk of the battalions were made up of part-time soldiers or reservists who could be called on in an emergency. Hancock joined the 26th Battalion, which operated in and around the Blayney area, and he was promoted to sergeant in March 1943.

On the day of the Breakout, 5 August 1944, the local VDC garrison swung into duty when a contingent of 25 men was ordered to guard the rail tracks and bridges around Blayney. The logical assumption was that now large numbers of prisoners were on the run, they would attempt to get to Sydney and, from there, onwards to rejoin their comrades on the battlefields of the Pacific, so it was imperative that rail facilities be closely guarded. This work became even more vital after the deaths of the two prisoners on the rail line on the night of 5 August. Tom Hancock was among the men called out to guard the railways, and he spent a cold and anxious night patrolling with his comrades before being given the all-clear and sent home to rest as the sun came up the following morning. The VDC members spent the day at home, recovering from their adventurous night and keeping a close ear to the wireless for updates on the escaped prisoners.

On the night of 7 August, the local representative for the Railways Department again contacted the Blayney VDC headquarters, asking for a guard to be posted to the rail lines. By this stage most of the prisoners had been rounded up, but there were still a couple of dozen on the run, and nerves were stretched at the thought that some or all of them could be trying to make their way to Sydney. The request came in at about 7.30 p.m., and Captain Erle Ewin, the commanding officer of the 26th Battalion's C Company, immediately started ringing houses and farms to rustle up the 25 men needed to form the guard patrol. One of the calls was to Corporal Norm

Gardiner, who had been on the patrol two nights earlier and was mates with several of the VDC men in the area. Ewin ordered Gardiner to round up the men who lived near him and report for duty at the Blayney VDC headquarters at 9 p.m. One of those men was Hancock.

Earlier in the evening, Gardiner had been speaking with a mate in the Blayney police force, who told him that the Japanese prisoners still on the run must be getting desperate by now, and were 'of a dangerous character'. Unsurprisingly this put him on edge so, for the first time in his VDC career, he loaded his Lee-Enfield rifle before he left home and placed it behind the seats of his ute with the safety catch on. The Lee-Enfield was a solid and reliable rifle, but the ones issued to the VDC had seen better days. They were of First World War vintage and had been kept in service through clever engineering and elbow grease – the safety catch on Gardiner's rifle was, in his words, 'a bit loose'.

At about 8.30 p.m. he picked up Hancock at his farm. Hancock kissed Hattie goodbye and told her he would see her in the morning. Gardiner noted that Hancock was wearing a clean uniform, but he looked weary. The two men climbed into the ute and headed off to pick up two other VDC blokes who lived nearby, then drove to the VDC HQ in Blayney.

At about 9 p.m. Gardiner parked on Adelaide Street, opposite the VDC headquarters. As the ute pulled up the tailgate fell open, so Hancock climbed out of the passenger seat to secure it. He had left his door open and, as he returned to close it, Gardiner grabbed his rifle by the buttstock and slid it towards him through the open driver's door.

Suddenly the night was shattered by an explosion – the dodgy safety catch on Gardiner's old rifle had failed and the gun had gone off. The muzzle was pointed squarely at the open door of the ute and, unluckily, the only thing in front of it was

Hancock. The bullet tore through his right buttock, leaving a gaping wound. 'Holy Ghost!' cried out Gardiner as he raced to Hancock's side. 'Where are you hit, Tom?' 'I'm not sure,' replied Hancock as he limped to a nearby petrol bowser and grabbed it for support. 'But it's bad.'

The gunshot had been deafening in the sleepy town. Lights were blinking on in windows along the street, and cautious heads peered nervously around doorways. One of the people who had heard the shot was the local doctor, D'Arcy Short, who threw on his coat and ran into the street. He saw a couple of soldiers frantically helping a hunched figure into the VDC HQ, and rushed to assist. He arrived to find Hancock in pain but relatively good spirits, and immediately drove him to the Blayney District Hospital in the back of his car, where Dr Short operated to clean up the wound.

At first Hancock did well. Over the next few days the wound seemed to be healing nicely, and he wasn't in too much pain. Hattie and the kids visited him in hospital every day, as did several of his VDC mates, who joked that only Hancock could be fool enough to get shot in the bum. On the 15th, however, Hancock took a bad turn. His temperature spiked and the wound turned nasty. Dr Short did what he could, but Hancock deteriorated rapidly. Late that night Dr Short called Hattie and told her she'd better come in. She stayed by Hancock's side until he died in the early hours of the following morning. The wound had turned septic, and Hancock had died of blood poisoning. In an era when antibiotics were still a novelty, and unlikely to be widely distributed to regional hospitals, there was nothing anyone could have done.

Hattie made funeral arrangements swiftly – the infection was causing rapid decomposition of the body – and Hancock was laid to rest in the Blayney Cemetery the next day. He was buried under a military headstone, and Hattie received more than £400 in compensation from the army, which she took as a lump sum rather than an ongoing pension. A military Court of Inquiry later found that Hancock's injury and death had been brought about 'indirectly by the escape of Japanese Prisoners of War from Cowra PW Camp on 5 Aug 44'. It found that he was serving as a member of the military forces and that he was on duty at the time of the injury that led to his death.

It all seems fairly straightforward, then – Hancock was an active member of the Australian military forces, and was on duty with those forces when he was accidentally shot. His injury and death were related to the Japanese breakout of the POW camp, and the army paid his widow compensation for his death, and even reimbursed her for the costs of the funeral. Today he lies under a military headstone in Blayney Cemetery, just like thousands of his comrades in cemeteries across the country who died during the war.

Why, then, is Tom Hancock not remembered as the fifth Australian to die during the Cowra Breakout? His name is not even recorded on the Roll of Honour at the Australian War Memorial in Canberra, which commemorates Australians killed in wars stretching back to the Sudan – even though Hardy, Jones, Shepherd and Doncaster are. It's certainly not because he was serving in the VDC instead of the regular army – 74 members of the VDC who died of illness or injury during the Second World War are listed on the Roll of Honour.

It seems that Tom Hancock has simply slipped through the cracks of history, overlooked both as part of the Cowra Breakout, and by the institutions tasked with making sure people like him are not forgotten. It's an inexcusable oversight, which hopefully will be remedied in time.

24

'MAXIMUM VALUE DIPLOMATICALLY': THE COVER-UP

From the earliest moments of the Breakout, the Australian military machine was concerned not just with what had happened at Cowra, but how much (or little) it was obliged to tell the wider world about it. Army HQ in Sydney first learned about the Breakout less than an hour after it began, when Colonel Brown issued a report via telephone at 2.40 a.m. 'P.W.Js broke out of "B" Compound at 0200 hrs,' he said. 'Exact numbers killed, wounded and missing not yet known. Position now in hand. In co-operation with Cowra Military Camp, local areas being patrolled to pick up any P.W.J. that has escaped.'[175] He was right about the situation being obscure – so obscure, in fact, that Brown's own report wasn't even correct. The military camp wasn't 'co-operating' with the round-up of prisoners – as already noted in the debacle that resulted in Harry Doncaster's death, the army camp wouldn't join the search until late the following day. It was also dangerously premature to claim that the position was now 'in hand'. Brown didn't even issue the order to cease unnecessary firing until 3.45 a.m., a good hour after he sent this report.

Unsurprisingly, Brown's report caused a flurry of activity at Army HQ, most of which was centred on two objectives: recapturing the prisoners as quickly as possible, and keeping news of the Breakout quiet. HQ's concerns at this early stage were understandable – until they had a better handle on exactly what was happening at the camp, it was imperative that they avoided a panic. It was clear that many people were already dead – God only knew what would happen if civilians started grabbing firearms and preparing do battle with the Japanese in the paddocks around Cowra. By 3 a.m. they had reached two conclusions: the local police would be kept updated about developments so they could assist in the round-up of prisoners, but there was to be a blanket ban on reporting of the Breakout in the press.

Most of the authorities who were aware of the Breakout agreed with this policy, but in some quarters it caused outrage. Lieutenant Colonel Sam Jackson, deputy director of security for New South Wales, was apoplectic. He argued, quite reasonably, that there were hundreds of potentially dangerous men roaming the countryside, and the citizens of Cowra had to be warned.

After several heated discussions, an unhappy compromise was reached: a report would be released announcing that prisoners had broken out of the camp, but it would not mention how many had escaped, how many had been killed or, most importantly, that the prisoners were Japanese. (It's clear that from the earliest moments army authorities and politicians were looking at the big picture – how and when to inform the Japanese government about the Breakout, and what potential implications this announcement would have for Australian prisoners in Japanese hands.)

In the early hours of Saturday morning, Army HQ issued a masterfully opaque statement to the news wires in time for inclusion in the morning bulletins:

> A number of prisoners of war escaped from an internment camp at Cowra at an early hour this morning. The district is being thoroughly patrolled by members of military and police forces. Individuals may attempt to secure assistance in evading capture. Any person approached for help should immediately inform military or police authorities.[176]

This brief statement did a good job alerting the people of Cowra to be on the lookout for escaped prisoners, but it also fired up media interest. Understandably, newspaper correspondents who had rushed to Cowra early on Saturday morning were anxious to report on the story, and the frosty reception they received from army authorities at the camp did nothing to dampen their enthusiasm. Senior army officials realised that the story was in danger of taking on a life of its own.

The most pressing concern was ensuring that the Japanese government didn't find out about the Breakout before the Australian authorities had a chance to cushion the blow. General Thomas Blamey, Commander-in-Chief of the Australian Military Forces, drafted a letter to the prime minister, John Curtin, stating that a Court of Inquiry to investigate the 'incident' should immediately be convened, and that its findings should form the basis for correspondence with the Japanese government.

No sooner had the decision been made than it was in danger of coming undone, when Sydney's *Daily Telegraph* ran a story in its Sunday morning edition that supplemented the brief statement issued by army officials with snippets of information gleaned from its correspondent in Cowra. 'WAR PRISONERS ESCAPE FROM CAMP,' screamed the headline, and it was followed by an article that covered most of the front page and gave the impression that prisoners (whose nationality wasn't revealed but were quite clearly Japanese) were roaming the countryside and terrorising the locals. ('Residents in homesteads and isolated districts have been warned to keep their children and womenfolk indoors at night,' a sub-heading breathlessly declared.)

The prime minister was furious, and asked his attorney-general whether the Commonwealth could take legal action against the newspaper for breaching censorship laws. In the end he settled for writing a sternly worded letter to the media imploring them to do better in future. Meanwhile, his office sent a flurry of cables to governments all over the world in an attempt to have the story hosed down before the Japanese government found out about it. In the end the Japanese got wind of the story but were suspicious that the whole thing was part of an inscrutable Allied propaganda ploy.

In an attempt to get ahead of the story, the army released another statement to the press on Sunday. An article in *The Argus* in Melbourne on Monday morning was typical of the coverage: 'An official Army spokesman announced tonight that all prisoners who escaped early on Saturday morning from the POW camp at Cowra had been accounted for. Military forces in the area have the situation completely in hand, and conditions in the area have been restored to normal, he said.'

This statement was so disingenuous as to border on fiction. On Sunday night up to 50 prisoners were still on the loose, and it was considered that these were potentially the most dangerous, as they were obviously the most determined of the escapees to avoid recapture.[177] The use of the term 'accounted for' was intended to be read as 'recaptured', a literary sleight-of-hand that may have calmed the nerves of anxious Australian Army authorities in Sydney, but caused real concern to the soldiers and police responsible for keeping the people of Cowra safe. The risk was considered so great that police constables were dispatched to households within a 50-kilometre radius of the camp to advise that the report was plain wrong, and that vigilance should be maintained. The local people of Cowra were so incensed at the army's obfuscation that the Shire Clerk wrote a letter of protest to the Minister for the Army (via his local Member of Parliament) the week following the Breakout, complaining about the army's 'deliberate misleading of the public', 'false reports' and 'laxity' in recapturing the prisoners. Included was a copy of an urgent telegram from local residents to the MP that had been sent on 11 August and read, 'Residents alarmed escaped Japanese POW from Cowra camp not yet recaptured seen in this vicinity. District rural work held up whilst women and children cannot be left alone. Please take immediate action to have efficient military search party organised. Awaiting reply.' Clearly the situation had hardly been 'restored to normal' if local farmers were still spotting prisoners roaming their properties six days after the Breakout. In spite of the army's assurances to the contrary, the last escapees were not recaptured until 14 August – nine days after the Breakout and a full week since the statement claiming they had all been 'accounted for'.

Given the perilous situation, it was imperative that a Court of Inquiry be convened as quickly as possible, and it was scheduled for Monday, 7 August, at a time when Japanese bodies were still being laid out at the camp.

In an outstanding essay about the Cowra Breakout, historian David Sissons (who had been a recruit at the Army Training

Camp during the Breakout and had joined the hunt for escapees) explains the rather convoluted reasons a Court of Inquiry was even held at Cowra.

In 1942 the British and German governments had agreed that an official inquiry would be held whenever a POW was killed or injured (this agreement would form the basis for the 1949 amendments to the Geneva Convention that spelled out rights for POWs). Several British servicemen had been killed in suspicious circumstances in German camps, and it was hoped that the extra scrutiny provided by a Court of Inquiry would encourage more prudent behaviour from guards in POW camps. Although Japan was not a party to the agreement, Allied powers hoped that the framework for the agreement would provide guidance to all nations who held prisoners during the Second World War and, by 1944, there were a lot of Allied prisoners in Japanese hands – more than 130 000 of them. So when Japanese prisoners were killed at Cowra, it was almost inevitable that a Court of Inquiry would be held to investigate.

The important question is of course *why* the Australian authorities thought it important to hold an official investigation. The answer is revealed plainly in a document circulated in Army HQ on 6 August, as plans for the Court of Inquiry were being put in place: 'Essential function of Court is to produce a report which will be of maximum value diplomatically and show that shooting was fully justified and that onus entirely on PW. Local administrative aspects should not be introduced on any account.'[178]

It doesn't get much more straightforward than that – before the court was even assembled, the required results had been spelled out. In order to dissuade the Japanese from retaliating against Australian POWs, the Court of Inquiry needed to lay the blame for the Breakout squarely at the feet of the Japanese prisoners and clear the Australians of wrongdoing.

Appointed as president of the court was Colonel Frederick Christison, a 53-year-old Scotsman who had emigrated to Australia as a young man and fought at Gallipoli in the 4th Light Horse, before being commissioned into the British Army. Sissons suggests that Christison was basically a yes-man who could be relied upon to deliver the verdict the army wanted. (In 1946 Christison would preside over a Court of Inquiry relating to the death of an Italian POW that was even more dubious than the one about to take place at Cowra.)

Whether that assessment is fair or not, there's no doubt that the Court of Inquiry was assembled in extreme haste and that Christison and the three other officers who presided over it were under no illusions as to the conclusions they were expected to reach. Even the timing put them under pressure – the court assembled at the camp on the morning of Monday, 7 August, while prisoners were still being rounded up and the smell of scorched wood, cordite and death still hung in the air. Nothing about the assembling of the court suggested that diligent judicial process was about to take place – the court had its orders and would facilitate them swiftly. They knew what was expected of them – everyone from the prime minister down was waiting anxiously for their findings so that the diplomatic pacification of the Japanese government could begin.

The members of the court spent Monday examining the site of the carnage, walking along Broadway, climbing up to the guard towers, inspecting the wire where the Japanese had broken out. On Monday evening they oversaw the burial of the first Japanese at Cowra Cemetery and then began formal proceedings on Tuesday in the YMCA hut at the camp. Over the next week they heard from 60 witnesses, including the camp commanders, soldiers who had been involved in the shooting and seven Japanese prisoners. The questioning was rudimentary, with no cross-examination, and little clarification requested. Most witnesses simply repeated the evidence they had given in their written statements.

On Tuesday, 15 August, the court wrapped up and the four officers decamped to Sydney to consider their findings. Exactly one week later, they delivered their conclusions to the government. Their findings presented a chronological account of the key moments of the Breakout, from the blowing of the bugle to the charge on the Vickers gun, from the attack on Broadway to the death of Harry Doncaster. They provided a grim statistical overview of the carnage: 231 Japanese had been killed (later increased to 234) and 108 were wounded; four Australians had died and another four had been wounded; 334 prisoners had been recaptured in the nine days following the Breakout, 25 of whom were dead. Crucially, the court assessed the number of rounds that had been fired by Australian guards (9141 rounds of .303, 2606 of 9 mm, 103 tracer rounds and 72 rounds of pistol ammunition) for a grand total of 11 922 fired rounds. Based on this maths and the evidence of witnesses that the firing was 'controlled', the court released its key finding:

> The firing was necessary. But for its use, the overwhelming numbers of escaping and escaped PW armed with lethal weapons would have been able quickly to overpower the guard, secure the Garrison's weapons and firearms and use them against the Garrison troops with considerable loss of life to military personnel and possibly the civilian population of the nearby town of Cowra … The firing was controlled and not excessive. Firing ceased at the earliest possible moment after control of the camp was assured.[179]

(The court seems to have placed considerable significance on the testimony of camp authorities such as Major Ramsay and Colonel Brown in its assessment that the amount of shooting was not excessive. It's difficult to see how either man was in a position to judge – they both spent the majority of the Breakout in their respective headquarters issuing orders, and did not witness the firing firsthand.)

The report went to great lengths to give the impression that Australian authorities had treated the Japanese with fairness and compassion, noting that the conditions in the camp prior to the Breakout were excellent (and the Japanese had never complained about them), wounded from the Breakout had been given immediate medical care, the dead had been buried with 'all due respect and reverence', and that Japanese prisoners had been invited to give evidence at the Court of Inquiry. The report also stated, 'In no case was an escaped PW fired on after recapture, nor is there any evidence of the illegitimate use of force during the recapture of escaped PW by the AMF patrols,' a statement that was questionable given the evidence the court had heard from several witnesses. The report also somewhat petulantly noted that the cost of damage to the camp had been estimated at £19 900.

The court found that the persons responsible for the Breakout were the camp leaders (including Kanazawa, Kojima and Toyoshima – the latter both deceased) and the Japanese prisoners who committed the violence. On the broader questions of the circumstances that led to the Breakout, the court was fairly noncommittal, expressing the view that the Japanese had been very well treated in the camp and had received adequate food, clothing, recreation facilities and the opportunity to communicate with their families back in Japan (a privilege that the Japanese never used). The court made the point that amenities provided to the Japanese prisoners were as good as those provided to the Australian guards, and often better. In short, the court concluded that the Japanese had had it pretty good at Cowra, and therefore had no valid reason to break out of the camp. (This conclusion, while superficially true, completely overlooked the true motivations for the Breakout – the desire of the prisoners to erase the shame of capture with violence. The court didn't reach this conclusion for the simple reason that it never considered it.)

The court briefly mentioned the impending move to Hay as a catalyst for the Breakout, but this reference was later removed from the report issued to the Japanese government. The court also stated that the uprising had been premeditated. Overall the findings had an air of self-justification, which is unsurprising when considering the terms under which the court had been assembled. The Australian military and government wanted a favourable result, and the court delivered.

Despite the court's dubious processes, there was little to argue with in its findings. At the end of the day it was correct: the Cowra Breakout was precipitated by the Japanese prisoners who planned and carried it out. The responsibility for the huge death toll lay with the men who launched the attack.

But it was the questions the court *didn't* ask, the aspects of the Breakout it *didn't* investigate, that represented its greatest failing. Not only did the court not draw any meaningful conclusions about steps that could have been taken to prevent the Breakout from occurring in the first place, it didn't even ask any questions about them. These were the 'administrative aspects' that the court had been directed to ignore, and it followed its instructions dutifully.

And there were many questions that should have been asked: Had adequate steps been taken to reduce overcrowding in the camp? Did the garrison have enough men to manage the large number of prisoners? Were the defences requested by Brown in June adequate? Were the perimeter fences effective? Were the machine-guns correctly sited? Did Army HQ follow up with Brown to ensure he had everything he needed? Why were the machine-guns not manned around the clock? Why did they not have supporting riflemen in place? Why were the prisoners given three days notice of the transfer to Hay? Why did the guards not notice the increase in activity in the camp in the hours leading up to the Breakout? How did the Japanese manage to assemble such a large arsenal of weapons, particularly knives and baseball bats? Why were more thorough searches of the camp not carried out? Why was F Tower only manned by one guard, who was armed so ineffectively? Why did it take most of the day for the Army Training Camp to provide search parties? Why were those search parties sent out with only bayonets? Why was Doncaster not armed at all? Why were some Japanese escapees shot on sight? Who shot or clubbed a prisoner to death in the field beyond the camp?

These questions needed to be investigated if the court had any chance of presenting fair and comprehensive findings. But for the time being, the prime minister and Army HQ had everything they needed to begin the delicate process of informing the Japanese of the disaster.

This was a complicated ballet, and there was considerable debate in the halls of Canberra about how best to accomplish it. Matters relating to prisoners of war would be passed on to the Japanese government by the neutral Swiss, known as the 'Protecting Power'. The timing was critical – Australian authorities were keen to demonstrate that they had nothing to hide by giving the Japanese time to examine the report on the Breakout, but not so much time that the Japanese could release a statement before the Australian government had the chance to. A memo labelled 'Top Secret' was distributed from the Prime Minister's Office to the Department of External Affairs (the department that was responsible for communicating with the Swiss) on 30 August. It spelled out in detail the intricacies of the timing of the release of the report to the Japanese, and gave advice on what information should be included and omitted. Crucially, it suggested that references to the separation of NCOs from other ranks at Cowra should be removed from the report, for the eminently sensible reason that 'it is not desired to cause the Japanese at this stage of the war to become unduly conscious of the fact that they have Allied and Australian officers, NCOs and men mixed together in some camps, which state of affairs is greatly to the advantage of the other ranks'.[180]

In addition, Australia's allies also had to be informed about the situation, particularly the USA, since it had been established that 118 of the dead had been captured by American forces and were being held in Cowra on behalf of the US government, a fact that had already been reported to General Douglas MacArthur, commander of US forces in the Pacific.[181]

On 2 September, after drafts and edits had been circulated in Canberra and run by the governments of Britain and the US, the report was submitted to the Swiss, with a request that it be passed on to the Japanese government. One week later, as soon as confirmation was received that the report had been passed on to Tokyo, Australian Prime Minister John Curtin released his official statement to the world. It was slightly sensationalist, but overall neatly summarised the findings of the court. It finished by reiterating the facts as the Australians saw them, that conditions at the camp were excellent, and that if the Japanese had a problem with them they should have spoken up. They had no reason to attack the guards, and the blame for the riot lay solely with the Japanese. In addition, the Australian guards had acted with restraint and, thankfully, their casualties had been light.

Given the scale of the casualties and the inherent drama in the whole episode, the story was embraced with relish by the world's press. From New York to London newspapers ran bold headlines and exuberant articles detailing the pitched battle between the fanatical Japanese and the courageous Australian guards. The country that responded most strenuously was, of course, Japan. The day after Curtin's statement, the Japanese issued a response that didn't mince words. 'WHAT IS THE TRUE STORY OF THIS AUSTRALIAN PRISON CAMP MURDER?' the headline screamed.

The document is a fascinating combination of feigned indignation, propaganda and convoluted logic:

Bursting with indignation at the cold-blooded murder of Japanese civilian internees, the Nippon people demand to know the true story of the midnight murder of more than 200 innocent Japanese, which Prime Minister Curtin belatedly reported more than a month after the incident occurred. It is perfectly clear to the Japanese people that these unfortunate Japanese who were murdered in the prison camp cannot have been prisoners of war, as John Curtin dishonestly claimed; they were internees, for it is a well known and accepted fact that the Japanese soldier never permits himself to be taken prisoner. His military creed is that death by his own hand is preferable to the dishonour and humiliation of capture by the enemy. Curtin may not care to admit it but the fact is perfectly obvious that the unfortunate victims of the midnight mass murder were internees, who had lived in Australia for long years before the war. They had become more or less accustomed to the Australian way of living and had a lot in common with Australians, probably they had Australian (friends) and girl friends.[182]

In spite of the outrage expressed in the statement and demands for further investigations, Australian authorities were relatively pleased with the Japanese response. The Japanese were offering them a get-out-of-jail-free card; by stating categorically that the victims could not have been prisoners of war, it was immediately clear that the Japanese would have no desire for the matter to receive undue coverage. And this was in fact exactly what happened – after this initial statement, the Breakout received little coverage in Japan. Japanese authorities well knew that the men held at Cowra were prisoners of war, but they were determined to avoid the embarrassment that would come with admitting that thousands of Japanese soldiers had ignored their 'military creed' and had allowed themselves to be captured. The risk of undermining the strict obedience to the Field Service Code that pervaded the entire Japanese military establishment was simply too great for the sake of a short-term propaganda win. As a result, the Japanese were as eager to sweep the whole affair under the rug as the Australians were, and the story of the Cowra Breakout quickly and quietly fizzled.

Even the novel Japanese strategy of declaring that the victims of the Cowra Breakout must have been civilian internees was soon abandoned. 'As far as is known,' an Australian intelligence report summarised, 'this too was broadcast only once, and apparently even this ingenious approach was considered unconvincing and too dangerous for repetition.'[183] In spite of Australian fears, there is no evidence that the Japanese retaliated against the Allied POWs held in their camps.

If the Australian government hoped that the Court of Inquiry was the only scrutiny the Cowra Breakout would attract, they were disappointed. Army commanders accepted that three members of the garrison had been killed while resisting the uprising, but they were deeply concerned that an unarmed officer had been bludgeoned to death while leading a search party. Army commanders called for an inquiry, and in mid-August a second military panel came together to investigate the circumstances of Harry Doncaster's death. Their findings make for interesting reading. Without the time constraints and political pressure the previous court had been subjected to, this new court was free to more thoroughly investigate Doncaster's death, and it didn't hold back. It called for more witnesses and probed the timing and reasoning for key decisions. In the end the court didn't formally censure any members of the military but it was extremely critical of many of the people involved, particularly Colonel Mitchell.

The court was particularly scathing about Mitchell's decisions regarding the rounding-up of prisoners. Under intense questioning, it became clear that Mitchell's sole focus had been the protection of his camp:

> The information given me … was that the Japanese had some intention to break out, circle round here and obtain arms and ammunition after having taken the camp and to do their mischief. It was therefore my first primary duty to protect this camp and to do that certain measures were taken.[184]

This was a perfectly reasonable position, given the information he had received, but he could not give a satisfactory explanation for his failure to plan for the round-up of prisoners.

During the conference with his battalion commanders on 9 June, the subject was briefly raised, but Mitchell's instructions caused consternation among his officers. It was at this time that he came up with the odd, and potentially deadly, order that if any troops from the training camp were called on to help recapture escapees, the men should only carry bayonets, and the officers leading them should carry no weapons at all. When grilled on the matter during the Court of Inquiry, Mitchell gave a rambling and tetchy response:

> [The Japanese] have got very many thousands of our troops over there prisoners of war and we have reason to believe in dealing with these very peculiar people that most severe reprisals would be inflicted on our prisoners when they learnt as they undoubtably would that numbers of their people have been killed in escaping ... Having regard to the facts that I have already told you and believing that if I, in my search for those added one more to the big number lying on the wire and over the fields, if I added one more to them I would probably be killing directly on the other side of the world perhaps up to ten of my own comrades in arms.[185]

Needless to say, this is a pretty big stretch. It's astounding that a mid-level officer of a recruit training camp in a sleepy Australian town would consider international diplomacy a more important consideration in a crisis than the personal safety of his own men. To quantify this opinion with raw numbers ('I would probably be killing ... up to ten of my own comrades') was bizarre, and obviously well outside Mitchell's abilities to accurately judge. Unsurprisingly, his response didn't go over well with the court.

Obviously not a man to quit while he's behind, Mitchell continued, apparently determining that the best form of defence was offence:

> I gave those orders, I alone am responsible for those orders and no one else and I can assure you in giving them I had completely thought out the whole situation. I gave them then and I would give them again if I were similarly situated and my instructions were actuated by the highest humanitarian motives of an extremely important international character. And if you understand that you will understand then everything I am trying to tell you … I particularly want what I have said to go down and I tell you it has already gone down in the big military Court that is going to Canberra.

Under further examination, Mitchell revealed that he had a second, and potentially more defensible, reason for not arming the patrols – he was concerned that if his troops carried rifles, they were so inexperienced that they would injure each other, or even civilians in the area (although the words he chose to explain this decision were decidedly odd): 'If you start firing bullets over this country the civilians get annoyed. I still can't trust these young fellows to fire bullets about. If the civilians get hit they start to get annoyed.'

This explanation was not only strange, it was simply wrong. The army camp wasn't just made up of raw recruits – of the camp's five battalions, three were comprised of recruits, but two were infantry training battalions, consisting of men who had completed significantly more training than their newly enlisted comrades. When pressed during the Court of Inquiry, Captain Frank Morris (who had organised the search parties on the evening of the breakout) went to great pains to clarify the matter, even returning to the witness stand to add additional details to his earlier statement. During this testimony he said, 'In view of those actual figures available on the 5th August as having completed all preliminary training in the D.P.4 syllabus [an army training standard that involved extensive training with firearms] the figures are 56 officers, 356 W.O.'s [warrant officers] and N.C.O.'s [non-commissioned officers] and 1159 O.R.'s [other ranks]'.[186] In spite of Mitchell's assertion that the men under his command were not capable of 'firing a bow and arrow',[187] in reality he had more than 1500 men in the camp who had been trained in the use of a rifle. This was reflected in the men selected for the search mission: 344 were drawn from the 14th Training Battalion, 109 came from the 19th Training Battalion and only 150 came from the 1st Recruit Training Battalion. These men were the best-trained soldiers in the camp, which was precisely why they had been selected. It should also be noted that the Australians of 1944 were much more proficient with firearms than those of today. Rifle shooting was a popular recreational activity, thanks to the ready availability of cheap firearms and ammunition, the high rate of service in cadet units and local militias, and the large number of returned servicemen from the First World War who had never lost the urge to shoot. Even on their first day of enlistment, a significant number of the recruits at Cowra would have been well versed in the safe handling of firearms. 'Most of us came from the country,' one recruit later said, 'and we could probably use rifles better than the officers.'[188] Given this, Mitchell's refusal to arm his men has never adequately been explained, and borders on gross negligence.

Mitchell's defensive and inadequate responses didn't paint him in a good light, and the court was highly critical of his actions in its findings. The Cowra Breakout effectively ended his career – he was swiftly removed as commander of the Army Training Camp and never held a command role again.

Just as the court was releasing these findings, yet another inquiry was being proposed. Australian law required that a coronial inquest be held in the event of the death of a prisoner of war and the New South Wales premier, Bill McKell, was determined an inquest be held as soon as possible. Throughout September and October he harangued the Prime Minister's Office in cables and telegrams, politely but forcefully reminding Curtin of his obligations under the National Security Regulations.

Finally, Curtin and the army relented, and an inquest was scheduled for 31 October, provided the coroner was advised to limit the scope of the inquiry to 'the bare essentials'.

In sittings held at the Cowra courthouse over six days in October, November and December, coroner Fred Arnold expanded on the work done by the military Courts of Inquiry to examine the reasons for the deaths of the Japanese prisoners and Australian soldiers. Arnold ruled that Hardy, Jones, Shepherd and Doncaster had died from 'the effects of injuries received in the execution of duty as members of the Australian Military Forces, feloniously and maliciously inflicted upon on the said date by some person or persons unknown to me, such persons being escaped Japanese prisoners of war'.[189]

He declared that the Japanese prisoners had died in a range of ways (including being shot, stabbed, run over by a train or by suicide) but that the wounds were 'lawfully inflicted by members of the Australian Military Forces … whilst unlawfully attempting to escape from such prisoner of war camp'.

The scope of the inquiry did not include detailed examination of why the Breakout occurred, and Arnold only briefly touched upon possible causes in his findings. He was, however, outspoken in his criticisms of the events that led to the death of Harry Doncaster:

I would refer particularly to the death of Lieutenant Doncaster. It is very much regretted, as from the evidence it appears that he was sent out to assist in capturing escaped prisoners of war and that he was unarmed and had no weapon of defence; that his death was a tragedy that should never had occurred, as at that time it must have been well known that those prisoners were desperate men.

On the subject of the conduct of the camp commanders, Arnold had high praise, particularly for Colonel Brown, who he said 'carefully handled a very difficult situation which may have been much worse but for his tact and firmness and that no blame whatever for the occurrence could be attributed to him or to his officers'. Given the complacency, oversights and foolish decisions that defined Brown's command in the days and weeks leading to the Breakout, this assessment from Arnold is difficult to reconcile.

The final, and most bizarre, chapter of this investigative phase of the saga took place in January 1945. Sergeant Major Kanazawa, the former camp leader, went on trial for murder. During the Breakout Kanazawa had spent a cold and aimless night heading vaguely north from the camp. Once he was through the wire he couldn't really contribute much, and he regretted having left the camp. His old war wounds ached and he couldn't keep up with the men around him. Eventually he just sat down and waited for the Australians to round him up, which they did, along with several other prisoners, late on Saturday afternoon.

On arrival back at the camp, Ramsay was waiting for him. 'I am to blame for the whole thing,' Kanazawa told him. 'I must be executed.' Instead, he was separated from the other prisoners and sent to the detention barracks, where a group of five officers and some enlisted men had been held since before the Breakout.

It was clear the Australians were seeking someone to blame for the incident, and Kanazawa, as camp leader (and the only member of the original cadre still alive), was the obvious target. Intelligence officers informed him that he would be required to make a written statement and appear before a military court to explain his actions. The night before he was due to give his statement, guards inspecting his cell found a long note, written on both sides of a metre-long strip of toilet paper, with instructions for Kanazawa from the officer group.

The note was effectively a primer for Kanazawa on the message the officers wished him to convey in any court appearance. It urged him to speak with 'caution and confidence' and to stick to a few key points about the Breakout. Much of it was convoluted, but the key instruction was that Kanazawa was to emphasise that the Breakout was spontaneous – a direct response to the announcement that NCOs would be separated from the enlisted men. Under no circumstances was he to suggest that the Breakout was a preconceived plan.

As Australian intelligence officers noted, this was a vitally important point. 'It is interesting to note,' Captain Kane observed, 'the insistence of the Japanese officers in priming Kanazawa to maintain that the escape was not preconceived, but spontaneous. If it had not been preconceived, it is difficult to understand the necessity for the officers to beg the question.'[190]

(The question of whether the Cowra Breakout was premeditated or spontaneous is an interesting one, and has been the subject of intense debate since the war. Warrant Officer Lionel Boorman, on the camp's intelligence staff, went to great lengths to state that the Breakout was not premeditated, drawing the sensible conclusions that the weapons used by the Japanese were simply what they had on hand in the compound, and that even the stacking of firewood under the huts was routinely carried out to keep it dry, and was simply a convenient fuel source when the decision to burn the huts was made. In spite of this, it's incorrect to conclude that the Breakout was completely spontaneous and that the blame should be placed solely with the Australian decision to move the prisoners to Hay. Takao Matsumoto's intelligence from several months earlier revealed that the Japanese had long been planning an uprising – this was the spark that prompted the transfer to Hay in the first place.)

Kanazawa gave a written statement and then verbal evidence at the Court of Inquiry, along with several other Japanese. On 24 January 1945, he went on trial for the murder of Ben Hardy. The case was a curious one, and there was much thrust and parry between the prosecution and defence as to whether the murder charge was even legal. (It's interesting to compare the zeal with which the legal arguments were pursued compared to the original Court of Inquiry held five months earlier – at one stage the cross-examination of a medical officer bogged down on the question of whether Hardy had even been murdered. The examiner suggested his injuries could have been caused by him being crushed by the machine-gun trailer.) The position of the prosecution was that, although Kanazawa hadn't killed Hardy with his own hands, he had actively participated in an unlawful act that resulted in Hardy's death, and therefore was guilty of murder. Kanazawa also faced a second charge, 'conduct prejudicial to good order and discipline among prisoners of war'. A second Japanese prisoner, Sergeant Major Hiroshi Yoshida, faced the same charges.

The murder trial basically swirled around one key legal concept: could a man who acted as part of a group of over 1000 people be held responsible for the actions of anyone else in that group? During the trial a couple of interesting points were raised. Firstly, Kanazawa stated categorically that the prisoners were not at all dissatisfied with the treatment they received from the Australians, and the Breakout was due entirely to the decision to separate the men from the NCOs. This statement effectively nullified the conclusions of the Court of Inquiry, and demonstrated just how far short that inquiry had fallen in getting to the bottom of the reasons for the Breakout. Secondly, Kanazawa mentioned in passing that, after the camp leaders' meeting on 4 August, he had informed Ramsay that the response from the group was that the separation of NCOs and men could not be allowed to happen and that the Japanese prisoners had elected to die. There is no mention of this important element in the evidence of the Court of Inquiry (although Moriki hints at the same thing in his memoirs – he says that after the camp leaders meeting the men in his hut were told 'the Camp leader is having a final discussion [with the Australians] about it now'). Even though both references to Ramsay being informed of the decision to break out are fleeting, they are vitally important – if it's true that Ramsay was informed, even peripherally, that a mass suicide was on the cards, his decision to do nothing about it is unforgivable.

After hours of legal argument and counter-argument, the court delivered its verdict: there was no legal basis to convict Kanazawa of a murder he hadn't actively participated in. On the first charge, Kanazawa was not guilty. On the second (conduct prejudicial to good order), however, the prosecution had a much more straightforward case. Kanazawa's own evidence in the Court of Inquiry and murder trial was damning. He had admitted that he was a key organiser of the Breakout, and that a demonstration of violence was a principal component of the plan. Kanazawa was found guilty. Fortunately for Yoshida, when giving evidence Kanazawa had been fairly dismissive of Yoshida's role in the plan, and couldn't recall if Yoshida was even in favour of breaking out. Yoshida was acquitted of both the murder and conduct-prejudicial charges.

To Kanazawa's disappointment, he did not receive the death sentence he was hoping for. Instead, he was given 18 months hard labour. The 'hard labour' component of the sentence was purely symbolic, but Kanazawa was transferred to Hay camp and detained in the detention barracks, separated from the other prisoners, until he was sent back to Japan in March 1946. In total he had been in solitary confinement since he returned to the Cowra camp the day after the Breakout – a total of 14 months. The physical burdens of hard labour might have been absent, but the psychological aspects were certainly there.

All in all, two military courts, one coronial inquiry and a murder trial had all given their opinions about why the Cowra Breakout occurred and who was to blame for it. Not only did none of them come close to finding the truth, their conclusions were not even made public. Filed away under the guise of national security, the findings from all four hearings were not released until researchers revealed them in the 1960s. It took more than 20 years to discover that there were still more questions than answers about the Cowra Breakout.

25

'YOU'RE A GHOST!':
AFTERWARDS

For three weeks the more than 800 Japanese survivors of the Cowra Breakout made the best of their extremely compromised living quarters in the remains of B Compound. Temporary accommodation was provided in the buildings that hadn't been torched, and tents were brought in to house the overflow, an unappealing predicament in the dead of a Cowra winter.

The Australian authorities were extremely edgy, and with good reason. The prisoners had demonstrated they were capable of just about anything, and a repeat of the Breakout at the earliest opportunity seemed a likely scenario. Rumours spread among the guards and townsfolk that another uprising was due any day, and a note found on a wounded prisoner being treated in the camp hospital exhorting his comrades to rise up again did nothing to dampen the speculation.

By and large, however, the fight was completely gone from the prisoners, and the evidence suggests that any discussion of launching a follow-up to the Breakout was isolated and not widely embraced by the majority of prisoners. This was partly due to the demographic restructuring of the camp that the Breakout had caused. Many of the hardliners who had lobbied for death had met that fate – the survivors naturally comprised a large number of men who had either gone along with the Breakout reluctantly or had not had the courage to meet an honourable death once the shooting had started. With the deaths of so many hardliners, the balance of power in the camp swung sharply towards more moderate voices. While the shame of capture had not been erased, many of the survivors felt lucky to be alive, having survived the perils of the battlefield and then the carnage of the Breakout. The Breakout had been an ordeal that most men were happy to leave in the past. There is also the fact that most of the prisoners were simply exhausted, and a lethargy descended on the prison population. One prisoner described the survivors as being 'as docile as a flock of sheep'.[191]

In this unusual atmosphere a strange irony now unfolded. The compound had been overcrowded when its buildings were intact. Now that most of them were in ruins there was no choice but to move the prisoners to a more permanent facility, and there was only one place that could possibly be used – the POW camp at Hay. The relocation of prisoners to Hay, the very situation that the Cowra Breakout had been launched to prevent, was now inevitable. On 30 August, the dejected prisoners in Cowra – NCOs and enlisted men together – boarded trucks for the long drive west to Hay (Japanese officers would remain in their compound at Cowra until February 1945, when they were transferred to Murchison camp in Victoria). They looked back with mixed emotions as the ruins of the camp, the scene of so much angst and bloodshed, disappeared from view. For most it was the last time they would see it.

As the convoy passed through small towns and villages, curious locals lined the streets. These were the first (and only) Japanese that most of them would see with their own eyes during the war, and the fact that these men were the instigators of the Breakout that they had heard so much about made the allure irresistible. At one point the breeze caught a Japanese prisoner's cap, which flew off his head and tumbled onto the roadside, where it was picked up by a local couple, Normand and Hazel Preston. They had obviously been well conditioned by propaganda which spoke of the uncleanliness of the Japanese, and they cautiously picked up the cap with a stick and then boiled it mercilessly in their kitchen copper to rid it of 'Jap germs', bleaching it from its original burgundy to an ugly grey-white. Today the cap is displayed in the Cowra Visitors Centre, one of the few original relics remaining from the Breakout.

Life for the prisoners is Hay was in many ways even more surreal than it had been in Cowra. The Cowra cadre was joined in Hay by a new batch of prisoners taken in New Guinea and the Solomons, but the two groups were separated, and the former Cowra inmates were watched with steely suspicion by the guard unit. 'A few pairs of guards with automatic machine-guns patrolled the barricaded area constantly, watching every movement of the Japanese POWs,' recalled Masaru Moriki. 'Under that guard, we, Cowra survivors, spent hopeless and gloomy days as "the worst Japanese POWs" with ruined spirits.'[192]

Over time the prisoners recreated the comforts they had established in Cowra, including vegetable gardens and a baseball field. They reformed the theatre company, in spite of the absence of several of its most important cast and crew, who had died at Cowra. Leading Seaman Ichijiro Do was elected camp leader and, although ideological clashes between hardliners and moderates continued, the hardliners were now firmly in the minority. After a request from the Red Cross, the more dexterous prisoners even participated in a program to build wooden toys for disadvantaged Australian children.

In response to Japanese outrage about the Breakout, the Swiss government commissioned Do and Moriki to compile a report from the Japanese perspective, apparently without informing Australian authorities about it. No copy of the report survives, but in his memoirs Moriki gives a concise summary, stating that he and Do explained the Japanese military code and its insistence that capture was an 'unforgivable sin', and that the goal of the Breakout was for as many men to die as possible. From that perspective the uprising was a failure. 'We said that however small in number, killing of Australian soldiers and burning down the buildings were regrettable,' Moriki recalled. 'However, we were proud of the fact that the escapees did not hurt any civilians and thanked the Australian Government for the perfectly fair treatment given to us.'[193] Crucially, the report stated categorically that the Breakout was not premeditated, but 'suddenly erupted after hearing of the planned move' to Hay, thereby completely undermining the results of the Court of Inquiry. It's unclear whether the Swiss passed the report on to the Japanese, but even if they did it seems to have elicited no official response.

A new air of detached resignation seems to have descended over the Cowra prisoners in Hay. As 1944 rolled into 1945, and new prisoners from one Japanese defeat after another continued to pour in, even the most loyal supporter of the Japanese cause found it impossible to conclude that the war would end with anything other than defeat. Strangely, this seemed to induce a calm in the prisoner population. 'Our feelings were complicated,' said Moriki. 'We had already experienced the Japanese force's retreat first hand at the end of 1942 in east New Guinea. For two years after that Japan continued retreat after retreat.'[194]

Finally, after hearing news of the devastation caused by the atomic bombings of Hiroshima and Nagasaki (events that were met with horror by the prisoners – many of their ranks hailed from those two cities), the camp leaders were ushered into the administration office one August morning. Moriki remembered the group gathering uneasily around Do as he addressed them solemnly:

'Everyone, the war has ended. Japan has surrendered to the allied forces unconditionally.' He said it in one breath and then tears rolled down his cheeks. Seeing that, we too covered our eyes and sobbed … The camp leader and staff stood in silence for a while with their heads lowered.[195]

Although not unexpected, the news was greeted with profound sadness by the prisoners. They had not even contemplated their place in a post-war Japan, and the end of the war forced each man into deep reflection. Theatrical events were cancelled and a collective mourning enveloped the camp. Even the arrival of peace was not enough to unshackle the prisoners from the unforgiving military dogma that had shaped their lives for so long:

We POWs had especially mixed feelings about the ending of the war. There must have been some of us who believed Japan would win right till the last moment but amongst the POWs who knew the current battle front situation there were some who predicted Japan's loss. Even those people thought, 'Because Japan will fight until every last solider is killed, Japan's loss will mean the disappearance of Japan as a nation. Most likely she will become a territory of the allied nations. Even if we went home to such a place we will be put to hard labour as slaves for the rest of our lives. Whatever we decide, POWs have no place to go. As long as we are POWs, it makes no difference to us whether [Japan] wins or loses.'[196]

The prisoners would have many months to reconcile their feelings. Repatriating POWs was a low priority in the grand machinations required to dismantle a world war, and it was not until March 1946 that shipping was made available to return the prisoners to Japan. During the month-long sea voyage the former POWs were understandably apprehensive – their families had been informed years earlier that they had died on the battlefield, and the news had not yet reached them that their sons and husbands were in fact alive and well, and soon to be reunited with them. A common topic of conversation was what each former prisoner would confess about his long absence – many elected to simply say they had come straight from the battlefields of New Guinea, despite the fact that most families in Japan were aware that the bulk of the fighting had ended there two years earlier. Moriki decided he had nothing to hide and would tell the truth about having been captured, but he lost his nerve at the first hurdle – when an old man greeted him at the port in Japan, he told him he had come direct from the battlefield.

The ship carrying the former prisoners, and their burden of shame, arrived in Japan in springtime. The cherry blossoms were flowering across a landscape that was torn and burned from years of relentless bombing raids. The prisoners said their final farewells and disbanded, beginning the long and intensely personal journey that would bring them to their hometowns and the families who long thought they were dead. For most there was uncertainty – they had never expected this moment to come, and were concerned that their families would reject them when they discovered the truth.

Marekuni Takahara, the flying boat tail gunner who had become Ichiro Takata after his capture, was greeted by his father with shock. 'You're a ghost!' he repeated several times – it took more than 30 minutes before he could be convinced his son was real.[197]

Moriki had telegraphed his family of his impending return when he had first arrived back in Japan. When he reached the station near his hometown of Ino several days later, there was no one there to greet him. Suddenly a neighbour appeared, pedalling furiously on a bicycle, and hugged him in disbelief. 'We had been told you were killed in action four years ago,' the neighbour said. 'This is like a dream!'[198]

Moriki's family were understandably shocked to see him, but they greeted him warmly, with no trace of the disgrace he had feared. His brother now had a wife, and Moriki didn't recognise his young sisters, who he had last seen as schoolgirls more than six years earlier. His elderly grandfather and parents were delighted to see him, and listened with interest and compassion as Moriki described the brutality of the battlefield, his life of captivity and the horror of the bloodshed at Cowra. A few days after returning home, he went for a long walk in the countryside and found himself at the local cemetery, where he had the unique and disquieting experience of standing in front of his own headstone. 'Grave of late Army Sergeant Masaru Moriki,' it read. 'Killed in action on the 11th of November 1942 at Bariibe, East New Guinea.' Moriki looked solemnly at the 20 or 30 new grave posts that dotted the cemetery. 'Many childhood friends had become grave posts,' he said. 'It was beyond tragedy.'[199] He thought of the comrades he had lost in New Guinea, and the eyes of dying men in their final moments. 'It was as if those eyes no longer felt any pain nor sadness.' Moriki thought sadly of the friends he had lost in Cowra, who had survived the horrors of jungle fighting only to perish on the wire or beneath the noose at the prison camp. It all seemed so unreal, so unnecessary. He stayed for a long time, until the sun was low in the sky. And then he turned, and began the long walk home.

26

'PRAYED FROM AFAR': REMEMBERING

By the late 1940s the people of Cowra had mostly moved on from the Second World War. The POW camp was gone, and with it that strange era when exotic men from Europe and Asia had briefly called Cowra home. Former soldiers from the district had returned from the war and gotten on with their lives, building careers and families; some harboured animosity towards their former enemies, but most were content to look forward, not back.

At the local cemetery, the small plot of Australian war graves (comprising the bodies of Hardy, Jones, Shepherd and Doncaster, plus 23 other servicemen who were killed in accidents or died of illness at the Army Training Camp) reflected the ambivalence felt by the community to the war. Officially it fell to the council to maintain it, but the task had mostly been taken on by the members of the local branch of the Returned Services League, who naturally saw it as their duty to maintain the resting place of comrades who had died in the war. Working parties regularly attended the cemetery to weed and prune; in 1948 they planted trees – gums, kurrajongs, wattles, pines and oleanders – and kept them healthy with water they carted in on trucks.[200] The adjacent Japanese plot was another story. More through a lack of adequate planning and accountability than a deliberate act of neglect, it had fallen into serious disrepair. 'The Australian graves didn't look too bad but the rest of the precinct was a disgrace,' recalled Alf Cowley, a future president of the Cowra RSL.

> The Japanese had a lot of four-by-two hardwood stakes driven in all over the ground. They had names on them. The thistles were about six or eight feet high and there were probably a few rabbit warrens around. I think probably that ex-servicemen didn't think it was good enough. A lot of us had seen war graves in the First World War run by the War Graves Commission which always, to my knowledge, have been excellent and the RSL I think had the general feeling that something should be done about the graves in Cowra.[201]

There wasn't any higher purpose to the decision – the blokes in the RSL just thought it was the right thing to do. This was remarkable given the strained relationship between Australia and Japan in the post-war years, and the general animosity felt towards the Japanese. This only increased with revelations of the atrocities committed against Allied servicemen, particularly prisoners, and the war trials that followed.

In spite of this, Keith Telfer, another RSL man, didn't detect much animosity directed towards the Japanese buried in Cowra. 'There was very little opposition [to the suggestion that Japanese graves should be maintained],' he said. 'It was mainly people who had had no service in any of the Army units that were against it because they had a hatred of the Japanese. But there were very, very few people like that.'[202]

The members of the Cowra RSL began a program to improve the Japanese plot, and to maintain it to the same standard as the Australian graves. It's important to recognise what a significant and compassionate decision this was – the men of the RSL were returned veterans, many of whom were well experienced with Japanese barbarity on the battlefield and in Asian prison camps. They were under no obligation to tend to the graves of their former enemies, particularly those who had died in an act that most Australians at the time considered the definition of Japanese fanatical insanity.

In short order the weeds were removed, rabbit holes filled in and headstones straightened. The Cowra Japanese cemetery received few visitors, but at least it now looked like a dignified last resting place.

In 1952 the Allied occupation force withdrew from Japan and diplomatic relations were re-established with Australia. A Japanese embassy opened in Canberra, and in 1955 a diplomatic envoy visited the Cowra cemetery to pay their respects to both their countrymen and the Australian war dead. Soon after, the Japanese ambassador, Tadakatsu Suzuki, visited the town and was hosted by Telfer as president of the RSL. This visit, and subsequent diplomatic visits from the Japanese embassy, did much to strengthen relationships between Japan and Cowra, but the cordial relations were felt only at the local level. Japan as a nation refused to acknowledge the presence of Japanese war dead in Cowra, an extension of the wartime policy which deemed men to be persona non grata once they had been taken prisoner.[203]

Suzuki was a deeply sensitive man and he was greatly moved by the dignity with which the people of Cowra had cared for his fallen countrymen. He began gently lobbying his government for a more formal recognition of the Japanese graves at Cowra. At about the same time, the Japanese government rejected a proposal from other officials in Australia that the bodies in Cowra should be returned to Japan, in line with the policy to repatriate Japanese remains en masse from battlefields and cemeteries across Asia and the Pacific. However, the Japanese government's obstinate refusal to acknowledge the existence of the graves of Japanese POWs in Cowra was about to have unintended, and far-reaching, consequences. Suzuki and his staff now determined that, if the Japanese bodies were to remain in Cowra, funds should be sourced to upgrade and maintain the cemetery. Thus emboldened, Suzuki put forward the extraordinary suggestion to his government that all Japanese nationals who had died during the war and were buried on Australian soil should be brought together in Cowra.

It would take several years for his vision to be realised, but, in 1962, after extensive negotiations, Australia and Japan agreed that a formal Japanese war cemetery would be established in Cowra, and that all 524 Japanese war dead in Australia – civilians who died as internees, airmen shot down in raids on northern Australia and, significantly, prisoners who had died in captivity – would be interred there. In a unique arrangement, funds were sourced from Japan for the cemetery's construction, but the cemetery would be maintained by the Australian Commonwealth War Graves Commission (now the Office of Australian War Graves) to the same standard as Australian military cemeteries. The entrance and ceremonial space at the cemetery were designed by Shigeru Yura, a Japanese architect who taught at the University of Melbourne. The Cowra Japanese War Cemetery was officially opened on 22 November 1964, with the guests of honour including the

Japanese ambassador, Saburo Ohta, and the director of the War Graves Commission, Brigadier Athol Brown, the man who had overseen the identification and interment of Japanese bodies after the Cowra Breakout 20 years earlier. It was (and still is) the only Japanese war cemetery outside Japan.

The other guests at the official opening were all diplomats and dignitaries; no families of the dead men attended. This was mostly due to secrecy – neither Japan nor Australia wanted to trumpet loudly to the world what had happened at Cowra. But shame also played a part. The families of the men who died at Cowra were still not reconciled to their sons' and husbands' fates; they didn't know whether to be proud or ashamed. And, of course, because these men were killed in the Breakout there had been no tearful reunions for their families, no years of contemplative conversation to learn that life as a POW was not as disgraceful as they had been led to believe. For the families of the dead, the concept of captivity was purely philosophical, and for many it would take years to find comfort and peace.

For most families attending the service was not an option, as they weren't told it was happening. Japanese authorities had made a half-hearted attempt to contact the families of the dead POWs in the post-war years to inform them of their relatives' fate, but soon abandoned the effort after being told by several families that 'it would have been better for them to have died in New Guinea'.[204] This memory apparently stuck with Japanese officials, and they made no effort to invite families of the dead POWs to the cemetery opening.

Mrs Tomoi Yonehara, whose husband, Tadashi, had died in the Breakout, wrote a heartfelt letter to *The Asahi Shimbun* newspaper after reading an article that questioned why families of the dead had not attended the cemetery dedication. In it she described how she had been moved to tears by news of the dedication, and how grateful she was that her husband had a peaceful resting place in Cowra. 'My only regret,' she wrote, 'is that no representatives of the surviving relatives have been permitted to visit the cemetery. I felt myself to be at blame in some way as I could not even send a bunch of flowers. It was natural that some Australians might criticise us for what they may consider to be an uncaring nature.' She went on to detail how some Japanese families still clung to the misguided doctrine of the Field Service Code two decades after the end of the war. 'My parents-in-law,' she wrote, 'have never believed that their son died in the Cowra riot, saying that "our son of all persons would never be taken prisoner". This being the attitude of his own parents, I could never disclose details of my husband's death to anyone. Above all, for quite a while, I feared that I might be treated as a coward.' She ended the letter hoping that her 'desire to visit Cowra will be realised in the very near future and so enable us to repay the goodwill of the Australian government and people' and that she had 'prayed from afar and with a happy heart for the repose of [her husband's] soul'.[205]

In response to letters similar to Mrs Yonehara's, and several newspaper articles expressing the same criticism, the Japanese Ministry for Health and Welfare sent a belated delegation of family members to Cowra in June 1965. Interestingly, these family members represented the three key interments in the war cemetery – the son of a civilian who died of illness in an internment camp, the widow of a navy pilot shot down in a raid over Darwin and the son of a prisoner who had died in the Cowra Breakout.

Not far from where they paid their respects were the graves of Ben Hardy and Ralph Jones, the two men who fought so courageously on the Vickers gun during the Cowra Breakout, and paid for it with their lives. By the time the adjacent Japanese cemetery was being formally opened, the original headstones on Hardy's and Jones's graves had been upgraded; the shiny new markers bore a shiny new inscription – the George Cross.

Introduced by King George VI in 1940 and equal in stature to the Victoria Cross, the George Cross is awarded by the British government 'only for acts of the greatest heroism or of the most conspicuous courage in circumstances of extreme danger'[206] that did not occur in the presence of the enemy (as the Japanese at Cowra were prisoners, they were no longer considered enemy combatants).

Ever since the smoke had cleared at Cowra, members of the garrison had lobbied for official recognition for the sacrifice of Hardy and Jones, but their efforts were stymied by the aura of secrecy and official embarrassment that swirled around the Cowra Breakout. But Hardy's and Jones's supporters were nothing if not persistent. In the face of constant rebuffs and redirections, former sergeant Syd Little was dogged – throughout the late 1940s he lobbied constantly for Hardy and Jones to receive a bravery award. Lieutenant Colonel Monty Brown had originally recommended the two men for the George Cross but, under pressure to do *something*, in November 1949 the Chifley government agreed to give the two men the significantly downgraded King's Commendation for brave conduct.

A month later, Ben Chifley was replaced as prime minister by Robert Menzies, who saw the award of the George Cross to Hardy and Jones as one of his key early priorities. He personally discussed the matter with the Minister for Defence and the Minister for the Army, and in April 1950 the recommendation for the George Cross was submitted to Buckingham Palace. The formal announcement of the awards was made in *The London Gazette* on 1 September 1950. Hardy's mother, Emily, had died just four days earlier. His medal was presented by

Governor-General Sir William McKell (the man who, as New South Wales premier in 1944, had lobbied the government for a coronial inquiry into the Breakout) to Hardy's sister Beatrice in January 1952. Jones's George Cross had been presented by the King to his brother Walter at Buckingham Palace a year earlier.[207]

For the family of Private Charles Shepherd, who died after being stabbed in the heart by a Japanese prisoner during the Breakout, there would be no official recognition. In many ways Shepherd is the overlooked victim of the Cowra Breakout. His death was not glorious; he didn't blaze away at the enemy from a Vickers gun like Hardy and Jones, or take on a group of escapees armed only with his bare hands and a will to stay alive like Doncaster. He simply ran down some steps, headlong into the path of an unidentified Japanese prisoner, who took advantage of this quirk of fate to add another Australian name to the tally of death.

After the war Shepherd's family struggled to find out what had happened to him. The Breakout was shrouded in secrecy and guilt, and rumours circulated freely. A comrade, evidently confused about who had done what, told the family that it was Shepherd who had disabled the Vickers gun. Another former soldier told them he thought Shepherd had been shot by a ricochet. Decades after the Breakout his family were still writing letters to the army trying to learn the true story. Shepherd's widow, Linda, never even received a pension – for reasons that are still unclear, and just as disgraceful today as they were in the 1940s, Shepherd was deemed to have not died in a combat zone, and was therefore not entitled to the benefits that would come to a man killed in action. Without the financial support of her husband, and abandoned by the government he had died serving, Linda was forced to give up her three children.

She died in 1952, never having learned the truth about her husband's death.

The Japanese survivors of the Breakout did their best to return to normal life back in Japan, but for most this would be a difficult challenge. Some embraced the story of their captivity, and saw it as their duty to their fallen comrades to make sure the story of the Cowra Breakout lived on. In 1964 Ichijiro Do, who had charged the fences near F Tower and then took over as camp leader after the move to Hay, helped form an association for survivors known as Cowra Kai. The group met regularly until the 1990s, and Masaru Moriki, the infantryman who had lain freezing in a ditch in Broadway and recorded his recollections of the Breakout in his excellent memoirs, took over as association leader when Do died in 1974. The group was active in fostering strong relationships between Australia and Japan, and made several trips back to Cowra in the decades after the war. But at its peak its membership only ever totalled a few dozen. The vast majority of the men who had survived that night of bloodshed in Cowra never joined Cowra Kai, and indeed never spoke of their imprisonment, even to wives and families. They simply got on with their lives, and faded into the shadows of post-war Japan. The last survivor of the Breakout, 98-year-old Teruo Murakami, made a final pilgrimage to Cowra for the 75th anniversary in 2019.

In 1971 the people of Cowra determined to solidify their strong ties with Japan on a site that reflected the nature of this unique relationship. Since the opening of the cemetery the town had arranged educational and cultural exchanges with Japan, but they now desired a location where visitors could reflect on the history of the Cowra Breakout and pay their respects to the men who died, both Japanese and Australian. An early suggestion was for a sound-and-light display in a disused bank on the main street, but this was quickly dismissed as too tacky. Soon after, Don Kibbler, president of the Tourist and Development Corporation, came up with the idea of a Japanese garden. He formed a committee and enlisted the help of a Japanese architect to build a model of a garden, which Kibbler carted around in the back of his station wagon to raise funds for the project.

After several years of planning and fundraising in both Australia and Japan, the first stage of the Cowra Japanese Garden opened in 1978. Comprising water features, a tea house and more than 6000 Australian and Japanese plants, the garden represents the coming together of the two nations after the bloodshed of that August night. It was designed by noted architect Ken Nakajima, who was captivated by the site after discovering that it was dominated by two large rocks, which are essential components of Japanese garden design. He felt such a strong connection to this garden in a rural corner of Australia that a portion of his ashes was scattered there when he died in 2000.[208] A second stage of the garden, which included the extension of a lake and the building of a bonsai house, was completed in 1986. Building a lush Japanese garden in the harsh Cowra countryside was always a slightly hare-brained scheme; it never should have gotten off the ground, and certainly should have struggled to remain open. But the garden has prospered, and receives tens of thousands of visitors each year – it is the tangible link between Australia and Japan that was forged by pain and sacrifice during the Breakout, and has become a living monument to the dead.

An avenue of more than 1000 cherry trees connects the Japanese Gardens to the war cemetery. Here, near a small Buddhist shrine, the dead from the Cowra Breakout lie in neat rows, the small plaque on each grave detailing the prisoner's name and date of death. Curiously, many men are buried under the false names they used in captivity, forever linking them to the shame they gave their lives to assuage. The names are only recorded in English, not Japanese, perhaps reflecting the attitude at the time of the cemetery's construction, that no Japanese visitors would want to come here.

Here, incongruously, in this quiet corner of rural Australia, lie the Zero pilot Hajime Toyoshima, the costume-maker Juichi Kinoshita, the firebrand Yoshio Shimoyama, the deputy leader Masao Kojima, the officer Ichiro Fujita and the 229 other men who died in the Breakout. Alongside them are nearly 300 other Japanese nationals: airmen and sailors, farmers and pearl divers, old people and young babies, all united by the simple fact that they were in Australia during the Second World War, and died here. Mrs Yonehara's wish, expressed in a letter to a Japanese newspaper in 1964, has been fulfilled, and Japanese visitors now regularly call at the cemetery. Prayers, said in hushed voices, waft over the small shrine and across the dark headstones in their neat rows.

Nearby, at the site of the former camp, it's hard to fathom the horror of what went on here. The sheep still wander and munch; the snakes still slither. Peppercorn trees sway in a gentle breeze over the rough concrete foundations of the former kitchens and ablutions blocks.

In a long-gone timber hut on this site, Shichihei Matsushima, the deep-thinking warrant officer who had thrown notes attached to sticks into Broadway in a misguided attempt to prevent a massacre, penned a short poem in the hours before the Cowra Breakout. As well as pledges to honour the Emperor and sorrowful recollections of his children, Matsushima included these lines, to succinctly capture his melancholy resignation to the violence he knew was only hours away:

The winding stream flows on,
And knows not to what it flows.
And on its surface float the fallen leaves of autumn.
They, too, are swept on, unknowing. Even such is our life.[209]

Although surely not the one of Matsushima's imaginings, today a winding stream does flow within earshot of the ruins of the camp. The Lachlan River, wide and muddy and unappealing to the thousands of Japanese eyes that saw it from the back of a truck, snakes lazily through the heart of Cowra. A group of boys are fishing on its lush banks, hoping to bag a yellowbelly or even an elusive Murray cod, but knowing deep down that the only fish they are likely to hook is the hated European carp. Even the carp aren't turning up today, and one of the boys soon grows restless. He puts down his rod and starts skipping stones across the water. It's hard to get a good ricochet in the swift current, but no matter: the *plop* as each stone hits the water is pleasing, peaceful. Soon the sun hangs low in the sky, and it's time to head home. The boys pull in their lines and scarper up the bank, leaving the river deserted. It flows on, as it's always done. The weeping willows cast flickering shadows over the ripples in the golden evening light. A frog chirps briefly in the tall reeds. Then all is quiet, but for the sound of the water.

REFERENCES

Reference notes have been condensed for brevity and to avoid website hyperlinks. Where multiple quotes are drawn from the same primary source (such as evidence presented at a Court of Inquiry), the source is noted following the first quote.

Abbreviations:
NAA: National Archives of Australia
NLA: National Library of Australia
AWM: Australian War Memorial
PHG: Papers of Harry Gordon, NLA.
COI-1: Proceedings of Court of Inquiry convened at No 12 Prisoner of War Group, Cowra on 8 August 1944. NAA.
COI-2: Proceedings of Court of Inquiry convened at Cowra Military Camp on 19 August 1944. NAA.
Cor-Inq: Proceedings of Coronial Inquiry convened at Cowra Courthouse on 31 October 1944. NAA.

1. 'Government and General Orders', *The Sydney Gazette and New South Wales Advertiser,* p1, 5 December 1818.
2. Peattie, Mark R., *Sunburst: The Rise of Japanese Air Power 1909-1941,* Naval Institute Press, 2013. (Information about Japanese carrier operations in this chapter is sourced primarily from two outstanding

accounts: Peattie; and Parshall, Jonathan and Tully, Anthony, *Shattered Sword: The Untold Story of the Battle of Midway*, Potomac Books, 2007.)

3. Tanner, Doris Brinker, 'Cornelia Fort: A WASP in World War II, Part I', *Tennessee Historical Quarterly*, Vol 40, No 4, p388, 1981.

4. Fort, Cornelia, 'At the Twilight's Last Gleaming', *Women's Home Companion*, p19, July 1943.

5. Mulholland, Jack, *Darwin Bombed*, Australian Military History Publications, p31, 1999.

6. *Ibid*, p32.

7. *Ibid*, p35.

8. *Ibid*, p28.

9. *Ibid*, p92.

10. *Ibid*, p95.

11. *Ibid*, p92.

12. *Ibid*, p95.

13. Lockwood, Douglas, *Australia's Pearl Harbour: Darwin 1942*, Cassel, p183, 1966.

14. *Ibid*.

15. 'Japanese Prisoner of War No. 1. Air Interrogation Report', 4 March 1942, AWM.

16. 'Japanese Prisoner of War No. 1. Army Interrogation Report', 1 March 1942, AWM.

17. Samuel Edgar Shallard, service record, NAA.

18. Sam Shallard letter to Harry Gordon, August 1980, PHG.

19. *Ibid*. [Translation sourced by author.]

20. Tadao Minami (Hajime Toyoshima) letter to Lionel Bell, March 1942 (copy included in letter from Bell to Harry Gordon, 9 April 1964), PHG. [Translation sourced by author.]

21. Information about internment in Australia is drawn from an outstanding account: Bevege, Margaret, *Behind Barbed Wire: Internment in Australia during World War II*, University of Queensland Press, 1993.

22. Piper, Bob, 'Point of No Return', *RAAF News*, p16, 1 May 1993.

23. *Ibid*.

24. Gordon, Harry, *Voyage from Shame*, University of Queensland Press, p29, 2010.

25. *Ibid*.

26. 'Information Derived from Japanese Prisoners of S.S. "Myoken Maru"', 9 March 1942, AWM.

27. *Ibid*.

28. Gordon, p32.

29. Moriki, Masaru, *Cowra Uprising: One Survivor's Memoir*, unpublished manuscript, p1, 1998?.
30. *Ibid*.
31. 'Cowra, POW Camp - Selection of Site', 1941, NAA.
32. Takahara, Marekuni, 'Senshisha no Kiseki', *Eimuzu*, Part 50, pp38-39. (Quoted in *Bridging Australia and Japan: The Writings of David Sissons, Volume 2*, Keiko Tamura and Arthur Stockwin (ed), Australian National University Press, p51, 2020.) [Noted as 'Sissons' hereafter.]
33. Bevege, p185.
34. Mario Soliani, interview with Ced Pratt, 6/8/1994, Cowra Tourism Corporation (courtesy of Cowra Breakout Association).
35. Intelligence Report No. 89, No. 12 PW Camp, Cowra, 4 June 1944 to 11 June 1944, NAA.
36. Statement by PWI 56437 Vivilecchia Eustacchio, PHG.
37. Intelligence Report No. 89, No. 12 PW Camp, Cowra, 4 June 1944 to 11 June 1944, NAA.
38. Intelligence Report No. 87, No. 12 PW Camp, Cowra, 21 May 1944 to 28 May 1944, NAA.
39. Moriki, pp20-21.
40. GHQ South-West Pacific Area, Allied Translator and Interpreter Section, Interrogation Reports, No. 161, AWM.
41. Bullard, Steven (translated by Keiko Tamura), *Blankets on the Wire*, AWM, p30, 2006.
42. *Ibid*, pp30-31.
43. *Ibid*, p31.
44. 'Japanese Policy Towards Own PW', Intelligence Report, Australian Attorney General's Department, 10 June 1944, NAA.
45. *Ibid*. [emphasis added].
46. Takahara, Part 63, p35. (Quoted in Sissons, p41.)
47. Moriki, p17.
48. *Ibid*, p19.
49. *Ibid*.
50. *Ibid*, p20.
51. David Sissons letter to Harry Gordon, 26 March 1984, PHG. [Noted as 'Sissons letter' hereafter.]
52. Gordon, p82.
53. Intelligence Report No. 89, No. 12 PW Camp, Cowra, 4 June 1944 to 11 June 1944, NAA.
54. Gordon, pp81-84.
55. LHQ to Aust Army Rep London, ML3792, 9 November 1943. (Quoted in Sissons, p38.)

56. Robert Ramsay, MC, service record, NAA.
57. O. E. Norvall letter to Harry Gordon, 20 August 1965, PHG.
58. Sissons letter.
59. Clarrie Mead, interview with David Hobson, 10 May 1991, Cowra Tourism Corporation (courtesy of Cowra Breakout Association).
60. Norm Beaman, interview with David Hobson, 17 September 1993, Cowra Tourism Corporation (courtesy of Cowra Breakout Association).
61. *Ibid.*
62. Military Court PWJA 145535 Sgt/Maj Kanazawa, Akira, NAA.
63. Field, Michael, 'POW still bitter over executions', stuff.co.nz, 24 April 2011.
64. Field, Michael, 'Last Coast Watcher remembers', stuff.co.nz, 25 April 2012.
65. Rowe, Don, 'Massacre at Featherston', *New Zealand Geographic,* Issue 138, nzgeo.com, 2016.
66. Ota, Yasuhiro, 'Shooting and friendship over Japanese prisoners of war', thesis, Massey University, Auckland, 2013.
67. *Ibid.*
68. *Ibid.*
69. '48 Japs Killed in Prison Camp Mutiny', *The Courier-Mail*, p1, 3 March 1943.
70. Allied Translator and Interpreter Section, South-West Pacific Area, Interrogation Report No 311-X, PWJA (USA) 147016, 7 August 1944, AWM.
71. Allied Translator and Interpreter Section, South-West Pacific Area, Interrogation Report No 311, PWJA (USA) 147016, 7 June 1944, AWM.
72. 'Copy of a report on a statement made by pw Matsumoto Takeo', Exhibit F, COI-1.
73. *Ibid.*
74. Intelligence Report No. 87, No. 12 PW Camp, Cowra, 21 May 1944 to 28 May 1944, NAA.
75. Gordon, p.105.
76. Lionel Boorman letter to Harry Gordon, 1965?, PHG.
77. Sissons, p34.
78. *Ibid*, p43.
79. Gordon, p203.
80. Stan Platz letter to Harry Gordon, 25 September 1994, PHG. [Noted as 'Platz Letter 1' hereafter.]
81. 'Alleged Intent to Escape from P.O.W. Camp. Report of Action Taken by Aust Recruit Trg Centre', 4 July 1944, NAA. [Noted as 'Training Centre Report' hereafter.]

82. Platz letter 1.
83. Beatrice Hardy, interview with Marion Starr, 4 January 1991, PHG.
84. Gordon, p147.
85. *Machine Gun Training* instruction manual, War Office, 1925, 'Machine Gun Drill'.
86. Training Centre Report.
87. Gordon, p.111.
88. Sissons, p.39.
89. Brown evidence, COI-1.
90. Ramsay evidence, COI-1.
91. *Ibid*.
92. Japanese actions and dialogue in this section are based on the recollections of Ryo Kanazawa, interviews with Harry Gordon, 20 April 1977 and 13 October 1993, audio recordings in PHG. [Noted as 'Kanazawa audio' hereafter.]
93. Takahara, Marekuni, *Kaura Monogatari*, Toyo Keizai Shinposha, 1987.
94. *Ibid.*
95. *Ibid.*
96. Kanazawa audio.
97. Moriki, p23.
98. *Ibid*, p24.
99. *Ibid*
100. *Ibid*
101. *Ibid.*
102. Kanazawa audio.
103. McKenzie, Walter, *Memories of the Cowra Breakout*, self-published, p2, 1990.
104. Moriki, p27.
105. *Ibid*, p28.
106. *Ibid*, p41.
107. Gordon, p133.
108. 'Examination of PWJA 145431 Matsushima, Shichihei', 17 August 1944, NAA.
109. Gordon, pp134-135.
110. Moriki, p44.
111. Rolls evidence, COI-1.
112. Aisbett evidence, COI-1.
113. Thomas Aisbett letter to Harry Gordon, 27 January 1979, PHG.
114. Timms, Edward, 'The Bloodbath at Cowra', *As You Were*, p179, 1950.
115. Takahara, Marekuni, 'Senshisha no Kiseki', *Eimuzu*, Part 67. (Quoted in Sissons letter).

116. Moriki, p29.
117. *Ibid.*
118. Alf Flynn, interview with David Hobson, 31 July 1993, Cowra Tourism Corporation (courtesy of Cowra Breakout Association).
119. Gordon, p162.
120. Beaman interview.
121. Wal McKenzie, interview with David Hobson, 5 August 1993, Cowra Tourism Corporation (courtesy of Cowra Breakout Association).
122. Mead interview.
123. 'Jap O/Rs Mass Escape' (undated, possibly a report submitted as evidence to a Court of Inquiry), PHG.
124. Ramsay evidence, COI-1.
125. Takahara, in Sissons letter.
126. Moriki, p30.
127. Small evidence, COI-1.
128. Kiichi Ishii, interview with Harry Gordon, 9 October 1970, audio recording in PHG.
129. Small evidence, COI-1.
130. *Ibid.*
131. Rankin evidence, COI-1.
132. Mancer evidence, COI-1.
133. McKenzie, p10.
134. *Ibid*, p11.
135. *Ibid.*
136. Moriki, pp36-37.
137. Gordon, p162.
138. Kanazawa audio.
139. Vincent Herbert Powis Patis, service record, NAA.
140. Patis evidence, COI-1.
141. Small evidence, COI-1.
142. Negerevich evidence, COI-1.
143. Leemon, J., Leemon, B. and Morgan, C., *War Graves Digger,* Australian Military History Publications, p72, 2010.
144. Report on the Directorate of Prisoners of War and Internees at Army Headquarters, Melbourne, 1939-1951: Volume 1, NAA.
145. McKenzie interview.
146. Gordon, p224.
147. Vern Northwood letter to Harry Gordon, 20 April 1979, PHG.
148. Rita Reid, interview with David Hobson, 9 October 1993, Cowra Tourism Corporation (courtesy of Cowra Breakout Association).

149. 'Message Lodged in Sydney by George Folster for the National Broadcasting Corporation of America', August 1944, NAA. [Noted as 'Folster' hereafter.]

150. Roy and Thelma Treasure, interview with David Hobson, 16 April 1993, Cowra Tourism Corporation (courtesy of Cowra Breakout Association).

151. Gordon, p185.

152. Jim Webb, interview with David Hobson, 8 June 1994, Cowra Tourism Corporation (courtesy of Cowra Breakout Association).

153. 'Escape of PsOW from Cowra Camp: Report that Japanese Escapee had reached Sydney', August 1944, NAA.

154. Folster.

155. *Ibid.*

156. Gordon, p245.

157. Northwood letter.

158. 'Service Casualties', *The Argus*, p7, 2 September 1944.

159. Platz Letter 1.

160. *Ibid.*

161. *Ibid.*

162. Stan Platz letter to Harry Gordon about Doncaster patrol (undated), PHG. [Noted as 'Platz Letter 2' hereafter.]

163. Platz evidence, COI-2.

164. Platz Letter 2.

165. *Ibid.*

166. *Ibid.*

167. *Ibid.*

168. Langley evidence, COI-2.

169. Findings of COI-2, in Harry Doncaster, service record, NAA.

170. *Ibid.*

171. *Ibid.*

172. Gordon, p213.

173. Alf Bourke written statement, Cowra police station, 14 November 1944, submitted as evidence to Cor-Inq.

174. Gordon, p276.

175. 'Report on Mass Escape - Ps.W.J. - Cowra 5 Aug '44', NAA.

176. 'Cowra prisoner-of-war escapes: Reports by Deputy Chief Publicity Censor and State Publicity Censor, Sydney', NAA.

177. Gordon, p.227.

178. Landforces to Milbase Sydney A69531 of 6 August 1944 (Quoted in Sissons, p46).

179. Memo from Department of the Army to Department of External Affairs, 'Mutiny of Japanese Prisoners of War', 29 August 1944, NAA.

180. *Ibid.*
181. *Ibid.*
182. Commonwealth of Australia Security Service, Listening Post report, 'News Commentary to Australia', 16 September 1944, NAA.
183. 'Japanese Policy Towards Own PW', Intelligence Report, Australian Attorney General's Department, 10 June 1944, NAA.
184. Mitchell Evidence, COI-2.
185. *Ibid.*
186. Morris Evidence, COI-2.
187. Mitchell Evidence, COI-2.
188. Mead Interview.
189. Cor-Inq, in 'Escape of Japanese prisoners of war from Cowra', NAA.
190. Gordon, pp252-253.
191. Asada, Teruhiko, *The Night of a Thousand Suicides: The Japanese Outbreak at Cowra*, Angus & Robertson, p110, 1970.
192. Moriki, p50.
193. *Ibid*, p51.
194. *Ibid*, p55.
195. *Ibid*, p56.
196. *Ibid.*
197. Gordon, p303.
198. Moriki, p63.
199. *Ibid*, p65.
200. Bullard, p92.
201. Keith Telfer and Alf Cowley, interview with Terry Calhoun, 17 March 2003, Australia-Japan Research Project, (ajrp.awm.gov.au).
202. *Ibid.*
203. Bullard, p92.
204. *Ibid*, p94.
205. Letter from Tomai Yonehara to *Asahi Shimbun* (1964/5?), PHG.
206. *The London Gazette*, Issue 35060, p622, 31 January 1941.
207. Gordon, pp305-308.
208. Bullard, p100.
209. 'Copies of exhibits used in the Court of Inquiry into Japanese breakout from Cowra Camp, 5 Aug. 1944', Exhibit L, COI-1.

ACKNOWLEDGEMENTS

No book about the Cowra Breakout could be written without tapping the vast resource of information that exists in the town itself. Thank you to the people of Cowra for keeping the history of this significant event alive, and for your commitment to remembrance and reconciliation. In particular, local historian Graham Apthorpe went above and beyond to assist with my research, providing invaluable information about the people who were involved in the Breakout, access to previously unpublished documents, and answers to my never-ending stream of questions. Graham is the leading authority on the Cowra Breakout and, under his care, the history is in safe hands. Thanks also to Lawrence Ryan from Cowra Council, who provided valuable insights into the Breakout and its effects on the people in the district. Thanks to the Cowra Breakout Association for giving me access to the interviews that had been conducted in Cowra in the 1990s, which became a key part of telling this story.

I owe a huge debt of gratitude to someone I never had the chance to meet: Harry Gordon wrote the definitive account of the Breakout in the 1970s, *Die Like the Carp!*, and followed it up in the 1990s with an updated version, *Voyage from Shame*. It was Harry who first lobbied the government to release information about the Breakout in the 1960s, which, up until that point, had been restricted under the pretext of national security. Harry was a wonderful journalist who had the ability to get people to completely open up to him. His interviews with both Australian and Japanese participants in the Breakout shed new light on the events of that cold August night and revealed vital aspects of the story that would otherwise be lost to us. Thank you to his family for giving me access to his papers in the National Library, where I found a trove of information that had not previously been published.

Thank you also to the group of historians who I regularly call on for advice and inspiration, including Karl James at the Australian War Memorial, who does brilliant work on all subjects relating to the Second World War, and David Howell, who gave me outstanding insights into the experience of army life during the war. Thanks also to Michael Molkentin, Aaron Pegram, Roger Lee, Richard B. Frank and Rebecca Hausler, who all contributed their thoughts to the construction of the story and steered me in interesting new directions for my research.

Thanks also to the family of the late Marion Starr, who revealed the story of Ralph Jones and his relationship with their aunt, Madeleine; one of those fascinating little sidebars of history that help bring a story to life.

This book wouldn't exist without the support of the amazing team at Hachette Australia, particularly Matthew Kelly, who first encouraged me to write my account of the Breakout many years ago, and Sophie Hamley, who was responsible for getting the project off the ground and who constantly supported me through the sometimes-rocky journey from idea to finished manuscript. Her dedication to presenting the history accurately, and her compassion for the people who had lived and died during the Breakout, were greatly appreciated. Thanks also to Stacey Clair, who worked tirelessly to edit and refine the book.

And finally, a huge thank you to the people in my life who support me on this sometimes-harebrained journey through the pages of history. My parents, Gil and Leonie, and sister, Lisa, who fostered this strange obsession in my early days and have supported it ever since; my dedicated assistant, Jess Stebnicki, who never runs out of energy or ideas; and my delightful children, Brooke, Heath and James, who give me faith that the future is in great hands. And finally my wife, Jess, a constant source of support and inspiration – this wouldn't have happened without you.

Mat McLachlan
Sydney
April 2022

INDEX